It's Raining Rock Cats and Sea Dogs:

A Fan's Guide to the AA Ballparks and Towns of the Eastern League

Steve Holcomb

Pax River Press
3540 Crain Highway, Box 229
Bowie, Maryland 20716
(301) 805-1757; Fax: (301) 352-8190
e-mail: 74273.310@compuserve.com

It's Raining Rock Cats and Sea Dogs:

A Fan's Guide to the AA Ballparks and Towns of the Eastern League

By Steve Holcomb

Library of Congress Data
Holcomb, Steve
    It's Raining Rock Cats and Sea Dogs: A Fan's Guide to the AA Ballparks and Towns of the Eastern League / by Steve Holcomb. - 1st ed.
        Includes bibliographical references.

    ISBN 0-9657765-7-3
    1. Sports - Minor League Baseball™
    2. Travel - United States

      Library of Congress Catalog Card Number: 97-91690

Pax River Press
3540 Crain Highway, Box 229
Bowie, Maryland 20716
(301) 805-1757 Fax: (301) 352-8190
e-mail: 74273.310@compuserve.com

It's Raining Rock Cats and Sea Dogs:

A Fan's Guide to the AA Ballparks and Towns of the Eastern League

By Steve Holcomb

Introduction.. 1

Overview of the Eastern League.................................... 8

Teams of the Northern Division

- Binghamton Mets; Binghamton/Cooperstown, New York...................... 11

- New Britain Rock Cats; New Britain/Hartford, Connecticut................. 37

- New Haven Ravens; New Haven, Connecticut.................................. 57

- Norwich Navigators; Norwich/Mystic/New London, Connecticut............ 81

- Portland Sea Dogs; Portland, Maine... 109

Eastern League Statistics.. 135

Teams of the Southern Division

- Akron Aeros; Akron/Canton, Ohio.. 143

- Bowie Baysox; Bowie/Annapolis, Maryland................................... 167

- Harrisburg Senators; Harrisburg/Hershey/Carlisle, Pennsylvania............ 195

- Reading Phillies; Reading/Berks County, Pennsylvania........................ 219

- Trenton Thunder; Trenton/Princeton, New Jersey............................. 245

Bibliography

For Diane

Introduction

Background

My interest in writing this book is mostly due to the fact that I live walking distance from Prince George's Stadium, home field for the Bowie Baysox. As a baseball fan all my life, and as someone who's had the privilege of attending games at Camden Yards, Fenway Park, Wrigley Field, and even Tiger Stadium, I find there's few things better than coming home from work on a hot summer night, and just walking across the street to grab a cold beer and a dog and see professional baseball for only a few bucks.

But that's not enough to explain a book about all the ballparks and towns of the Eastern League. What happened was after attending well over two dozen games a season since Prince George's Stadium first opened in 1994, I began wondering about some of the visiting ballclubs and their hometown communities. Specifically, did they have ballparks that were as nice as the one my family had begun to include regularly in our summertime entertainment budget? Towns like Binghamton, Harrisburg, Portland and New Haven, not to mention Hardware City (a.k.a. New Britain), were towns I'd never visited before, so I knew little about these visitors called the Mets, Senators, Sea Dogs, and Ravens, not to mention the Rock Cats. I knew almost as little about the hometowns of the Norwich Navigators, the Canton-Akron Indians (a.k.a. the Akron Aeros), the Reading Phillies, and the Trenton Thunder. Since, at the time, I couldn't find any books on the subject, that's when I began my plans to write this book about the stadiums, teams, and towns of the Eastern League.

So, I wrote the book I would've bought, if I could've found it. My methodology is further explained below under the heading General Disclaimer, but basically what I've tried to provide in ten chapters, one for each team, follows two different prongs. First, the ballpark sections. In these sections you'll find such information as club name and address (mailing, office, and Internet, where applicable), club affiliation, ownership, and detailed stadium information. The stadium information is further broken down into stadium dimensions and characteristics, concessions and souvenirs, admission prices as available at the time of printing, picnic and group information, ticket outlet information, team history, mascot, the name of the visiting hotel for visiting teams, and directions to the stadium. Secondly, the town section of each chapter is not only meant to provide local information about the community, but also places to stay and things to see while you're waiting for the game. These sections cover the history of the town, information on local Chambers of Commerce and Convention Bureaus, a guide to historic sites and museums, daytime entertainment possibilities ranging from aquariums to zoos, a list of public golf courses (my favorite), local shopping malls, seasonal events, and nearby hotel accommodations.

The Trip and Some Thoughts Along the Way

The Trip

Once I settled on what I wanted to write, then came the question of how to go about it. The easiest way would have been just to call the local Chamber's of Commerce, request their free informational brochures, and work from there. However, I wasn't sure that would give me a real flavor of the towns. I probably could have called the teams and requested to purchase a souvenir program over the phone, but that wouldn't give me a proper sense of the stadiums. No, the solution was, of course, a road trip.

Not just any road trip, though. I came up with the idea for this book around Independence Day, 1996. In order for me to cover the other nine teams in the Eastern League (I had a pretty good handle on what I wanted to include about the Bowie Baysox already), I had to try and make it to towns as far away as Akron, Ohio and Portland, Maine before Labor Day. Not only that, but I had to schedule my trip in the coming two months so that I would be in each of the nine towns when the ballclub was at home. With that hurdle ahead of me, I began to doubt whether I could pull this off before the end of the season. Fortunately, I had received the 1996 schedules from all of the teams at this point (the teams will mail you a free schedule if you call ahead), so I could lay them all out and plan my trip. In the end, I determined the best way was simply to follow the Bowie Baysox on the road the rest of the season. Their away schedule fit in nicely with my plans, and if I followed them on the road, I realized I could cover six of the other teams quite easily. I could schedule the other three teams when the Baysox were at home, therefore allowing me to complete my round trip before the playoffs began in September. All this with the blessing of my better half, and just barely enough room on the credit cards to make sure I had a home to come back to when I was done!

I won't bore you anymore with the details of the road trip, but I do want to include some general observations to try and give you a sense of what it's like to follow a Minor League team on the road. First and foremost, if you're going to do it, make sure you have the stamina to endure plenty of long drives and a few days and nights in new and different towns. I don't know how these young guys can manage the long bus rides from town to town, living their entire summer out of hotel rooms, then having the energy to go out and play nine innings of baseball almost every day! Although some of the bus trips can be short, especially for the three Eastern League teams located in Connecticut, other trips can take all day. In the Overview, before I begin talking about each of the individual teams, there's a mileage map showing the distance between each of the towns. Each of these teams play at least two series against each other during the season. That means, for example, that the Portland Sea Dogs have to travel to play both the Akron Aeros (744 miles), and the Bowie Baysox (553 miles), and vice versa! That's a long ride if you're just coming off a tough and exciting series against another Eastern League opponent. Compare that with a match-up between the New Britain Rock Cats and the New Haven Ravens (35 miles).

The other aspect of Minor League travel that amazes me, is the life living out of hotel rooms all summer long. I was fortunate enough to have my own room on the trip, but I imagine, with Minor League expenses being what they are, these guys have to double up and share. And because there's so much movement in AA ball, the roommate you start with at the beginning of the season, probably is not going to be the one you end up with at the end. They're your teammates just the same, but c'mon, ... some personalities inevitably will clash on the road. In addition, I'll tell you up front that a few of the hotels designated as the Visiting Hotel for the team aren't exactly luxury resorts. Most of them in this league are really quite adequate, especially if all you're doing is sleeping there and then going to play baseball in the afternoon. Some of these even offer room service, which I gather would be a welcome break to a player who'd spent all summer having just doughnuts and coffee for breakfast. But, there are a few hotels which, for want of being nice, leave a lot to the imagination. This is why I've listed more than one hotel for each city. More on that later.

However, when all is said and done, I think most of these guys, even the ones that don't make it all the way to the top, will look back on this part of their careers with fondness, even humor. It takes a lot of talent and skill to play at this level, much more than any of us who think we're the best softball players in the world will ever have, and paying your dues like this in The Minor Leagues is not only a way to hone those skills, but it's an honest way to build professionalism and character. As for the average baseball fan who takes on to follow a team, I can't say it does much to build your character, however, it is a worthwhile and entertaining experience that will give you days of baseball memories that will last, at least until the next season comes again.

The Fans

One thing I discovered about home team loyalty on the trip, is that it's much different at this level. Given the rate that these guys move through the leagues, you don't have very long to get to know the players. It's just really hard to get attached to a player who probably won't be with the team all season. And anyway, if they're doing their job right, you expect that they will get moved up at least to the next level, AAA, if not all the way to the Show! They want it, and you want it. If they're not doing their job right, they'll be sent back down to A-ball, or shipped out altogether. That's why the AA level probably sees the most movement. If there is any loyalty at this level, it really isn't attached to particular players. Loyalty extends to the club itself. That, and the fact that pro-ball is being played at a decent stadium just around the corner from your house.

And, I've noticed that most people don't take AA baseball too seriously. This is for fun, not for rabid fans waiting to see their team in the World Series. Almost everyone who follows Minor League ball follows it for just one reason. It doesn't matter so much that the team win or lose. It doesn't matter if the pitcher has a good curve or a slider yet. It doesn't matter if the biggest, strongest designated hitter on the club has ten or even twenty homers. All that matters is that it's baseball, and you've got a great seat at the game.

Two other things come to mind while I'm on the subject of fans: one, many fans will leave the game at 9:30 p.m., no matter what the score, and two, people in this league do like to talk baseball. If you've never been to a game at this level, don't be afraid to ask the guy or gal next to you about the next hitter coming up to bat, or the next pitcher coming in from the bullpen. There's no doubt in my mind that you'll make a friend for the night. Baseball at this level isn't about rivalries centuries old, (even though the Eastern League is 75 years young), baseball at this level is just about the game itself.

Don't get me wrong, the fans throughout the Eastern League do take their home teams quite seriously. Anytime you see someone wearing a ball cap, t-shirt, or jacket with the team logo, I'll give you even money there's three other fans showing off their team spirit in the same way. And, in most towns in the league, the loyalty to the team even garners attention by the local and regional media outlets. In some towns, like Portland and Trenton for example, local coverage isn't limited to scores and stats in the daily paper. These towns regularly send out television crews to provide nightly reports on the local evening news (What's interesting to watch is when the local sportscaster completely fumbles on the pronunciation of a player's name. There are no Ripken's, Boggs, or Vaughn's in AA ball, just a lot of young whathisname's that may or may not become famous in their own right someday). For me, a fan of the Bowie Baysox, this television coverage came as a surprise. There is weekly coverage of the Baysox in a small local paper, but the nationals, like the Washington Post, at best only provide box scores. And forget about the nightly news, since the Bowie Baysox are simply located too close to the major media markets of Washington, D.C. and Baltimore to warrant such attention.

Kids and AA Ball

As for getting fans through the door, one of the neatest admission gimmicks, if you will, occurs at the Bowie Baysox games. Little leaguers in uniform are admitted free at Prince George's Stadium. This makes a lot of sense. First of all, admission for a kid of Little League age is only $3.00 anyway. If you get them in the door for free, the stadium is easily going to make up twice that amount in concession sales for every young fan. I don't know why the other stadiums don't follow this example.

However, all the stadiums in the Eastern League are specifically geared toward families. Most even remind folks prior to the game that there are a lot of families in the audience so please watch your language and behavior. I saw a couple rowdies, who bordered on too much to drink, but even these guys weren't unconscious of the audience around them. Everyone knows to check the four letter words at the gate, and everyone realizes that while the game is good fun for fans of all ages, the game has always been for and about kids.

Another no-nonsense draw for fans of all ages, chances are greater at Minor League games to obtain autographs. Who knows, maybe one day the AA player in your home town will be starting in the show? Let your children collect their signatures while they can, and come out to the park early with a ball or a bat, and a good marker or pen. You can't imagine what it must mean to these young boys and girls. I know I can't begin to convey the looks I saw on the faces of every young fan who got close enough to their favorite ballplayer. I just saw that same expression on kids everywhere.

It's not what you'd expect, ...that is, pure and simple wonder. These young fans look like it's two weeks before Christmas: they know they'll probably get something they want, but they're not sure if they've been good enough to deserve it. There's plenty of concern and way too many furled brows you don't expect to see on kids 12 and under. They're all worrying about getting that signature on their scorecard, on their hat, on their ball, on the free souvenir they received as they came through the gate. The great thing about the Eastern League, most of the time, these ballplayers are more than eager to accommodate their youngest fans.

It all happens as soon as the youngsters can see the grass on the diamond. They'll immediately start spying for that player who at one moment is talking to a reporter, and in the next, up against the fence making souvenirs. When kids spot a player with a pen, they dash through empty bleachers, criss-crossing and zig- zagging to get in line before the player has to go off to take some infield or batting practice. If a kid is lucky enough to get that prized acquisition, the smile you'll see is worth twenty home runs (well, not really, but it's great to see the grins on these kid's faces who still aren't old enough to need major dental work yet.)

The only bad thing I can think of associated with player autograph time, is when some parents start collecting signatures for themselves by using their children. One guy I saw had a Louisville Slugger covered with autographs. His little daughter was trying to work her way through the crowd up to the fence. When she finally got close to the player she liked, her dad said, "No, not him. We already have his." The poor girl, who just seconds before looked genuinely happy being this close to a ballplayer, looked utterly confused after her father said those words. Hey, who are the autographs for, Dad? You or your daughter?

But, if there's one thing I learned on my trip, it's that good giveaways get them in the door, great games will keep them there. With bad and boring games, the long endless pitcher duels on a hot summer night for example, there needs to be diversions in between innings to keep the fans in the stands, and that's especially true for families. Kids may be fascinated with the game, with players autographs, even with that first hot dog, but if the third inning goes on for a half hour, the natives will get restless. That's what most of the teams in this league are good at though. Most of them, with only a few exceptions, know their audience, and they know how to keep them interested.

In fact, I've noticed that kids are much more excitable at Minor League games for some reason. You don't see too many twelve year old's running lose at Yankee Stadium, Fenway Park or Camden Yards, but at the AA level, I've seen plenty of displays of adolescent restlessness. There are a few stadiums in the Eastern League that make accommodations for this exuberance, the ones with playgrounds, giveaways, contests, and mascots, ...other places obviously can't. Suffice it to say, most young fans I saw are committed to the team and the game, however, there are those few that need these diversions. The stadiums that can provide those distractions seem to be the ones that consistently draw the repeat business.

The Stadiums

Strange as it may seem, I like to think these ballparks and towns are all connected somehow. Although all are different in their own ways, there is much in common. Superficially for instance, there are five cities which either are, were, or are close enough geographically to state capitals. Trenton and Harrisburg are the capitals of New Jersey and Pennsylvania, respectively, Portland used to be the state capital of Maine, and New Britain and Bowie are both a very short drive away from the state capitals of Hartford and Annapolis. Also, Binghamton, Harrisburg, and Bowie are connected by the great Susquehanna River, with Bowie situated only a few miles away from the Chesapeake Bay.

On a more concrete level, many of the stadiums in the Eastern League are what I'll call "Stay Alert" parks (a phrase I'm borrowing from Prince George's Stadium Announcer, Bud Freeman). What this means is that at these open Minor League stadiums, where almost everyone is close to the action, there's a higher probability percentage-wise that you're going to be near a foul ball. (Of course, I'm creating this statistic totally out of intuition. Maybe future editions will include real statistics on Foul Ball Catches per capita at each of the Eastern League ballparks.) Anyway, as you probably already know, some of those fouls coming off the end of the bat aren't just delicate lobs into the audience. These batters are trying to knock a hit at least out of the infield and that means they're swinging hard and fast. That's how some foul balls come into the stands. You can be seriously hurt if you don't "Stay Alert!"

Speaking of stadium announcers, I think all of them in this league do a great job. Part statistician, part baseball fan, and part cheerleader, the Eastern League stadium announcers know what the fans want and expect out of the game. When there's a lull in the action for instance, the announcers and staff are always on the ball, and inevitably you'll notice the graphic displays on the scoreboard encouraging you to make some noise on behalf of the home team. But, I'm not so impressed with this aspect of the cheerleader in the booth, as I am with their wonderful singing voices heard nightly during "Take Me Out to the Ballgame." If they're not always on key, at least they're the loudest ones in the park.

Also in common at all these stadiums, you'll be hard pressed to find a bad seat anywhere. At only one park, Yale Field, do you really have to contend with obstructed views, and there's only a few of those anyway. If by chance you do wind up with a bad seat, don't worry, I've noticed that after about the 7th inning, it is so much easier to sneak on down to the box seats, as opposed to in the major leagues. But, you didn't hear that from me.

The Growing Difference between The Minor Leagues and Major Leagues

It's no secret that in recent years there has been a movement back towards Minor League Baseball. One doesn't have to speculate on many factors to see why this is so: the high costs of attending and enjoying major league games; the childish and unsportsmanlike conduct of some major league ballplayers and owners; and, of course, the strike that canceled the 1994 World Series. Anyone of these alone could explain why attendance figures have dropped in the big leagues, but does that necessarily correlate with the increase in attendance in the minors? Maybe, maybe not. There's probably plenty of statistical analyses and marketing demographics out there which is much more scientific than my anecdotal observations, but as for the Eastern League as a whole, attendance figures seemed to really starting taking off around 1994.

In fact, after 1994, when the Eastern League drew a then record total attendance of 2,554,570 fans, the fans turned out again in 1995 and topped that record by drawing another record total of 3,057,051! In 1996, this figure dropped off slightly to a total of 2,960,648, only 39,352 fans shy of the three million mark (With average daily attendance in the Eastern League hovering around 4,450 fans per game, they probably could have made it to three million with one or two more games per club). In fact, four of the ten teams listed here, the Binghamton Mets, the New Britain Rock Cats, the Canton-Akron Indians (a.k.a. the Akron Aeros), and the Reading Phillies saw increases in attendance from 1995 to 1996. (Reading broke their own single season attendance record in 1996 for the ninth consecutive year!)

Maybe the fact that both the 1994 and 1995 major league seasons were written off by most baseball fans is an explanation why people came out and discovered the Eastern League all over again. Maybe the major league's recovery after Cal Ripken broke Lou Gehrig's record in September 1995 somehow relates to a slight decline in attendance in The Minor Leagues during 1996. Or, maybe it was just bad weather this year, who knows? In any event, it's clear that the Eastern League provides great family entertainment for all ages, and much more affordably than the big leagues do, or ever can, for that matter. After all, what better and more wholesome entertainment value can you find anywhere? The movies? I don't think so. There's simply nothing like the game.

General Disclaimer

The limitations of this book are based on personal subjectivity and time. Although every effort was made to ensure that the information contained herein was as accurate as possible, I only had so much time to spare in each town, so I apologize if I've left anything or anyone out. With that disclaimer, the reader should know however, that I did spend an inordinate amount of time investigating the following places and attractions. The ones I thought would be enjoyable, admittedly based solely on my subjective tastes, are included. If I didn't see the attraction at all, or if I simply didn't care for it, despite the attraction being recommended in local visitor informational brochures, chances are it's not included in this book either. I hope to correct these deficiencies in future editions. (Note also that schedules and hours listed are subject to change.) Meanwhile, if you want further information about a town, I'd suggest you contact one of the visitor organizations I've listed. I've found them all to be helpful and willing to send you more free information than you probably will ever have time to read.

Further, this book was researched during the summer of 1996. To the best of my knowledge, the information contained is as accurate as possible. However, that being said, I recommend that upon arrival at any of the stadiums discussed in this book, you do yourself a favor and purchase a Souvenir Program. These ten clubs all produce high quality professional programs, with detailed up to date information about the stadium, background statistics on the current team with player profiles, the scorecard for that day's game, as well as information about local merchants and attractions. Not to mention, in most cases the clubs sponsor some form of signature contest with promotions and giveaways tied to either signatures or stamps located inside random individual programs. If you want a chance to catch a freebie (other than the occasional foul ball), nine times out of ten, you're going to need to purchase a souvenir program.

Also, please note that there are no aerial photos in this book (Not that I wouldn't have wanted to include them. I just couldn't afford them on my budget.) All the photos you see were taken by me, an amateur photographer (I'm not too proud to admit it) looking for ways to convey the typical fan's view of the stadium. I didn't always get shots on the best summer's day or night. More importantly, I had no special access to any parts of the stadium that any other average person couldn't obtain as well. I'm just a fan. So, like I say, these shots may not be the best example of what the stadium looks like, but they are an average example.

As for my concession recommendations, please understand that I do not boast to being a food critic (although my present girth belies that fact). I am a baseball fan. I'm drawn to baseball games of any size and shape for three reasons: the sport, the beer, and the dogs, not always in that order. So I apologize to all the legitimate food critics out there when they read my reviews of the best hot dog in the Eastern League. This book is not about the science of gastronomy. My research methods were not based on some objective rules involving taking one or two bites of a sausage sandwich and then trying to describe the texture, taste and presentation of the concession in multisyllabic words. No, I'm just a fan. I rushed through the gates, bought a dog and a beer, found my seat, and then devoured both as hungrily and as quickly as possible.

Let's face it, there aren't that many ways to describe a stadium hot dog. There really are only a couple factors to consider: whether it's grilled, boiled or roasted; whether it's dry and cold or hot and juicy; and, finally, whether it's the normal, store-bought size, or a foot long. (By the way, the best hot dogs in the Eastern League are in Harrisburg - grilled, hot and juicy, foot long.) Trust me, ask any restaurant critic you know, and they too will admit it's hard to describe a stadium hot dog smeared with mustard as "elegant", "scrumptious", "magnificent", or even as "luscious". However, how can any normal American enjoy a decent ball game without the required seven inches of tasteless meat, covered in bad, gallon-jug, stadium mustard, way over-pickled relish, and then served on a powdered and processed, white bread bun? I know I can't.

In regards to town information, a note about accommodations is required. I stayed in hotels this trip, and I'll probably always stay in hotels on future trips. I'm just not a bed and breakfast type of guy, it's that simple. However, I recognize and admire the appeal of these establishments, so where I thought relevant, I've included some sort of B&B information. Also, I did not devise a rating system for the accommodations in the interest of time. I always list the visiting hotel for the ballclub first, and then, in general, I list the rest in order of personal preference.

Also, you will not find any information about restaurants in this book. My expectation is that you'll have breakfast somewhere, then store up for the concessions on sale at the ballpark. That being said, when you peruse the hotel listings, note that I have indicated whether the hotel has a restaurant or whether they serve a complimentary continental breakfast. Where you do not see that information, you should assume that you're on your own when it comes to the first meal of the day.

And finally, just one note to all the Minor League ballplayers: If you're reading this to try and find something exciting to do during the day, instead of waiting around in your hotel watching soap operas, here's my advice: "All My Children" is on at 1:00 p.m. in most cities. What are you reading this part of the book for, anyway? You should be resting and then arriving at the ballpark early to practice, practice, practice! You don't have time to go to Cooperstown, or the Football Hall of Fame, or Great Adventure, or the Outlet Mall, or the waterfronts and seaports, or even to the L.L. Bean. Rest up so WE can have fun while you're working! Now, let's Play Ball!

All schedules, times, dates and prices are subject to change without notice. Any updated information and/or comments are welcome.

Eastern League rules prohibit bottles, cans, food containers and alcoholic beverages from being brought into any Eastern League stadium.

Overview of the Eastern League

The history of the Eastern League officially dates back 75 years to the first game played on May 9th, 1923 in the town of Williamsport, Pennsylvania, the present home of the Little League World Series and the Little League Hall of Fame. However, the early history of baseball reveals there was another league originally called the Eastern League. According to an excellent resource on The Minor Leagues[1], an Eastern League existed as early as the 1880's, and included teams such as those from Newark and Syracuse. This league continued play through the turn of the century with various other teams from Binghamton, Buffalo, Hartford, and the famous Baltimore Orioles team from 1903 to 1911. It was in the year 1911 that this version of the Eastern League became the International League, known today for AAA baseball.

The present Eastern League grew out of the Class B New York-Pennsylvania League, and officially was designated a AA league in 1963[2]. The oldest ballclub among the ten current teams in this Eastern League is the Reading Phillies, a team which has been in the league at various times since 1933, and consistently in the Eastern League from 1967 to the present day. The newest ballclub is the Norwich Navigators who began play in 1995 after the Yankees affiliate moved from Albany, New York. The New Haven Ravens play in the most historic stadium, Yale Field. Built in 1927, Yale Field oversaw both the retirement of Babe Ruth, as well as the play of a young ballplayer who made good, President George Bush.

The Eastern League also saw the early play of such future Hall of Famer's as Jim Palmer, Warren Spahn, Whitey Ford, Ralph Kiner, and Mike Schmidt. And, current Major League Stars such as Rafael Palmeiro, Albert Belle, Jim Thome, Charles Nagy, Darren Daulton, David Cone, Jeff Bagwell, Mo Vaughn, Roger Clemens, Doc Gooden, as well as Greg Luzinski, Ryne Sandberg, Julio Franco, Sid Fernandez, and Andy Van Slyke have, at one time or another, passed through the gates and played in an Eastern League stadium.

Eastern League Directory				
Club	**Affiliation**	**Stadium**	**Capacity**	**Age**
Binghamton Mets	New York Mets	Binghamton Municipal	6,000	1992
New Britain Rock Cats	Minnesota Twins	New Britain Stadium	6,100	1996
New Haven Ravens	Colorado Rockies	Yale Field	6,200	1927
Norwich Navigators	New York Yankees	Thomas J. Dodd Memorial	6,200	1994
Portland Sea Dogs	Florida Marlins	Hadlock Field	6,400	1994
Bowie Baysox	Baltimore Orioles	Prince George's County	10,000	1994
Akron Aeros	Cleveland Indians	Canal Park	9,000	1997
Harrisburg Senators	Montreal Expos	Riverside	6,300	1987
Reading Phillies	Philadelphia Phillies	Reading Municipal Memorial	8,000	1950
Trenton Thunder	Boston Red Sox	Mercer County Waterfront Park	6,400	1994

---

[1] Chadwick, *Baseball's Hometown Teams: The Story of the Minor Leagues*, Abbeville Press, New York.

[2] Adelson, Beaton, Koenig and Winston, *The Minor League Baseball Book*, Macmillan, New York (1995).

On the Road in the Eastern League

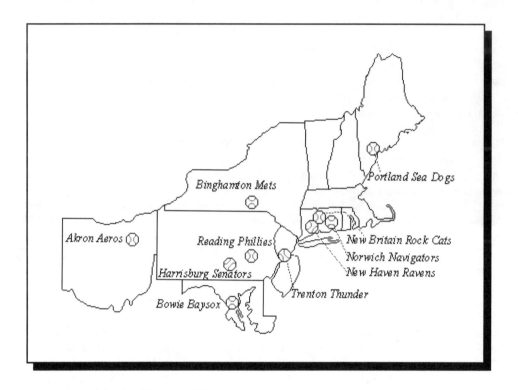

Eastern League Mileage Chart									
	BNG	BOW	AKR	HAR	NBR	NH	NOR	POR	REA	TRE
Binghamton	X	285	367	179	210	207	259	370	154	172
Bowie	285	X	349	109	335	310	362	553	133	167
Akron	367	349	X	289	537	524	571	744	345	431
Harrisburg	179	109	289	X	274	255	298	489	57	136
New Britain	210	335	537	274	X	35	47	215	231	167
New Haven	207	310	524	255	35	X	56	242	213	142
Norwich	259	362	571	298	47	56	X	339	195	205
Portland	370	553	744	489	215	242	339	X	446	384
Reading	154	133	345	57	231	213	195	446	X	78
Trenton	172	167	431	136	167	142	205	384	78	X

Source: Binghamton Mets Baseball Club (Mileage figures are approximate.)

Binghamton Mets

Team: **Binghamton Mets** (Northern Division)

Stadium: **Binghamton Municipal Stadium**

        Office Address: 211 Henry Street, Binghamton, N.Y. 13901
        Mailing Address: P.O. Box 598, Binghamton, N.Y. 13902
        Phone: (607) 723-METS
        Fax: (607) 723-7779
        Web Site(s):   http://www.spectra.net/mall/bmets

Team Ownership:

        Operated by: Binghamton Mets Baseball Club
        Principals: David Maines, William Maines, R.C. Reuteman (General Manager), George
                      Schere, Christopher Urda, Michael Urda (President)

Affiliation: New York Mets

Years in Eastern League: 1923-64; 1967-68; 1992-Present

Stadium Physical Characteristics:

        Age, Built in: 1992
        Stadium Owner: City of Binghamton

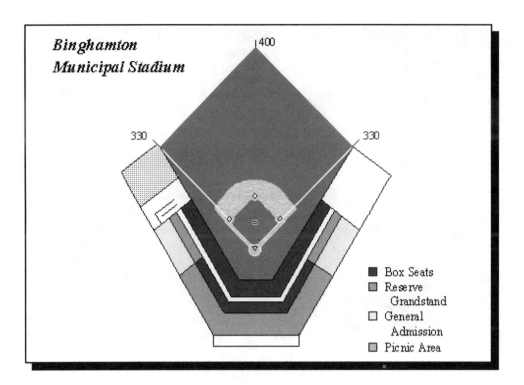

Binghamton
Municipal Stadium

400

330   330

■ Box Seats
■ Reserve
   Grandstand
□ General
   Admission
▨ Picnic Area

Bullpens: Behind the fences, and outside of foul territory. (Although not on the playing field, these
                 bullpens run parallel to the very ends of the foul lines and are visible from the stands.)

Playing Surface: Natural grass

Characteristics:

The fence around the outfield has two tiers to it. I noticed a number of gaps in the second tier, all
the way around. Through these gaps, you will see the occasional locomotive whistle by the
ballpark, several times during the course of a game. If you're concerned about avoiding foul balls,
the screens behind home plate extend all the way to the dugouts at Binghamton Municipal.
However, there is no overhead screen, so you still might be able to catch a few soft pop-ups.
Flags line the stands pretty much all the way around, so it's relatively easy to gauge which way the
wind blows during the game. Finally, Binghamton Municipal Stadium is a concrete park, and
probably one of the nicest buildings in all of Binghamton. The stadium rises from the field level
up a very slight incline, but still you'll feel high off the ground if you're seated in the upper
bleacher seats. Another characteristic of note is that there are no vertical divisions or gaps

between sections. That means you can walk uninterrupted around the entire stadium on the walkway between box seating and the reserved grandstands. In sum, no matter where you sit at Binghamton Municipal, you'll be close to the game.

Capacity: 6,000

	1995	1996
Attendance	200,077	206,589

1996 Average Attendance:
No. of openings 1996: 68
Daily Average 1996:   3,038

All Time Attendance Records:
Daily: 6,847 on July 3, 1995
Seasonal: 259,284 in 1992

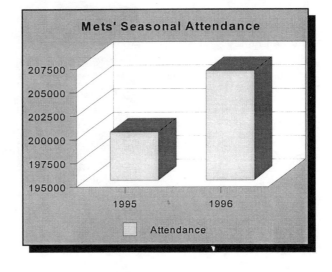

Skyboxes: Six (6)

Type of Seating: All seats at Binghamton Municipal Stadium are comfortable, have plenty of room, and include armrests. Cupholders available for Diamond Club members in box seating only. If you want to get really up close to the game, reserve a box seat. At Binghamton Municipal, Box Seating begins at field level and extends on the first level (Boxes 1 through 18) all the way from right field to left field, and on the second level (Boxes 100 through 108) from first base to third. Reserved Grandstand seating is just above Box Seating and also extends all the way around the stadium (Sections 110 through 114, and 200 through 208). Finally, General Admission seating is located in six sections behind the Reserve Grandstand from first base out to right field (Sections 210, 212, and 214), and from third base out to left field (Sections 209, 211, and 213).

Covered Seating:

Available high behind home plate, Reserve Grandstand sections, in a few rows near the Press Box. (Sections 200 through 206).

Restrooms:

Ladies: Two (2)
Men: Two (2)
Changing tables: Yes

**Customer Service
Window:**

Located on the concourse
behind home plate, near the
"On Deck Circle".

Smoking Policy:

Smoking not permitted in the
stands, however, during the
1996 season it was permitted
on the concession concourse.

First Aid:

Any fan injured or in need of
medical assistance should
promptly contact any member of the Mets staff or the nearest usher. A First Aid area is located behind
home plate on the first base concourse, and emergency medical service is provided by Lourdes Hospital
and United Health Services. Medical transport provided by Superior Ambulance Service.

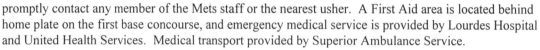

**Wheelchair
& Handicapped Seating:**   Yes. The concession areas near left and right field are both at ground
level. In addition, wheelchair and handicapped seating is available
behind Box 1 and 2. Handicapped seating tickets, as well as
companion seats, are for sale at the advance ticket windows.

Telephones: Two pay phones are located near the entrance gate in right field, and across from the "On
Deck Circle" on the third base concourse.

ATM: None.

Scoreboard: There is a graphic scoreboard located in right center field. Easy to read Binghamton's
scoreboard from anywhere in the stadium.

Game Clock: Digital clock located on
bottom of the scoreboard.

Sound: A quality sound system is
located around the tops of
the stands.

Sunsets?   The sun sets behind third
base.

Autographs: The home team players give
autographs before each
game along the first base
side.

Concessions and Souvenirs

Best stadium food:

By far the best stadium food at Binghamton, and for that matter, the entire Eastern League, are the Spiedies from Lupo's Spiedies Pit near right field. Spiedies are local to the Susquehanna Valley, and they were described to me best by the following jingle: "It's a tasty treat of marinated meat, charbroiled and fed on crispy Italian bread." It's hard to beat that description, but with no disrespect intended, the best way I

can describe this grilled delicacy is that it's like a shish-ka-bob sandwich. Hot off the grill, a spiedie is tender and juicy on the inside, with just the right amount of crispiness on the outside. You have your choice of either chicken or pork, and they can be served with peppers and onions. (This is a combination worth recommending.) You can spread a little sauce on your spiedie, but it's a dandy on its own. As a side, do yourself a favor and order the salt potatoes. They're hot; they're swimming in butter; and they're great!

As for other concession options, the Warner's Bullpen BBQ Area is usually reserved for group outings, however, after the ballgame begins, you'll find a fantastic menu of ethnic foods which also are worth the trip. Included on the Warner's menu are the following: German bratwurst, cheesebrats, Knockwurst & white hots; Polish Kielbasa, fried bologna, Piroghis & Holupki; Italian coiled sausage sandwich and meatball subs; Greek gyros; Western BBQ sandwich, and marinated BBQ chicken. You also find a nice selection of imported beers.

One last local item to look for, Binghamton serves up fresh and hot grilled pretzels at Vinnie's pretzel carts located around the concession concourse. If you like soft pretzels (and who doesn't?), they don't come any fresher than this!

Concessions

in stands: You'll find vendors serving the following items in the stands: Hot dogs, peanuts, cotton candy, beer and soda.

Hot Dog: The hot dogs served at Binghamton are all regular sized. (No foot longs) They are not grilled, but nevertheless, still remain juicy and hot on the inside. I found that the dog had faint hints of pepper or smoke which enhanced the flavor. All in all, Binghamton serves up some pretty good dogs.

Peanuts: $1.25 for regular; $2.25 for a large.

Beer: Two (2) beer limit per valid photo ID. Minimum drinking age is 21. Beer sales suspended at end of seventh (7th) inning.

On tap:	Labatt's, Molson Ice, Bud, Bud Light. (Three sizes available)
Bottles:	Sam Adams, Heineken, Beck, Peroni (Italian)
In stands:	Labatt's, Bud, Bud Light, Red Dog.
Microbrews:	Sam Adams.
Non-alcoholic:	Sharp's, Odoul's.
Wine:	Not available
Other:	Non-alcoholic pina coladas and daiquiris's are available at Lupo's Spiedie Pit.

Desserts: Soft serve ice cream cones; Souvenir helmet sundaes; cotton candy.

View of Field from Concession Stands:

There are primarily two concession areas at Binghamton Municipal Stadium where you can still watch the ballgame while you're waiting in line. That is Lupo's Spiedie Pit near right field, and Warner's Bullpen BBQ in left. Otherwise, most of the concessions are located underneath the stands, and if you find a line, unfortunately you will miss part of the game.

Best to go in between innings, or wait for a vendor to come to your section if you don't want to miss any of the action.

Picnics: Warner's Bullpen BBQ Picnic area is reserved for private outings 1 ½ hours prior to game time. However, the picnic area is then open to the public. There are also picnic tables located in Lupo's Spiedie's Pit along the right field line.

Gift Shop: The "On Deck Circle" is Binghamton Municipal Stadium's gift shop. Located behind home plate towards the third base side, the gift shop has an excellent selection of memorabilia, ranging from autographed souvenir balls to Binghamton Mets official windbreakers and sweaters. There is also a smaller souvenir window located along the first base concourse. In addition, when I was there in mid-July, the "On-Deck Circle" was conducting a clearance sale on a number of attractive souvenir items. Take some time between innings to browse through Binghamton's "On Deck Circle." The "On Deck Circle" is also open during the season from 10 a.m. to 6 p.m Monday through Friday.

Admission*:

Prices	
General Admission	$4.50
Reserved Grandstand	$5.50
Box Seats	$6.50

Special rates for Kids and Seniors:

Senior citizens 60 and over, as well as children 14 and under receive a $1.00 discount per ticket.

Season Ticket Plans Available:

$390.00 per season for all 71 Mets home games gives you admission as a Diamond Club member. This is a 15% savings off ticket prices. You'll receive special privileges including exchange of unused ticket for general admission on Diamond Club nights, cup holders in the box seats, free subscription to "Box Seat" newsletter, V.I.P. card, annual Diamond Club Cookout with players, specialized Diamond Club merchandise.

Group Information:

Group Rates:

Special group rates are available for groups of 25 or more, from Sunday through Thursday. For larger groups of 100 or more, Friday and Saturday dates are available. Your group will be acknowledged by the Mets on the scoreboard in right center field, and also over the stadium sound system, and your group leader will be entitled to two complimentary tickets to a future Mets game.

Group discount rates:	
Box Seats:	$5.50
Reserved Grandstand:	$4.50
Early Bird group discounts (April and May only):	
Box Seats:	$4.50
Reserved Grandstand:	$3.50

Picnic Area: Groups of 25 or more may also schedule an all-you-can-eat barbecue picnic at the Warner's Bullpen BBQ Picnic Area along the left field line. The picnic starts when the gates open, 1 ½ hours prior to game time, and conclude at the scheduled starting time.

Three menus are available:

Hot Dogs	$6.95
Hamburgers and Hot Dogs	$8.95
Chicken, Hamburgers and Hot Dogs	$10.95

There is a $2.00 discount for Children 14 and under.

Included are a choice of salad (potato, macaroni, or cole slaw), potato chips, watermelon, and unlimited soft drinks. You may also purchase beer at a special discount. Menu prices do not include the price of a game ticket.

Ticket orders for all groups have to be made at least one week prior to the game, and the Mets request you have a firm number commitment at that time. No later than 48 hours prior to the game, your group leader must pay for and pick up the tickets by cash or check only. Group tickets are non-refundable and non-exchangeable. Group rates not available Opening Day, fireworks, Fan Appreciation Day, exhibitions, playoffs, or other restricted games.

Special Ticket Plans:

Birthday Parties:

The Mets are proud to offer special birthday plans for children's groups. The birthday package includes a reserved seat ticket, helmet ice cream sundae, hot dog and soda, and a Mets souvenir. In addition, the birthday child takes the field with a Mets mascot in between innings so the crowd can sing 'Happy Birthday'. The cost is $10.00 per child with 8 children minimum.

Field of Dreams:

Little league teams are encouraged to contact the Mets to schedule a special day at Binghamton Municipal Stadium. The Little Leaguers are invited into the dugout to meet the Mets just prior to the ballgame. Then, your young players accompany the Mets out onto the field during the playing of our National Anthem. Truly, a special opportunity for any young baseball fan.

[***1996 Data: Prices subject to change. Call (607) 723-METS for more information.**]

Ticket Sales:

Address: P.O. Box 598, Binghamton, NY 13902
Phone: (607) 773-TIXX ($1.00 service charge)
Credit Cards: Visa, MasterCard

Hours Ticket Window Open:

Advance ticket windows are open at Binghamton Municipal from 10 a.m. to 6 p.m. Monday through Friday. When the Mets are at home, hours are extended, and the windows will also be open Saturdays and Sundays.

Mets tickets are non-refundable and non-exchangeable.

Rain Check Policy:

"In the event 4 ½ innings are not

played on any given date due to inclement weather (3 ½ innings for a 7 inning game), tickets may be exchanged for any non-restricted regular season game, based on availability. No Cash Refunds will be given."

Game times:

Weekdays:	7:00 p.m.
Saturday:	April-June 1: 1:30 p.m.; June 1-September: 7:00 p.m.
Sunday:	1:30 p.m.

(See schedule for day games. All game times subject to change.)

Time Gates open:

1 ½ hours before game time.

Parking: Parking at Binghamton Municipal Stadium is $3.00 per car. If an official game is not played because of rain or other inclement weather, parking vouchers may be exchanged for another regular season game, depending upon availability. No Cash Refunds .

Other

For the kids:

Find out how fast you can throw at the Speed Pitch Cage along the right field concourse.

All kids 14 and under are invited to become members of Buddy's Knot-Hole Gang. For 1996, your $10.00 membership got you admission to every regular season Sunday home game; a special edition Buddy t-shirt; membership card; newsletter; and participation in pre-game educational seminars and an annual baseball clinic. Call 723-METS for more information.

Promotions and Giveaways:

In 1996, the Binghamton Mets hosted a vast array of promotional nights and special giveaways. There were seven scheduled nights of post-game fireworks spread throughout the season. In addition, the Mets gave out schedule magnets, batting helmets, bats, baseballs, team photos, lapel pins, sports bags, Sunday caps, beer tankards, checkbook covers, baseball gloves, mini bats and much more at scheduled home games.

In 1996, every Tuesday was Two for

Tuesday sponsored by Labatt Beer, Pepsi and WKGB. Every Wednesday was Kellogg's Raisin Bran night, where fans could cash in two box tops of Kellogg's Raisin Bran with $2.00 for four tickets to any Wednesday home game. Every Saturday during the season, except fireworks nights, kids could run the bases during the Sylvan Learning Center Fun Run Around the Bases. And finally, every Sunday in 1996, special promotions were held for members of Buddy's Knot-Hole Gang. Check the Binghamton Mets Schedule for updated promotions during future seasons.

In between innings:

There are a number of special contests in between innings at every Binghamton Mets home game. If you're lucky, you'll be picked for the "Let's Make a Deal" contest and have the chance to win some fabulous, and quite expensive, prizes. Other on-field contests include a dizzy bat contest and a race around the bases with Buddy.

However, if you want the best chance to win a prize, you'll need to purchase a Binghamton Mets Souvenir Program. Contained inside every program are Lucky Numbers stamped on random advertisement pages. If your Lucky Number matches the one announced periodically between innings over the sound system, you can pick up your prize at the Customer Service Window located on the concourse behind home plate.

What song played during 7th inning stretch?

"Take Me Out to the Ballgame"

Radio Station Broadcasting Game: WNBF 1290 AM

Eastern League Information:

League Standings and the Starting Lineups for the game are posted on the concourse wall behind home plate on the first base side.

Binghamton's Mascots: Buddy the Bee and Ballwinkle

Team Information

Binghamton Mets
(Northern Division)

History:

Baseball in the Binghamton area dates as far back as 1892 with the original team known as the Bingo's. That team moved to what is now Johnson City and became the Triple Cities, shortened in later years to the Triplets. The Triplets played at Johnson Field, built in 1913, named after George F. Johnson, Endicott-Johnson founder. Games were played at Johnson Field until 1968, when the state demolished the historic stadium in order to build the eastbound lanes of Route 17. But there were many great seasons at Johnson Field, and the Triplets became an affiliate of the New York Yankees soon after the installation of one of the first lighting systems in professional sports back in 1932. A number of great ballplayers played in the Susquehanna Valley before being called up to The Show, the most famous of which have to be Hall of Famer's Wee Willie Keeler and Whitey Ford, who played a stellar season here in 1949, as well as Eddie Sawyer, Tommy Holmes and Bill Hallahan.

Baseball returned after 24 years to the city when Binghamton Municipal was built for a mere $3.9 million in 1992 and the franchise moved from Williamsport, PA. Since that time, well over twenty Binghamton Mets have made the transition to major league ball, including such notables as Jason Isringhausen, Curtis Pride, Edgardo Alfonzo, Bobby Jones, Alberto Castillo, Bill Pulshiper, and Butch Huskey. Other big leaders who have walked through the locker rooms at Binghamton Municipal include Doc Gooden, Sid Fernandez, and Ryan Thompson, all sent here during rehab.

Eastern League Championships:

1994 Eastern League Champions

    Binghamton over Harrisburg (3 games to 1)

1992 Eastern League Champions

    Binghamton over Canton-Akron (3 games to 2)

(1996:   Binghamton reached the Semifinals, defeated by Portland (3 games to 2))

AA All Stars:

1994: Binghamton Municipal Stadium hosted AA All-Star Game

Notable Players who went on to the Major League:

Jason Isringhausen (1994, '95); Curtis Pride (1992); Edgardo Alfonzo (1994); Bobby Jones (1992); Alberto Castillo (1994); Bill Pulshiper (1994); Butch Huskey (1993); Doc Gooden (rehab -1994); Sid Fernandez (rehab - 1993); Ryan Thompson (rehab -1995).

New York Mets Minor League Organization			
Team	**League**	**Level**	**City & Phone**
New York Mets	National League	Major League	Flushing, NY (718) 507-TIXX
Norfolk Tides	International League	AAA	Norfolk, VA (804) 622-2222
Binghamton Mets	Eastern League	AA	Binghamton, NY (607) 723-6387
St. Lucie Mets	Florida State League	A	Port St. Lucie, FL (407) 871-2100
Capital City Bombers	South Atlantic League	A	Columbia, SC (803) 256-4110
Pittsfield Mets	New York-Penn League	Short A	Pittsfield, MA (413) 499-6387
Kingsport Mets	Appalachian League	Rookie	Kingsport, TN (423) 378-3744
Gulf Coast Mets	Gulf Coast League	Rookie	Port St. Lucie, FL (407) 871-2132
Dominican LGE Mets	Dominican Summer League	Rookie	Santo Domingo, Dominican Republic.

Approximate distance from Binghamton Municipal to Shea Stadium: 182
(Source: Rand McNally TripMaker, Version 1.1 1994; Binghamton, NY to New York, NY.)

Mascot(s):   Buddy the Bee and Ballwinkle
Team Colors: Light navy and warm red.
Visiting
Hotel: Holiday Inn Arena, 2-8 Hawley St., Binghamton, NY 13901 (607) 722-1212

Fan Club: Binghamton Mets Booster Club, P.O. Box 26, Castle Creek, NY 13744

Directions to stadium:

Exit 4S off I-81, take New York Route 7 south. Follow towards U.S. Route 11, turn on Henry Street. Binghamton Municipal is located at 211 Henry Street, at the corner of Henry and Fayette.

Binghamton/Cooperstown

Background

Although Binghamton, New York (1990 Pop. 53,008) and Cooperstown, New York (1980 Pop. 2342) are not usually considered in the same breath, I figured how complete could an Eastern League travel guide be without mentioning Cooperstown, considering that its National Baseball Hall of Fame is only about an hour and a half away from Binghamton Municipal Stadium? What baseball fan could pass up that sort of a prospect? Therefore, this chapter is divided in two. In keeping with the overall spirit of this book, Binghamton is discussed first, then the second half of the chapter is devoted to Cooperstown.

Broome County Court House, Binghamton, New York.

Binghamton, the Broome County seat, is an industrial city located in what's locally referred to as a "Valley of Opportunity" near the beautiful Chenango and Susquehanna Rivers. It was first settled in 1785 as Chenango Point, and then was named for Senator William Bingham (PA), who owned land in the region. In 1837, economic prosperity grew as Binghamton first was connected to Utica and the Erie Canal, and then even more so when the railroad arrived in 1848. The canals were so important to local commerce that what is now State Street in downtown was originally a canal until 1875. It was during this boom time when industries in the Triple Cities of Binghamton, Johnson City, and Endicott produced footwear, cigars, finished goods, furniture, wagons, and carriages. Throughout the Industrial Age and on into the early twentieth century, the region saw the first flight simulator invented here by Edwin A. Link, Endicott Johnson shoes became a household name, and a small company called the Bundy Time Recording Company from Endicott became International Business Machines (IBM). Today, the major industry seems to revolve around support of the State University of New York at Binghamton, founded in 1965.

As for sightseeing possibilities before the ballgame, I'll just say that if it's rainy out, downtown Binghamton is no picnic. However, when the sun is shining, and if you enjoy marveling at historic buildings, Binghamton is the city for you. With a twelve block area of downtown listed on the National Register of Historic Places, every which way you turn, you're surrounded by fantastically restored buildings from the 19th century. You can also see historic Washington Street Bridge, one of the last, and the longest triple parabolic arch bridges left in New York.

Finally, sporting and recreation have always played an important role to the valley. Not only home to the two-time Eastern League champion Binghamton Mets, in the 1950's the Triplets played at historic Johnson Field (since torn down to make way for a freeway), and that team included such Hall of Famer's as Whitey Ford and Thurman Munson. As for golf, the Broome County B.C. Open has been drawing golf lovers to the area for over twenty five years. And finally, Broome County is known as the "Carousel Capital of the World." This accolade goes back to the touching generosity of George F. Johnson. As a child from a poor family, George F. was denied a ride on a carousel in his youth. When he finally made his fortune in later years, he donated six beautiful carousels to the region and decreed that rides would be free in perpetuity. Therefore, you and your children can still enjoy George F's legacy at any of six parks located throughout Broome County.

Old Perry Building, now M&T Bank - One of the few remaining all cast iron buildings in the United States. U.S. Dept. Of Interior Historic Site.

Information

Chamber of Commerce/Tourist Bureau

Broome County Convention & Visitors Bureau/Broome County Chamber of Commerce
P.O. Box 995TG
Binghamton, NY 13902-0995
(607) 772-8945 or (800) 836-6740

Web Site(s):

http://www.spectra.net/bcc

Daytime Entertainment

Museums and Zoo

Ross Park Zoo
60 Morgan Road
Binghamton, NY 13903
(607) 724-5461 or (607) 724-5454

Fifth oldest zoo in United States. American Bison, Cougar, Arctic Fox, Timber Wolves, Endangered Red Wolves, Endangered Spectacled Bears, Endangered Bald Eagle, Siberian Tiger, Rocky Mountain Goats. Carousel, concessions, gift shop.

April through October, 10 a.m. - 5 p.m.

Discovery Center of the Southern Tier
60 Morgan Road
Binghamton, NY 13903
(607) 773-8661

This hands- on museum for the children include exhibits on markets, retail stores, ecology, geology, archaeology, dentists, and fire station. Classes, special events, museum store.

Summer Hours: Mon. to Sat. 10 a.m. - 5 p.m.; Sun. Noon - 5 p.m.

Roberson Museum and Science Center
30 Front Street
Binghamton, NY 13905-4779
(607) 772-0660

Regional museum exhibits art, folk art, history, science and technology. 19th century mansion, planetarium, theater, research library & shop.

Parks and Carousels

Broome County Carousel Parks

There are six carousels located throughout the Susquehanna Valley which offer free rides thanks to the beneficence of George F. Johnson (1857-1948). All the classic wood carved carousels, or merry-go-rounds, were built by the Allan Herschell Company in a country fair style. The six carousels are located in the following parks:

C. Fred Johnson Park

C.F.J. Boulevard, Johnson City, NY
(607) 797-9098

Largest carousel listed here includes 72 figures, 4 abreast. Installed in 1923. Most decorative carvings, pagoda-style house. Fountains pavilion, tennis courts, ballfield, playground. Summer carousel hours: Weekends Noon - 8 p.m.; Weekdays from Memorial Day to mid-June 4 p.m. - 8 p.m.

George W. Johnson Park

Oak Hill Avenue, Endicott, NY
(607) 757-2427

1934 installation, restored 1994. Carousel has 36 horses, 2 chariots. Swimming pool, picnics, ballfield, playground. Carousel hours Noon - 5 p.m., 6 p.m. to 8:15 p.m.

West Endicott Park

Page Avenue, Endicott, NY
(607) 754-5595

From 1929, carousel includes 36 animals with one pig and one dog. Kiddie pool, tennis courts, playground, picnic area. Carousel hours 10 a.m. - Noon, 12:30 p.m. - 5 p.m., 5:30 p.m. - 8:30 p.m.

Recreation Park

Beethoven St., Binghamton, NY
(607) 722-9166 or (607) 772-7017

60 jumping horses, chariots, and original Wurlitzer Military Band Organ with bells from 1925. George F. Johnson statue, Rod Serling Memorial, pools, tennis courts, playground. Summer carousel hours: Memorial Day to mid-June, Weekdays 3 p.m. - 7:45 p.m., Weekends Noon - 7:45 p.m.; mid-June to Labor Day, Noon - 7:45 p.m.

Ross Park

Morgan Road, Binghamton, NY
(607) 724-5461

From circa 1920, restored carousel has 60 jumping horses, 2 chariots with one monkey, restored Wurlitzer Military Band Organ. Zoo, museums, playground, picnic pavilion. Summer carousel hours: Noon - 5 p.m.

Highland Park

Hooper Road, Endwell, NY
(607) 754-5595

1925 carousel was relocated from En-Joie Park, 36 animals includes one pig and one dog. Swimming pool, picnic area, playground, tennis courts, volleyball, horseshoes. Carousel hours: 10 a.m. - Noon, 12:30 p.m. - 5 p.m., 5:30 p.m. - 8:30- p.m.

Chenango Valley State Park

153 State Park Road
Chenango Forks, NY 13746
(607) 648-5251

This beautiful park, no more
than twenty minutes or so
north of downtown, is a real
find. In fact, I thought it was
so nice, you might seriously
consider camping for your
local accommodations. The
park was officially opened in
1930 and spans over 1,000
acres. There are two glacial
ponds, Lily Lake and
Chenango Lake. During the season, swimming, fishing, and small boat rentals are permitted on Chenango
Lake. There is a great 18 hole golf course, with all the amenities including a clubhouse and restaurant.
Picnic areas and pavilions, playgrounds, and nature trails.

Public Golf courses and Sports Park

Chenango Valley State Park Golf Course

153 State Park Road
Chenango Forks, NY 13746

(607) 648-9804

18 hole golf course first built in 1935, located in Chenango Valley State Park. Tee times
accepted three days in advance, Pro Shop opens at 7 a.m., can call at 6 a.m. Clubhouse,
restaurant, locker rooms, driving range, practice green. Statistics:

Blue Yardage 6271, Rating 69.95, Slope 124, Par 72
White Yardage 5878, Rating 68.9, Slope 120, Par 72
Red Yardage 5246, Rating 69.5, Slope 120, Par 73

Ely Park Golf Course

Mount Prospect, Ridge Road
Binghamton, NY
(607) 772-7231

18 holes overlooking downtown
Binghamton. Restaurant, locker rooms,
driving range, practice greens, only
course in the city. Call for directions.
Statistics:

Blue Yardage 5637, Par 70
White Yardage 5292, Par 70
Red Yardage 4925, Par 73

Conklin Players Club

1520 Conklin Road
Conklin, NY 13748
(607) 775-3042

1991 18 hole course designed by Rick Rickard. Tee times accepted two weeks in advance, Pro shop opens 7 a.m. Driving range, clubhouse. Statistics:

Blue Yardage 6772, Rating 72.5, Slope 127, Par 72
White Yardage 6128, Rating 69.5, Slope 121, Par 72
Red Yardage 4699, Rating 67.8, Slope 116, Par 72

Conklin Sports Park

942 Conklin Road
Conklin, NY
(607) 771-7526

Only four miles from downtown, this large and open recreational park includes Grand Prix go-karts, golf lessons and driving range, miniature golf, indoor batting cages, indoor basketball court, Pro Shop, nearby spiedie and ice cream shop.

Open 11 a.m. - 11 p.m.

Ely Park Golf Course

Shopping Malls/Outlets

Oakdale Mall

Harry L. Drive
Johnson City, NY
(607) 798-9388

JC Penney, Sear's, Bradlee's, The Bon Ton, Montgomery Ward, and over 100 specialty stores, restaurants.

Hours: Mon. - Sat. 10 a.m. - 9 p.m.; Sun. 9 a.m. - 9 p.m.

Seasonal Events

Dates are approximate, contact regional tourism offices listed above for updated schedule information.

Friday afternoon Farmer's Market on Court Street, downtown

May: Two Rivers Ethnic Festival, Sunday in the Parks

June: Vestal Festival, Greek Festival, Carousel Festival

Lunchtime near the Court House, downtown Binghamton

July: JulyFest, Fourth of July Extravaganza, Broome County Fair, Sounds on the Susquehanna, Spiedie Fest & Balloon Rally (featuring Hot Air Balloon Launches, Antique-Classic-Streetrod-Motorcycle Show, and Spiedie Cooking Contest)

August: Annual Chris Thater Memorial Criterium, Frito-Lay Pro-Tennis Tournament, Irish Festival, AMA National Moto-Cross Championship

Accommodations/Other

Hotels and Motels

Visiting Hotel for the Binghamton Mets :

Holiday Inn Arena
2-8 Hawley St.
Binghamton, NY 13901
(607) 722-1212 or (800) HOLIDAY
Restaurant & Lounge, Indoor Pool, Complimentary use of YMCA, pets ok, shops, Entertainment discounts (Also, on summer Friday nights after the game, join over 1,000 people for live music and dancing at the ever-popular Party on the Patio.)

Best Western Binghamton Regency
Hotel & Conference Center
One Sarbro Square
Binghamton, NY 13901
(607) 722-7575 or (800) 723-7676
Restaurant & Lounge, Indoor Pool, workout room, sauna

Historic Hotel de Ville
80 State Street
Binghamton, NY 13901
(607) 722-0000
Restaurant & Lounge, pets ok, Entertainment discounts. (Originally City Hall, built in 1897. Across street from popular nightclubs, bars and restaurants.)

Holiday Inn at the University
4105 Vestal Parkway East
Vestal, NY 13850
(607) 729-6371 or (800) HOLIDAY
Restaurant & Lounge, Outdoor Pool, pets ok. (Near SUNY)

Residence Inn by Marriott
4610 Vestal Parkway East
Vestal, NY 13850
(607) 770-8500
Continental breakfast, Outdoor Pool, kitchens. (Near SUNY)

Days Inn
1000 Front Street
Binghamton, NY 13905
(607) 724-3297
Continental breakfast, Outdoor Pool, pets
ok. (North of downtown.)

Comfort Inn
1156 Front Street
Binghamton, NY 13905
(607) 722-5353
Continental breakfast, pets ok. (North of downtown.)

Campgrounds

Chenango Valley State Park
153 State Park Road
Chenango Forks, NY 13746
(607) 648-5251

216 Trailer and Tent campsites, 51
w/elec., bathrooms with hot showers
nearby, trailer dump stn. 24 Cabins, 9
w/fireplace, rest with wood stove, elec.,
cold wtr., ref., gas cook stove, toilets.
Beach, nature trails, 18 hole golf, boat rentals, playgrounds. Convenience store before entrance.

New York State Camping Reservation System: (800) 456-CAMP

Hospitals

Binghamton General Hospital
10-42 Mitchell Avenue
Binghamton, NY 13903
(607) 762-2200

Transportation

Binghamton Regional Airport	(607) 763-4471
Greyhound Bus	(607) 724-5542
Short Line Bus	(607) 722-7553
Avis Rent a Car	(607) 729-6001
Enterprise Rental	(607) 748-5005
National Car Rental	(607) 797-2417
Thrifty Car Rental	(607) 723-7368

Cooperstown

Background

Located in the heart of Leatherstocking country, Cooperstown, New York is a quaint summertime village nestled up against the fragile beauty of Otsego Lake, the headwaters of the Susquehanna River. The town was settled in the 1780's by the father of the American novelist, James Fenimore Cooper, author of *The Last of the Mohicans* (1826), among other works. A popular tourist destination, the streets of Cooperstown retain a real Victorian-era charm with its delightful shops and restaurants, romantic inns, and, of course, its modern museums. For as every baseball fan knows, Cooperstown is home to the National Baseball Hall of Fame and Museum. It is also the focus of an ongoing historic controversy over the game. Many believe Abner Doubleday invented baseball here in 1839, which is the primary reason the Hall of Fame was established here one hundred years later in 1939. However, just as many people, or even more, believe that the game of baseball didn't begin until the first recorded game was played on June 19, 1846 at Elysian Fields in Hoboken, New Jersey. But, this book is not about settling that great debate, it's a guide for fans of the game. And, there's just no more marvelous a place than Cooperstown for you and the entire family to revel in fantastic baseball memories.

Information

Chamber of Commerce/Tourist Bureau

Cooperstown Chamber of Commerce

31 Chestnut Street
Cooperstown, NY 13326
(607) 547-9983

The Chamber publishes an excellent and thoroughly comprehensive 72 page Visitors' Guide and I recommend you call ahead for your free copy.

Web Site(s):   http://cooperstown.net

Daytime Entertainment

Museums

The National Baseball Hall of Fame and Museum

(Baseball Hall of Fame Continued)
P.O. Box 590
25 Main Street
Cooperstown, NY 13326
(607) 547-7200

The ultimate baseball experience for any fan, you'll lose yourself in these amazing hallways as you remember all the great heroes of the diamond. From Lou Gehrig's locker to future Hall of Famer Cal Ripken's jersey, the displays are not only historic, but also surprisingly current at the same time. You'll see three floors of baseball wonder and magic, in addition to the revered plaques of all the legendary inductees enshrined in the Hall of Fame Gallery. My favorites, of course, were the third level displays on The Minor Leagues, and the history and development of the modern Ballpark, but you'll find your own favorite among such exhibits as: the Longest Games; No-Hit Games; Baseball at the Movies; Scribes & Mikemen; the Records Room; Today's Stars; Babe Ruth and Hank Aaron; Women in Baseball; Negro Leagues; Scouts; the Evolution of the Uniform; Baseball Music; Baseball Cards; and finally, the multi-media baseball presentation in the new Grandstand Theatre.

National Baseball Library & Archive
(607) 547-0313

Includes comprehensive research materials on baseball. Literature, periodicals, newspapers, statistics, autographs, scorecards, poetry, recordings, film, video and microfilm. Open to the general public, however due to limited research space, advance appointments are recommended. Library & Archive open Monday through Friday 9 a.m. to 5 p.m.

Hall of Fame Museum Shop
(607) 547-2445 or (888) HALL-OF-FAME

Includes an extensive collection of baseball souvenir memorabilia and great gift ideas. Call for a free catalog.

Hall of Fame Hours:

May through September: 9 a.m. - 9 p.m.;

October through April: 9 a.m. - 5 p.m.;

Fall Weekends:

October through December:
Fri. & Sat. 9 a.m. - 8 p.m.

(Closed Thanksgiving, Christmas & New Year's)

Fenimore House Museum and the American Indian Wing

Lake Road, P.O. Box 800
Cooperstown, NY 13326
(607) 547-1400

Neo-Georgian mansion dating from the 1930's, this museum includes displays on the family of James Fenimore Cooper, vast collection of American folk art, paintings from the Hudson River School, rare books, vintage photographs, and American quilts. The American Indian Wing displays from the over 700 piece Eugene and Clare Thaw Collection of American Indian Art. Exhibits cover the Eastern Woodland, Northwest Coast, Eskimo, Great Lakes, Southwest and Prairie Native American cultures.
Spring/Summer Hours: April Tues. - Sun. 10 a.m. - 4 p.m.; May Daily 10 a.m. - 4 p.m.; June to Labor Day 9 a.m. - 5 p.m.; Labor Day through Oct. 31 10 a.m. - 4 p.m.

The Farmer's Museum and the Village Crossroads

Lake Road, P.O. Box 800
Cooperstown, NY 13326
(607) 547-1450

Farmstead working museum, recreating rural life from the mid-19th century. Workshops and presentations, hands-on activities for children, special events. Located one mile from center of town on Lake Road/Route 80.
Spring/Summer Hours: April Tues. - Sun. 10 a.m. - 4 p.m.; May Daily 10 a.m. - 4 p.m.; June to Labor Day 9 a.m. - 5 p.m.; Labor Day through Oct. 31 10 a.m. - 4 p.m.

Performing Arts

Glimmerglass Opera

Route 80
P.O. Box 191
Cooperstown, NY 13326
(607) 547-2255

Summer opera festival runs from late-June through August at the 920 seat, Alice Busch Opera Theater, located about eight miles north of town. Call for schedule.

Public Golf course

Leatherstocking Golf Course

The Otesaga Resort
Nelson Avenue
Cooperstown, NY 13326
(607) 547-5275

18 holes resort golf course opened in 1909 and was designed by Devereux Emmet. Rated 4 stars by 1996-7 Golf Digest. Public welcome, but will pay more in greens fees than resort guests. Pro Shop opens at 7 a.m., tee times accepted six days in advance, practice green, restaurants. Statistics:

> Blue Yardage 6324, Rating 71.0, Slope 124, Par 72
> White Yardage 6053, Rating 69.3, Slope 120, Par 72
> Red Yardage 5254, Rating 69.2, Slope 116, Par 72

Miniature Golf

Cooperstown Fun Park
Route 28
Cooperstown, NY
(607) 547-2767
Mini- golf, driving range, go-karts, bumper boats, arcade. Summer Open 11 a.m. - 11 p.m.

Lake Tours

Classic Boat Tours
Fair Street
Cooperstown, NY
(607) 547-5295

One hour tour of Lake Otsego. Charters and catering available upon request. From Mid-May through Columbus Day, call for hours.

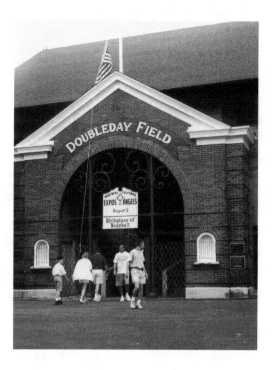

Seasonal Events

Dates are approximate, contact National Baseball Hall of Fame, or the Cooperstown Chamber of Commerce for updated schedule information. Note: On select Saturdays and weekends throughout the summer, local and semi-pro baseball games take place at Doubleday Field.

August: Baseball Hall of Fame Induction Ceremonies; Hall of Fame Game at Doubleday Field

Accommodations/Other

As discussed elsewhere in this edition of the guide, listing of accommodations primarily focuses on hotel lodging, just because of entirely subjective purposes at this time. I have only listed five hotels and inns below, but by no means are these the only places to stay in the village. There are over two dozen

hotels and motels in the area, and around a half-dozen areas to camp such as Glimmerglass State Park. However, of all the towns covered in this book, I think you should consider a Bed & Breakfast as your choice accommodations in Cooperstown. Many of them are not only charming, and hopefully romantic, but also, most of the B&B's are centrally located so you can walk to all the major attractions and restaurants in town.

Cooperstown has over thirty five Bed & Breakfasts for your consideration, and they are all listed and carefully described in the Cooperstown Chamber of Commerce Visitors' Guide, available free by calling the Chamber at (607) 547-9983. (Once you obtain that guide, as a general rule I'd recommend you focus your attention on those lodgings located closest to the heart of this historic village. Hopefully, future editions of this guide will include updated information on Cooperstown B & B's.)

Hotels and Inns

Otesaga Resort Hotel
60 Lake Street
Cooperstown, NY 13326-0311
(607) 547-9931 or (800) 348-6222
Lakeside Resort hotel, Restaurants & Lounge, Golf Course, heated outdoor pool, tennis courts, sports center access, game room.

The Cooper Inn
Main & Chestnut Streets
P.O. Box 311
Cooperstown, NY 13326
(607) 547-2567 or (800) 348-6222
Complimentary continental breakfast, twenty rooms, all Otesaga Resort facilities available to Cooper Inn guests.

Best Western Inn at the Commons
Route 28, Commons Drive
Cooperstown, NY 13326
(607) 547-9439 or (800) 528-1234
Complimentary Continental Breakfast, heated indoor pool, whirlpool, exercise facilities, laundry, game room. (Built in 1994, only 3 ½ miles south of town.)

The Inn at Cooperstown
16 Chestnut Street
Cooperstown, NY 13326-1041
(607) 547-5756
Complimentary continental breakfast, 17 guest rooms with private baths, off street parking.

Bassett House Inn
32 Fair Street
Cooperstown, NY 13326
(607) 547-7001
Continental breakfast, restored inn across street from Hall of Fame, private baths.

Hospital

Bassett Healthcare
1 Atwell Road
Cooperstown, NY 13326
(607) 547-3456

Transportation

Park and Ride the Trolley
Cooperstown Village Offices
Cooperstown, NY
(607) 547-2411

During the summer, parking is scarce in the village so it is highly recommended that you take park outside of town and ride the trolley. Look for the signs on Routes 28 and 80 to the trolley parking lots. Weekends from Memorial Day through end of June, daily from end of June to Labor Day, weekends from Labor Day to Columbus Day. Hours: 8:30 a.m. to 9 p.m.

Directions to Cooperstown

Located in central New York on southern shore of Lake Otsego, one hour northeast from Binghamton, seventy miles west of Albany, thirty miles south of the N.Y. State Thruway.

From west: Exit 30 off N.Y. State Thruway (I-90), take Route 28 South.

From east: Exit 25A off N.Y. State Thruway, I-88 to Route 20 West, follow 20 West to Route 80 West to Cooperstown.

From south: Take I-88 East to Oneonta, then Route 28 North.

New Britain Rock Cats

Team: **New Britain Rock Cats** (Northern Division)

Stadium: **New Britain Stadium**

    Office Address: New Britain Stadium, Willow Brook Park, South Main Street, New Britain, CT.

    Mailing Address: P.O. Box 1718, New Britain, CT. 06050

    Phone: (860) 224-8383

    Fax: (860) 225-6267

    Web Site(s):   http://gs1.com/Rock/Cats.html; http://www.klx.com/guide/hardware_city.html; http://www.minorleaguebaseball.com/teams/hardware-city/; http://www.courant.com/sports/minor/rocprev.htm

Team Ownership:

    Operated by: Buzas Enterprises, Inc.

    Principals: Joe Buzas, Chairman; Gerald R. Berthiaume, VP-General Manager

Affiliation: Minnesota Twins (Since 1995)

Years in Eastern League: 1983-Present

Stadium Physical Characteristics

    Age, Built in: 1996

    Stadium Owner: City of New Britain, CT. and State of Connecticut

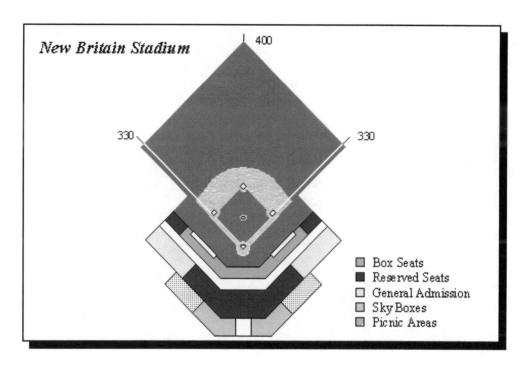

New Britain Stadium

400

330   330

☐ Box Seats
■ Reserved Seats
☐ General Admission
☐ Sky Boxes
▨ Picnic Areas

Bullpens: Inside the fences, and in foul territory.

Playing Surface: Natural grass

Characteristics:

New Britain Stadium is a great venue for watching a professional baseball game. With the exception of Canal Park in Akron, New Britain Stadium is the newest stadium in the Eastern League and it shows. All the views of the field are unobstructed; the state of the art scoreboard features quality graphic and video displays; the stands are clean, comfortable and easily accessible; and the field is kept in immaculate condition by a thorough and dedicated grounds crew. New Britain Stadium is also a fantastic

place for group outings. Groups of 25 or more have the option of reserving one of two picnic areas located along either the first base and third base lines. Although these picnic areas are at the top of the stands, this is actually much closer to the field than other stadiums where you'll usually find the picnic grounds way out in the outfield. In fact, New Britain Stadium ranks right up there as one of the better stadiums for groups in the entire league.

Capacity: 6,200

	1995	1996
Attendance	124,560	160,765

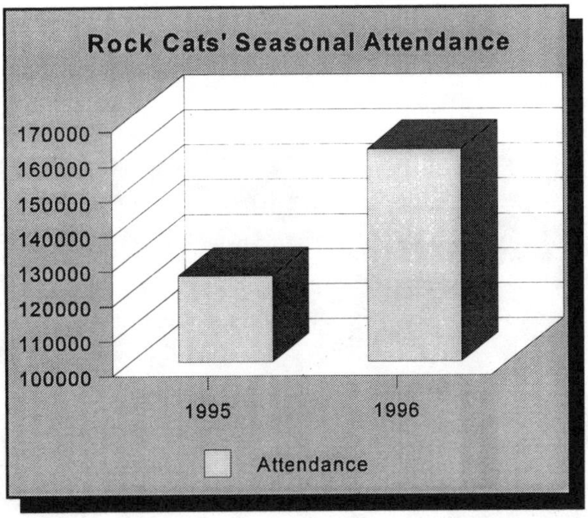

1996 Average Attendance:

Number of openings: 62
1996 Daily Average: 2,593

All Time Attendance Records:
Daily: 6,146 on April 12, 1996
(Opening Day at New Britain Stadium)

Seasonal: 160,765 in 1996

Skyboxes: 12

Rock Cats' Seasonal Attendance

Type of Seating: New Britain has some very comfortable seating available in both the Field Box Seats and Reserved Seating. Wide and somewhat roomy, all the seats in these sections provide armrests. General admission areas provide aluminum bleachers.

Covered Seating: Limited covered seating is available high behind home plate in the Reserved Sections. The concession concourse area under the stands also provides cover.

Restrooms:
Ladies: 2 (with 35 separate fixtures)
Men: 2 (with 35 separate fixtures)
Changing tables: Yes. There is also a Family Restroom located near the First Aid office behind home plate.

Customer Service Window: Located near the Rock Cats Souvenir Store behind home plate. Open after the third inning.

Smoking Policy:

Smoking is not permitted in the stands at New Britain Stadium. However, two areas are reserved for smoking, one out past the Rock Cats Clubhouse near right field, the other past the Visitor's Clubhouse near left.

First Aid:

Located behind Home Plate on the first base side.

**Wheelchair
& Handicapped Seating**:

Yes, there is ample room for wheelchair access on the stadium concourse dividing Box Seats from Reserved. Ramps are located at the end of the stands.

Telephones:

Located near the front gate to New Britain Stadium.

ATM: None.

Scoreboard: New Britain has one of the best scoreboards in the Eastern League. Located in left field, outstanding computer graphics and video displays will contribute to your entertainment.

Game Clock: On top of the scoreboard.

Sound: Good, hi-quality sound system broadcasts from the top of the stadium.

Sunsets?   Out between Left Field and Third Base.

Autographs: The Rock Cats are happy to sign autographs near their dugout along the first base line until the umpires take the field. There is also a reserved booth set up behind home plate for autographs before the game, but you may have a better chance out near the dugout.

Concessions and Souvenirs

Best stadium food:

         I think the best concession item at New Britain has to be the regular old traditional hot dog. The Jumbo is a better choice since it is at least another two inches longer than the regular dog. It was hot and juicy inside, of a decent size, and of an exceptional value. The only other concession I really can recommend here are the French Fries. As for the other concessions, I was disappointed. By this point in the book, you've gathered my rule that grilled food is the best ballpark food. Unfortunately, New Britain Stadium doesn't sell any grilled items to the

general public (The picnic area reserved for groups does have a grill, however.) There is a specialty ethnic sausage booth, but frankly, I was unimpressed. In fact, the buns were so stale and hard when I was there, I think the sausages may have been tastier without it.

Concessions in stands:

Very limited selection. Two nights I was there, only sold cotton candy. (This creates long lines at concession booths underneath the stands. Half the fun of a game is being able to order a beer and a dog, or a soda and a pretzel given your tastes, from your seat. That wasn't available during the games I attended.)

Hot Dog: Oven roasted and served hot, the Dogs, both regular and Jumbo are the best concessions at New Britain Stadium.

Peanuts: $1.75

Beer:

On tap:	Coors, Molson Ice, Molson Red, Killians Red, Miller, Miller Lite, Coors Light
In stands:	Not available (This was a problem since lines were so long during the game.)
Microbrews:	None
Non-alcoholic:	Coors Cutter
Wine:	White Zinfandel (Blossom Hill and Glen Ellen); Bacardi Breezer Wine Coolers

Desserts: Ice cream, sno-cones, cotton candy

View of Field from Concession Stands:

No, however you can hear the live radio broadcast of the game while you are waiting.

Third Base Gift Shoppe:

New Britain has a very nice Souvenir Store located on the main concourse underneath the stands. I was impressed by the selection, as well as the service. The store was open well after the game, and sold not only Rock Cats' merchandise, but also merchandise from other Minor League clubs. There was also a nice array of memorabilia on display under glass counters.

Admission*:

Ticket Prices (Per Person)				
	1-24	25-99	100-499	500+
Box Seats	$7.00	$6.00	$5.75	$5.50
Reserved	$6.00	$5.00	$4.75	$4.50

General Admission (Per Person)				
	1-24	25-99	100-499	500+
Adult	$5.00	$4.00	$3.75	$3.00
Children 12 & under	$2.00	$1.50	$1.25	$1.00
Senior 62 & over	$3.00	$2.00	$1.75	$1.50

Season Ticket Prices	
Field Box Seats	$450.00
Reserved Seats	$400.00
Adult General Admission	$300.00
Senior General Admission (62 & Over)	$150.00
Child General Admission (12 and under)	$100.00

Special Ticket Packages:

New Britain offers more types of Ticket Packages than any other club in the league. You have eight (8) different options to choose from, all designed for your convenience.

Rock Cats Ticket Packages						
Plan	Description	Box	Reserved	Adult G.A.	Child G.A.	Senior G.A.
Weekender	36 games - All Fri., Sat, & Sun games & Mem. Day & Labor Day	$252	$216	$180	$72	$108
Nutmegger	18 games - against Conn. rivals	$110	$95	$80	$30	$45
Two-Fer-Tuesdays	10 games - Buy 1 to all Tues., get 1 free to each game	$70	$60	$50	$20	$30
Once Around the League	9 games - against all 9 EL opponents	$63	$54	$45	$18	$27
Summer Sampler	9 games - June through Aug.	$63	$54	$45	$18	$27
The Opener	6 games in April	$42	$36	$30	$12	$18
May Madness	5 games in May	$35	$30	$25	$10	$15
Holiday Package	5 games on Summer Holidays	$35	$30	$25	$10	$15

Group Information:

Group outings are spectacular at New Britain Stadium. I believe this may be the best feature of the entire park. There are two pavilions located at the top of the stadium, one along the first base side, the other along third. From both vantage points, your group will have an outstanding view of the field, your choice of premium all-you-can-eat concession menus (by far, the best in the park), not to mention specialized treatment for you and your guests.

The Rock Cat Cafe can accommodate groups of 25 or more (minimum required). Every member of your group will receive one Reserved Seat ticket with your reservation. Reservations must be made at least one week in advance, and there is a $100.00 non-refundable deposit required. The Picnic fun begins 1 ½ hour before game time, and continues until the first pitch of the game. Alcohol is not included in the following prices, but can be ordered for an additional charge by calling (860) 832-4518.

First Base Dugout Prices	
Adults	$20.00
Child (12 & under)	$15.00
Infant (4 & under)	Free

First Base Dugout Menu
Boneless Chicken
Hot Dogs
Hamburgers
Corn on the Cob
Baked Beans
Potato Salad or Cole Slaw
Watermelon
Beverage

Third Base Dugout Prices	
Adults	$20.00
Child (12 & under)	$15.00
Infant (4 & under)	Free

Third Base Dugout Menu
Boneless Chicken
Hot Dogs
Hamburgers
Corn on the Cob
Baked Beans
Potato Salad or Cole Slaw
Watermelon
Beverage

Taxes are included in Picnic Prices, Menus subject to change.

Luxury SkyBox Rentals:

Why not watch the game from one of New Britain Stadium's luxurious skyboxes? When you want to entertain that all-important group, for only $225.00, you can enjoy the game from a furnished skybox, complete with heating and air conditioning, cable television, waiter and waitress service, and a complete catering menu. If you want to book a SkyBox, call the Box Office at (860) 224-8383. To find out about New Britain's delicious catering, call (860) 832-4518.

Birthday Parties:

Have your special birthday party for that special young fan at New Britain Stadium. For only $12.95 per person (10 person minimum) you can let the Rock Cats host your party. Each member of the party receives one reserved seat, a hot dog, soda, popcorn, and cupcake, and one General Admission ticket for a future Rock Cats game. In addition, the birthday child receives the following:

Special Birthday Child Gifts from the Rock Cats
Rock Cats Logo Baseball, and Baseball Cap
Rock Cats Scorebook and Pencil
Happy Birthday Scoreboard Announcement
The Birthday child is allowed on the field to have a picture taken with a Rock Cats Player. The picture is then made into an autographed souvenir Birthday Card.

Book your Birthday Party early by calling 832-4518.

[*1996 Data: All Prices subject to change. Call (860) 224-8383 for more information.]

Ticket Sales:

Address: P.O. Box 1718, Willow Brook Park, New Britain, CT 06050
Phone: (860) 224-8383
Credit Cards: American Express, MasterCard, Visa, Diner's Club
Hours Ticket Window Open: 10:00 a.m. to 5:00 p.m.

Rain Check Policy: If a game is canceled due to inclement weather, or if 4 ½ innings have not been played, the ticket is good for one ticket of equal or lesser value to future Rock Cats regular season games, subject to availability.

Game times:

Weekdays:	7:00 p.m.
Saturday:	7:00 p.m.
Sunday:	2:00 p.m.

(See schedule for day games. All game times subject to change.)

Time Gates open:

One hour before game time.

Parking: $2.00

Other

For the kids: There is a special Rocky's Fun Page in the Official Souvenir Scorebook Magazine.

Promotions and Giveaways:

The Rock Cats' 1996 promotional schedule included two special nights of Fireworks at New Britain Stadium. In addition, the club made efforts to bring out the fans by giving away such items as baseballs, schedule magnets, seat cushions, and tote bags. There were also special promotional nights reserved for groups and organizations, especially a high number of nights for the Little Leaguers in the New Britain area. And finally, during 1996, every Tuesday home game was Kellogg's Raisin Bran Night were fans could bring 2 box tops from Raisin Bran and $2.00 to receive 4 General Admission tickets to the game.

In between innings:

You'll find many in-game giveaways during any regular season Rock Cats home game. These include such fun activities as the Dizzy Bat Race, where two contestants have to spin around a bat ten

times and then try to run about twenty feet without falling down (Believe me, it's much cooler than it sounds), there is also a race with Rocky around the bases for the kids. But, the best chance to win a giveaway at New Britain Stadium only comes if you buy a Souvenir Scorebook Magazine. Inside some lucky random programs, you might find a signature or a stamp which guarantees you some great prizes provided by local merchants who support the team.

In all, although it's difficult to compare the Rock Cats' promotional schedule with other clubs in the Eastern League, the organization seems aware that one of the main draws for Minor League professional baseball is the family atmosphere that you just don't get at the major league level anymore. Given what I've read in the local New Britain and Hartford press, the Rock Cats' family is committed to bringing more fun-filled entertainment to you and your family in the coming seasons. Therefore, my information probably is a little incomplete here, since I expect the club to schedule even more promotions and sponsored giveaways in the future. Call the ticket office today and receive your free Rock Cats' schedule for more information.

What song played during 7th inning stretch?   "Take Me Out to the Ballgame"

Radio Station Broadcasting Game: WMRD 1150 AM

Eastern League Information: No updated information on stats, averages, etc.. posted.

Team Information

New Britain Rock Cats
(Northern Division)

History:

The New Britain Red Sox began play at Beehive Field in 1983, a very successful season which culminated in the Eastern League Championship. Since that time, New Britain has had some trouble getting back to where it all began. The last time they made the playoffs was in 1985. However, this doesn't mean they haven't produced quality players. These include such stars as Roger Clemens, Mo Vaughn, Jeff Bagwell, John Valentin, and Brady Anderson.

The relationship with Boston continued until the end of the 1994 season when New Britain began its affiliation with the Minnesota Twins. There is a player development contract between the club and the Twins at least through 1998. With the new affiliation, New Britain then changed its name and began the 1995 season as the Hardware City Rock Cats. The name originated with New Britain's history as an industrial city dedicated to hardware manufacturing. The world headquarters of the famous Stanley Tools Company still is located in town. This nickname still stands, but the team has changed its name one more time to the New Britain Rock Cats, demonstrating its commitment to the area.

In addition to these changes, the City of New Britain, the State of Connecticut, and owner Joe Buzas made a commitment to keeping professional baseball in the area with the design and construction of New Britain Stadium, located next to Beehive Field in Willow Brook Park. The new $10 million stadium has an increased capacity totaling 6,200, and boasts significant fan comforts as unimpeded views, graphic scoreboard displays, a dozen sky boxes and two picnic pavilions for group outings, a concession concourse with improved facilities over the old outdoor carts at Beehive Field, and a year round souvenir store. New Britain also is one of three teams to participate in the People's Bank Connecticut Cup, awarded to the Connecticut team with the best record against the other two Eastern League teams located in the state. In addition, for all his dedicated years of service, the Eastern League MVP Trophy is named the Joseph J. Buzas Trophy honoring the current owner of New Britain Rock Cats.

Finally, despite the new stadium, and despite the fact that the club set a seasonal attendance record in 1996, the New Britain Rock Cats are suffering from one of the poorest overall attendance records in the league. This has been attributed to a number of factors, including the change in affiliation, poor performance by the team, lack of promotions and giveaways, and inadequate advertising. However, my impression is that there is a sincere commitment by all players, the city, the state and the ownership to turn this around. After all, they've got the most important requirement guaranteed to boost attendance already in place - a clean, comfortable, brand new stadium which is unequivocally a great place to come out and watch the national pastime.

Eastern League Championships:

1983: Eastern League Champions   (First year of the franchise.)

1996:   Won the Connecticut Cup.

Players who went on to the Major Leagues:

Jeff Bagwell (1990); Mo Vaughn (1989); John Valentin (1990-91); Roger Clemens (1983); Brady Anderson (1987); Ellis Burks (1985-86); Aaron Sele (1992); Todd Walker (1995); Matt Lawton (1995); "Oil Can" Boyd (1989 - rehab).

Minnesota Twins Minor League Organization			
Team	**League**	**Level**	**City & Phone**
Minnesota Twins	American League	Major League	Minneapolis-St.Paul, MN (800) 33-TWINS
Salt Lake Buzz	Pacific Coast League	AAA	Salt Lake City, Utah (801) 485-3800
New Britain Rock Cats	Eastern League	AA	New Britain, CT (860) 224-8383
Ft. Myers Miracle	Florida State League	A	Fort Myers, FL (813) 768-4210
Ft. Wayne Wizards	Midwest League	A	Fort Wayne, IN (219) 482-6400
Elizabethton Twins	Appalachian League	Rookie	Elizabethton, TN (615) 543-4395
Gulf Coast Twins	Gulf Coast League	Rookie	Fort Myers, FL (813) 768-4280

Approximate distance from New Britain Stadium to Metrodome: 1302 miles
(Source: Rand McNally TripMaker Version 1.1 1994, New Britain, CT to Minneapolis, MN)

Mascot: Rocky the Rock Cat
Team Colors: Black, scarlet and silver.
Visiting Hotel: Ramada Hotel, 65 Columbus Blvd., New Britain, CT. 06051 (860) 224-9161
Fan Club: Rock Cats Booster Club, call Angela Beebe @ (860) 225-6266 for more information.

Directions to stadium:

Take Interstate 84 to Exit 35 (Route 72 East). Proceed on Route 72 to Route 9 South, then take Exit 25 (Ellis St.) Turn left onto Ellis, then at the first stoplight, turn left onto South Main Street. New Britain Stadium is located in the middle of Willow Brook Park, which is a little over ¾ of a mile on the right.

New Britain

Background

New Britain, Connecticut (Pop. 75,491) is best known for local production of hand tools and machinery. This reputation grew in the late 19th and early 20th centuries with the advent of toolmaking giants like Stanley Works, American Hardware, North & Judd, Fafnir Bearing, and Union Manufacturing. The city's motto, written by Elihu Burritt, the Learned Blacksmith, is "Industria Implet Alveare et Mele Fruitur" or "Industry Fills the Hive and Enjoys the Honey," which has recently been updated to the "Home of the American Dream", and the city's nickname remains the "Hardware City."

However, the early history of New Britain did not anticipate this reputation. New Britain was once a small, rural farming community, originally settled in 1686 and named by its earliest settlers for their native lands in Britain. It was part of nearby Farmington until the early 18th century, and then became its own ecclesiastical society with the founding of the parish of New Britain in 1754. Religion, in fact, has always played a major influence in this town of many cultures, beginning with the organization of the First Church of Christ in 1758. The town of New Britain eventually incorporated in 1850, and then officially became a city in 1871.

Main Street, downtown New Britain

Other influences in the region might be attributed to contact with nearby communities like Southington, Berlin, Meriden, and the towns of the Farmington Valley. Most notably however, New Britain's proximity to Hartford, established as the capital of the Connecticut Colony in 1662, should be considered as Hartford is located but a mere twelve miles away. Hartford, recognized since the later 18th century for its service industries like the insurance trade, has also in the past attracted luminaries of art and literature such as Mark Twain, Harriet Beacher Stowe and Noah Webster.

Recently, New Britain has been a city in transition. The city's multiethnic population grew steadily throughout the early 20th century, most of them coming straight from Ellis Island to work in the hardware factories, until growth peaked at 83,441 according to the 1970 census. Since then, there was a noticeable decline in population, but with somewhat modest gains through the late 1980's up until today. Apparently, this transition is largely due to changes in the city's traditional economic manufacturing base. The largest employers today are no longer the famous toolmakers, like Stanley Works which opened its World Headquarters here in 1984, but the New Britain General Hospital, which includes the George Bray Cancer Center, and the Tomasso Critical Care Tower.

As for visiting the New Britain/Hartford area, there are many cultural sites to explore during the day while you wait for the Rock Cats to take the field. However, of all the activities to do and all the things to see, if you only have time for one thing other than the ballgame, overall I'd recommend you bring your golf clubs. You'll find plenty of great public courses nearby.

Information

Chamber of Commerce/Tourist Bureau

New Britain Chamber of Commerce
55 West Main Street
New Britain, CT. 06051
(860) 229-1665

Vision New Britain
185 Main Street, Room 429
New Britain, CT 06051
(860) 225-3335

Central Connecticut Tourism District
One Grove Street
New Britain, CT 06051
(860) 225-3901

Greater Hartford Convention & Visitors Bureau, Inc.
One Civic Center Plaza
Hartford, CT. 06103
(860) 728-6789 or (800) 446-7811
(Including the Greater Hartford Sports Commission)

Memorial in Central Park, New Britain

Farmington Valley Visitors Association
P.O. Box 1015
Simsbury, CT 06070
(860) 651-6950 or (800) 4-WELCOME

Web Site(s):   http://www.ntplx.net/~nbv

Daytime Entertainment

Guided tours

Connecticut State Capitol Tours
Capitol Information and Tours
210 Capitol Avenue
Hartford, CT 06106
(860) 240-0222

The Hartford Guides
P.O. Box 231194
Hartford, CT 06123-1194
(860) 522-0855

Heritage Trails
P.O. Box 138
Farmington, CT 06034-0138
(860) 677-8867

Museums

New Britain Museum of American Art

56 Lexington Street
New Britain, CT 06052
(860) 229-0257

This is the oldest museum in the country solely devoted to the exhibition of American Art. The collection of over 5,000 works includes art from the colonial period, the Hudson River School, genre paintings, the American Impressionists, the Ash Can School, early moderns, and contemporary art. There are special programs for children, including Art Explorers and Second Saturday Family Fun, as well as the delightful Cafe on the Park during the summer months.

Open Tuesday through Sunday from 1 p.m. to 5 p.m.

New Britain Industrial Museum

185 Main Street (Second Floor)
New Britain, CT 06051
(860) 832-8654

An interesting collection worth viewing. Includes products and artifacts produced in New Britain by such toolmakers as The Stanley Works, Fafnir Bearing, American Hardware, and Landers, Frary & Clark. The staff is very knowledgeable and most helpful, and no doubt you'll come away with a better understanding of the history of hardware.

Open Monday through Friday from 2 p.m. to 5 p.m., and by appointment.

Twain-Stowe-Day Houses at Nook Farm

The Mark Twain House

351 Farmington Avenue
Hartford, CT 06105
(860) 493-6411

This High Victorian style house was built by Samuel Langhorne Clemens in 1874, and the Clemens family lived here until 1891. While living here, Twain wrote seven major works, including *Tom Sawyer*, *The Prince and the Pauper*, *Life on the Mississippi*, *A Connecticut Yankee in King Arthur's Court*, and, of course, the greatest American novel ever, *The Adventures of Huckleberry Finn*. There are fine examples of period art and architecture, and the entire house has been meticulously restored to its original 19th century standing. The Mark Twain House is a National Register Historic Landmark, and has won two awards from the National Trust for Historic Preservation. (Of note, during August of 1996, The Mark Twain House, WFSB Channel 3, and the Hartford Courant sponsored Mark Twain Days which included three days of concerts, performances, exhibitions, and contests. The Mark Twain Days is an annual event, so you might call the House for more information.)

Summer Hours, open Mon. - Sat. 9:30 a.m. to 5 p.m.; Sun. Noon - 5 p.m.

Harriet Beecher Stowe House/
Katherine S. Day House
71 Forest Street
Hartford, CT 06105
(860) 525-9317

The Stowe House was the last residence for the successful 19th century writer of *Uncle Tom's Cabin*, and *American Woman's Home*. Built in 1871, this 19th century Victorian cottage has been restored in order to display the comfortable lifestyle of the Stowe family during the late 19th century. The nearby Day House, also offers Victorian interiors with changing exhibits from the holdings of the Stowe Center and the Stowe-Day Library.

Summer Hours, open Mon. - Sat. 9:30 a.m. to 4 p.m.; Sun. Noon - 4 p.m.

Wadsworth Atheneum
600 Main Street
Hartford, CT 06103
(860) 278-2670

Founded in 1842, this is the oldest public art museum. Houses over 50,000 works from the U.S. and abroad, including Egyptian, Greek, and Roman bronzes; Renaissance and baroque paintings; European decorative arts; 17th and 18th century decorative arts; French and American Impressionists; the Hudson River School landscapes; and 20th century masterpieces.

Open Tuesday through Sunday, 11 a.m. to 5 p.m.

Parks and Gardens

Walnut Hill Park

West Main Street, behind the New Britain Museum of American Art

The primary park in New Britain, this large open park offers a family friendly environment, with areas to picnic, walk, bike, and rollerblade. There's a nice, easy on the feet exercise trail, two ballfields, a grand ampitheater, and restrooms.

Iwo Jima Memorial Monument

Iwo Jima Memorial Expressway (Route 9)
Exit 29 Ella Grasso Blvd
New Britain/Newington Town Line

More a memorial than a park, this small dedication along the public highway is a fitting tribute to the 6,821 Americans who gave their lives in the Battle of Iwo Jima during World War II. If you'd like more information, write Dr. George Gentile, Iwo Jima Survivors Association, Inc. P.O. Box 310516, Newington, CT 06131 or phone (860) 666-5521.

Bushnell Park

Bushnell Park Foundation
P.O. Box 31173
Hartford, CT 06103

Located near the State Capitol Building, Bushnell Park offers the Carousel, Corning Fountain, the Soldiers and Sailors Memorial Arch, the Spanish War Memorial, and Bushnell Park Pond.

Public Golf courses, miniature golf

Stanley Golf Course
245 Hartford Road
New Britain, CT 06053
(860) 827-8144

Built in 1931, there are twenty seven holes grouped into three sets of nine by the colors Red, White and Blue. (There are two different tees on the 7th hole of the White Course which explains the variance in yardage below.) Tee times accepted 3 days in advance, call as early as 6:30 a.m., Pro Shop opens 7 a.m. Lockers, lessons, chipping & putting green, 19th hole, Zabbara's Restaurant. Statistics:

	Yard	Rtg	Slope	Par
Blue&Red Course Blue Tees	6453	71.1	115	72
White Tees	6067	69.4	111	72
Red Tees	5681	72.0	122	73
Red&White Course Blue Tees	6156/38	69.0	108	71
White Tees	5757/42	67.2	104	71
Red Tees	5359/46	70.1	114	72
Blue&White Course Blue Tees	6329/11	69.8	112	71
White Tees	5757/42	68.0	108	71
Red Tees	5359/46	71.3	118	73

Tunxis Plantation Country Club

87 Town Farm Road
Farmington, CT 06032
(860) 677-1367

There are two 18 hole courses and one 9 hole course. Tee times accepted 3 days in advance, Pro Shop opens 7 a.m., takes calls at 6 a.m. Range, Lessons, Locker Rooms, Tavern on the Green Bar and Restaurant. Statistics:

	Yard	Rtg	Slope	Par
White Course Blue Tees	6638	71.0	121	72
White Tees	6241	69.2	117	72
Red Tees	5744	71.5	116	72
Green Course Blue Tees	6424	70.0	120	71
White Tees	6008	68.1	117	71
Red Tees	4903	71.0	115	71
Red Course Blue Tees	3297	70.8	123	36
White Tees	3076	68.8	119	36
Red Tees	2790	N/A	116	36

Goodwin Golf Course

1130 Maple Ave
Hartford, CT 06114
(860) 956-3601

Two courses, one 18 holes, one 9 holes. Tee times accepted one week in advance. Pro Shop opens 7:00 a.m., Driving Range, Practice Green, lessons, 19th Hole. Statistics:

	Yard	Rtg	Slope	Par
Goodwin Course Blue Tees	5929	67.8	110	70
White Tees	5638	66.7	108	70
Red Tees	5343	69.6	109	70
North Course White Tees	2544	N/A	N/A	35
Red Tees	2544	N/A	N/A	35

Farmington Miniature Golf Course

1048 Farmington Ave., Route 4
Farmington, CT 06032
(860) 677-0118

Traditional Miniature Golf, Ice Cream Parlor and Yogurt, Snack Bar. Located adjacent to Tunxis Plantation Country Club.

Goodwin Golf Course, Hartford, Connecticut

Shopping Malls

Westfarms Mall
Route 71, New Britain Avenue
Hartford, CT
Customer Service (860) 561-3024; Answer Line (860) 561-3423

Nordstrom's, JC Penney, Filene's, Lord & Taylor, and over 100 specialty stores.
From State Route 9 to
Westfarms - take Exit 30 and
proceed north on State Rt. 71.
From I-84, take exit 39A south
(Route 9), proceed to Exit 30
and follow Rt. 71 to the mall.

Seasonal Events

Dates are approximate, contact
regional tourism offices listed above
for updated schedule information.

Statue of Lafayette and Bushnell Hall, site of 1996 Presidential Debate, Hartford

April: Spring Fling

May: Dionysos Greek
Festival; Memorial Day
Parade; Mayor's Fun
Day in Walnut Hill
Park.

June: Main Street, U.S.A.; Annual New Britain Criterium Bicycle Race; Strawberry Festival; Berlin
Spring Crafts Festival; Southington Victorian Garden Party; Puerto Rican Festival.

July: Independence Day Fireworks; Nutmeg State Antiques and Collectibles Show.

August: Mark Twain Days in Hartford; Festa Italia-Italian American Feast; Dozynki Polish Festival;
Berlin Summer Crafts Festival; Plainville Hot Air Balloon Festival; Southington Grange Fair.

Cafe on the Park at the New Britain Museum of American Art (Wednesdays 5:30 p.m.-7:30 p.m. Still
enough time to catch a ballgame afterwards.); and, the Summer Music Festival (Walnut Hill Park, Monday
and Wednesday Evenings July to August (860) 826-3360.) Early Summer: The Canon Greater Hartford
Open, Tournament Players Club at River Highlands.

Accommodations/Other

Visiting Hotel for the New Britain Rock Cats:

Ramada Inn & Conference Center
65 Columbus Boulevard
New Britain, CT 06051
(860) 224-9161
Lounge, Pets OK, Entertainment Discounts (Middle of downtown)

Farmington

The Farmington Inn
827 Farmington Avenue
Farmington, CT 06032
(860) 677-2821 or (800) 648-9804
Complimentary Continental Breakfast,
Restaurant, Valet, Secretarial Services,
AAA and Entertainment Discounts (Located
in a charming, historical area not far from
New Britain. Close to Golf Courses.)

Hartford Marriott Farmington
15 Farm Springs Road
Farmington, CT 06032
(860) 678-1000 or (800) 228-9290
Restaurant & Sports Lounge, entertainment,
Indoor and Outdoor Pools, Exercise Room,
Tennis Courts, Jogging Trails, AAA and
Entertainment Discounts (Designed for the
business traveler. Near Golf Course)

Downtown Hartford

Sheraton Hartford Hotel
315 Trumbull Street
Hartford, CT 06103-1186
(860) 728-5151
Restaurant & Lounge, Indoor Pool, Health Club

Meriden

Hampton Inn-Meriden
10 Bee Street
Meriden, CT 06450
(203) 235-5154
Continental Breakfast, located at Exit 16N/17S on I-91.

Residence Inn by Marriott
390 Bee Street
Meriden, CT 06450
(203) 634-7770 or (800) 331-3131
Continental Breakfast, Kitchens, Pets OK, Outdoor
Pool, Exercise Room, located at Exit 16N/17S on I-91.

Hospitals

New Britain General Hospital
100 Grand Street
New Britain, CT
(860) 224-5011

Hospital for Special Care
2150 Corbin Avenue
New Britain, CT
(860) 223-2761

Transportation

Bradley International Airport   (860) 292-2000
Exit 40, I-91 (12 miles north of Hartford)

Airport Connection, Inc.   (860) 627-3400
(Shuttle Service to Bradley International)

AMTRAK (Hartford)   (800) USA-RAIL

CTTRANSIT   (860) 525-9181
(Bus service, over 30 routes around greater Hartford)

New Haven Ravens

Team: **New Haven Ravens** (Northern Division)

Stadium: **Yale Field**

Address:	252 Derby Avenue, West Haven, CT 06516
Mailing Address:	63 Grove Street, New Haven, CT 06510
Phone:	1 (800) Ravens-1; (203) 782-3140; (203) 782-1666
Fax:	(203) 782-3150; (203) 782-1555
Web Site(s):	http://www.ravens.com (official); http://www.minorleaguebaseball.com/teams/new-haven; e-mail ravens@connix.com

Team Ownership:

Operated by:	New Haven Ravens Baseball Club
Principals:	Edward Massey
General Manager:	Charles Dowd

Affiliation: Colorado Rockies

Years in Eastern League: 1916-32; 1994-Present

Stadium Physical Characteristics

Age, Built in:	1927
Stadium Owner:	Yale University

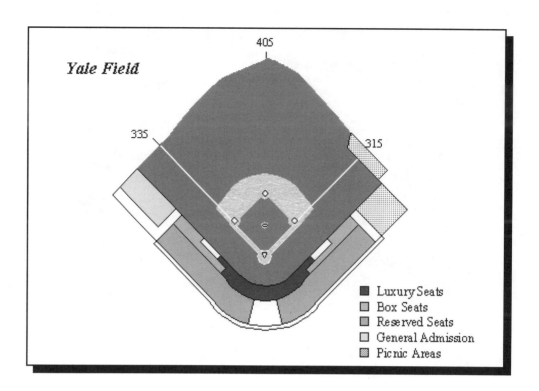

Yale Field

405

335   315

Luxury Seats
Box Seats
Reserved Seats
General Admission
Picnic Areas

Bullpens: Inside the fences, in a very large foul territory.

Playing Surface: Natural grass

Characteristics:

One word. Loud. That's the best way to describe Yale Field. An all metal stadium built in 1927, fans here like to shake and stomp the place apart whenever the home team does anything even remotely positive. If a Raven batter draws a walk, they stomp; if they get a hit, they stomp; if a Raven pitcher throws a strike, they stomp; if a coastal breeze blows in on a hot summer night, they stomp. (I don't know who's more intimidated by all the noise, the opposing teams, or non-stomping fans trying to keep their beer from tipping over.)

Once you get used to the noise, you'll begin to appreciate the intimate surroundings of this historic park. From the weathered concrete facade and large, open archways around the circumference of the stadium, to the steel columns supporting the canopy which protects Reserved and Box Seats from the elements, you'll think you've step back in time to some sort of field from your dreams. There's an old

scoreboard in center field, still somewhat hand operated, which they call the Green Monster. (As a matter of fact, I understand that the Green Monster is made out of World War II battleship scraps.) Yale Field keeps the trend towards parks of the past alive, while at the same time offering a lot that is new. There was a $3 million renovation in 1994 after the Ravens became one of two expansion teams in the Eastern League, along with the Portland Sea Dogs.

As for the actual field itself, you'll immediately notice that unlike other parks in the Eastern League, your seat is some distance away from home plate. In fact, foul territory at Yale Field is huge. In left field, it's so big the opposing team probably could take infield practice during the game. Despite this, the gentle slope of seating down to the dugout level gives the fan an impression of being much closer to the game than at other parks.

Finally, one other unsupported characteristic. Because of the dimensions of the field, the fact that the breeze seems to be blowing in all the time, and the huge foul territory, it is no exaggeration to say that Yale Field is a pitcher's park. I don't have the stats, but I would guess there are many pitchers in the EL eager to come to New Haven and drop their ERA a few notches.

Capacity: 6,200

	1994	**1995**	**1996**
Attendance	276,316	283,766	254,064

1996 Average Attendance:

No. of 1996 openings: 62
1996 Daily Average: 4,098

All Time Attendance Records:

Daily: 7,011 on August 24, 1996
Seasonal: 281,076 in 1995

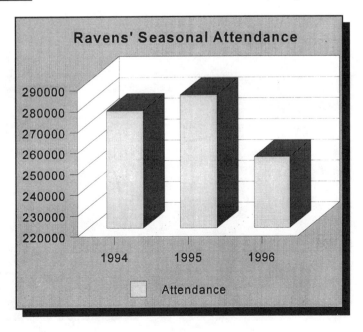

Type of Seating:

The Luxury Seats at Yale Field are some of the best in the league. Not only do they provide armrests, but they have trays and cupholders built in between the seats. There is also a waitress service for these special luxury seats. If you can't afford Luxury seating, the regular box seats also offer armrests and cupholders for the fan. As for the rest of seating, reserved and general admission are aluminum bleachers. One thing to note, on a sellout night, and there are more than a few, the stands get kind of cramped. If you need to stretch before the middle of the 7th, there is a nice sized walkway behind you, which extends around most of the stadium at the top of the reserved sections. Trust me, you won't be the only one standing up there, and you will still have a pretty good view of the field.

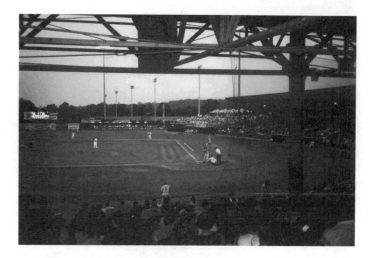

Covered Seating: Except for General Admission and the Picnic Area, all seats in Yale Field are under cover. This makes for pleasant viewing on hot summer days, or during short rain delays. Unfortunately, it also means that some views are obstructed.

Restrooms:
Ladies: 2
Men: 2
Changing tables: Yes.

Customer Service Window: Customer Service is located on the main concourse near the main gate.

Smoking Policy: Smoking appears to be allowed in the concourse area, but definitely not in the stands.

First Aid: Located behind Section 5 in the St. Raphael's Healthcare room.

Wheelchair & Handicapped Seating:

Yes, there is a walkway that extends around the top of the reserved sections. The access ramp is located on the rightfield side of the stadium.

Telephones: Four.

ATM: None.

Scoreboard:

There are a total of three scoreboards at Yale Field. There is an electronic scoreboard in right center showing updated stats and out of town scores, a high quality color graphic scoreboard in left center, and the "Green Monster" in center. This last is an historic scoreboard which is still updated the old fashioned way, manually. In addition, only three players in history have ever hit a dinger over the Green Monster, the most recent being Jose Malave of the New Britain Red Sox in 1994.

Game Clock: Small clock above the scoreboard which is difficult to read. However, from time to time, there is a digital readout on the board in left center.

Sound system: Surprisingly good.

Sunsets? Just to the right of home plate.

Autographs:

Unique to the league, Yale Field has an autograph corral for the kids near the first base line. This is only open for fifteen minutes prior to the game so get there early. However, if you want a visiting player's autograph, note that the entrance to their dugout is just near the speed pitch on the concourse. Stand nearby and you might just surprise a friendly player from the other team.

Concessions and Souvenirs

New Haven has some outstanding concession items. The only concern is the location. Most everything is located underneath the stands. As you will no doubt find out, this area can become quite congested during the game. If you don't have Luxury Box Seats with Waitress Service or if you are even slightly claustrophobic, then I recommend either you arrive early and get your concessions before the game, or try out the more open space area behind the General Admission bleachers near left field.

New Haven Ravens   61

Picnic Pavilion overlooking Right Field

Best stadium food:

I believe the best items are at the grill area out in the Left Field Concession Area. My favorites were the Red Hots, the Sausage with Peppers, and the Cheeseburger, in that order. Red Hots are a hot and spicy sausage, grilled, and served on a warm, tasty bun. If you like spicy food, this is the one for you. My mouth was so on fire afterwards, not even the coldest of beers could put out the flames. (That's a compliment, by the way.) Next, I truly enjoyed the Sausage with Peppers, also for sale in Left Field. This sausage had to be at least nine to ten inches long and was quite a bargain. Served again on a warm, soft bun, this concession was so good, it didn't even need the traditional dab of mustard I usually prefer with stadium food. Finally, I'm not much of a Cheeseburger fan, but the burgers at Yale Field were grilled, hot, juicy, and extremely difficult to pass by. Also, you'll be sorry if you forget to try McCain's French Fries. I think with these choices, and of course, the Hummel Hot Dog, you'll find all sorts of tasty treats to tempt any palate at Yale Field.

Concessions in stands: Except for the lack of beer sales in stands, Yale Field has one of the widest selections for fans watching the game. These include Hot Dogs, Pizza, Pretzels, Peanuts, Sodas, Ice Cream, and Cotton Candy.

Hot Dog: The Dogs at Yale Field are always a good choice because they're just really, really good.

Peanuts: $2.00

Beer:
On tap:	Miller, Miller Lite, Red Dog, Rolling Rock
In stands:	None.
Microbrews:	Blackbird Ale (best choice), Elm City Connecticut Ale
Non-alcoholic:	None.
Wine:	Bacardi Breezers; Red or White Wine available in Luxury Seats

Desserts: Fried Dough, Funnel Cake, Slush Puppies, Ice Cream, Italian Ice, Cotton Candy, Sno-cones.

View of Field from Concession Stands:

No. (Some stadiums broadcast their play by play in this type of situation, but New Haven does not.)

Gift Shop:

The Ravens have an outstanding selection of merchandise for sale at a number of locations. First of all, there is the Ravens Souvenir Store located near the main gate. You have a choice of over eighty items like souvenir Rally stuffed toys, Rally caps, Ravenswear t-shirts, windbreakers, shot glasses, baseballs, mugs, even stadium blankets for those cool, crisp Connecticut evenings. If the store inside is too crowded, the Ravens set up stands outside Yale Field during the game. Finally, if the shopping whim strikes you when the Ravens are out of town, try The Dugout Store, located at 63 Grove Street, downtown New Haven.

Admission*:

Prices	
Luxury Box Seats	$15.00
Box Seats	$8.00
Reserved	$6.00
General Admission:	
Adult:	$4.00
Senior (65 and older):	$2.00
Child (6 - 12 yrs):	$2.00
Infant (5 and under):	Free

Season Ticket Prices	
Luxury Box Seats	$945.00
Box Seats	$490.00
Reserved Seats	$350.00
General Admission	
Adult:	$225.00
Senior/Child:	$125.00

Ticket Books Available	
General Admission (10 games)	$36.00
Reserved (10 games)	$54.00

Weekender Plans	
Box Weekender	$275.00
Reserved Weekender	$200.00

Ticket books are undated coupons which can be used for any home game during the regular season. Reserved ticket coupons must be redeemed on game day, and prior to the game for an actual ticket, subject to availability. Coupons may be redeemed at either the Ravens Ticket Office at Yale Field, or at the Dugout Store, 63 Grove St., New Haven the day of the game.

Benefits of Season Tickets and Weekender Package Holders:

Same great seats. Discounted ticket prices. Options on discounted parking. Playoff and Renewal Priority. Staff and Player Picnic. Recognition page in Program. 25% off merchandise. Premium gift. Off season party. Priority on 1998 AA All Star Game. Referral incentives.

10-Game Plans	
Seat Selection:	
Box Seats	$80.00 per seat
Reserved Seats	$60.00 per seat
Plan Selection:	
Ty Cobb Plan	All Friday Games
Mickey Mantle Plan	All Saturday Games
Cy Young Plan	All Sunday Games
Stan Musial Plan	Weekday Games

Group Information:

Groups are treated very special at Yale Field. In addition to the ability to choose from a wide array of special discount plans, your group will receive recognition over the Ravens Public Address System, the Ravens Message Center Board, and you will be permitted to display your company or group banner. Your group will also receive a group photo on the day of your outing. And finally, your group will always receive professional, courteous service by the Ravens staff.

Group Ticket Prices		
	Reserved	General Admission
25-99	$4.00	$2.50 Adult $1.50 Senior/Child
100-499	$3.50	$2.25 Adult $1.25 Senior/Child
500 +	$3.00	$2.00 Adult $1.00 Senior/Child

Ravens Group Merchandise Plans				
	Baseballs	Pennants	Minibats	Hats
25-49	$3.00	$1.50	$2.50	$6.00
50-99	$2.50	$1.25	$2.25	$5.00
100 +	$2.00	$1.00	$2.00	$4.00

Merchandise prices in addition to Group ticket sales. The Ravens Staff can also personalize select merchandise at your request.

Group Sales Including Food Coupons		
	Reserved	General Admission
	Hot Dog, Soda + Ticket	Hot Dog, Soda + Ticket
25-99	$6.75	$5.50 Adult $4.25 Senior/Child
100-499	$6.25	$5.00 Adult $4.00 Senior/Child
500 +	$5.75	$4.75 Adult $3.75 Senior/Child

Other Food Coupons available, including Pizza, Beer & Ice Cream; CALL for prices.

The Ravens also offer a wide variety of all-you-can-eat entertainment packages for groups of 30 or more at either the terraced Party Pavilion near the right field line, or at the Short Porch Cafe behind the right field wall. The Party Pavilion is a terraced picnic area which can accommodate groups ranging from just 30 all the way up to 325 persons each game. Groups of 300 or more can obtain exclusive use of the Party Pavilion. The Short Porch Cafe offers similar amenities, but is smaller and can only accommodate groups of 30 to 125. Groups of 100 or more can reserve the Short Porch exclusively. Because of their outstanding location and appeal, both of these special group areas book fast so call and reserve early.

Party Pavilion and Short Porch Cafe Menus	
Hot Dogs and Hamburgers	$12.50
Barbecued Chicken & Ribs	$17.50
All Four Items Above (Pavilion Only)	$20.00
N.Y. Strip Steak (Short Porch Cafe Only)	$20.00

All menus include corn on the cob, potato salad, watermelon, peanuts and soda. Prices are per person, and include game ticket. Children 4 and under free.

The Ravens also can accommodate larger groups ranging in size from 300 to 2,000 at a New Haven Ravens Pre-Game Festival. The staff can set up tents, tables, food and drink, and whatever it takes to make it a special day for you and your organization. Pre-game Festivals can begin as much as three hours before game time on the grass field adjacent to the stadium. There is an all-you-can-eat menu available which may include all the great menu selections listed above, and beer sales can be made on a cash basis as well. Call ahead and arrange your large group outing with the Ravens Staff today.

Finally, the Ravens are proud to host the Birthday Bash celebrations for groups of ten or more. What a great way to spend a birthday. The price for the Birthday Bash is only $12.50 per person, and every guest at the party receives the following:

Reserved Seat Ticket
Hot Dog, Soda, Popcorn, Ravens cupcakes
Souvenir Ravens Pennant
Buy 1, Get 1 Free Speed Pitch Coupon
Coupons good for 10% off Ravens souvenir merchandise
Gift Certificates good for $2.00 off Kids Club Membership
Chance for Autographs during Pre-Game Signing Session
Gift from Milford Amusement Center

In addition, the Birthday Boy or Girl receives:

Name "In Lights" on Message Board
Special Ravens Baseball Hat
Ravens Logo Baseball
Name in the Nightly Roster/Stats Insert
Autographs during Exclusive Pre-Game Signing Session

Special: The New Haven Ravens also sponsor special fundraising sales, which appear to be unique to the league. Prospective fundraisers can help raise money for local organizations, Little Leagues, civic groups, etc... by selling Reserved Seat ticket vouchers. Home games Monday through Thursday in April and May are set aside for the fundraising program. Organizations can receive Reserved Seat ticket vouchers to sell on a consignment basis in books of ten for $6.00 per voucher (face value). After the drive is completed, participating organizations receive $3.00 times the number of vouchers sold, provided unsold vouchers and money returned to Ravens by June 1, 1997. Call the Director of Group Sales, at (203) 782-1666 for more details.

[*1997 Data: Prices subject to change. Call (800) RAVENS-1 for more information.]

Ticket Sales: Available at the Ravens Box Office one half hour before the gates open, or advance sales at the address below.

    Address: New Haven Ravens, 63 Grove St., New Haven, CT 06510
    Phone: (800) RAVENS-1; (203) 782-1666
    Credit Cards: Visa, MasterCard, American Express
    Hours Ticket Window Open: 1 ½ hour before game time.

Rain Check Policy: A game is official if after 4 ½ innings the Ravens are leading, or after 5 innings and play is suspended. If a game is called because of inclement weather, then tickets may be exchanged at the box office. No refunds.

Game times:

Weekdays:	7:05 p.m.
Saturday:	7:05 p.m.
Sunday:	2:05 p.m.

(See schedule for day games. All game times subject to change.)

Time Gates open: 1 hour before game time.

Parking: Lot # 1, X/Y Dr: For Pre-Paid Customers and Handicapped Only.
Lot # 2, Marginal Drive on RT 34 across from CT Tennis Center for $2.00
Other: Inside the Yale Bowl on the corner of Yale Ave and Chapel St - $1.00

(Parking is somewhat of an inconvenience at Yale Field, especially if you arrive late or if there is an expected sellout. Some homeowners in the area will sell you a spot in their driveway if there is an overflow, however. Do yourself a favor and come out to the stadium as early as you can.)

Other

For the kids:

There is a Speed Pitch along the third base line where kids of all ages can test their arms. (Find out about special coupons for birthday parties at Yale Field.) In addition, there was one video game out past the Left Field Concessions.

Promotions and Giveaways:

Looking at the 1996 Ravens Promotional Calendar, there was one night I'm sorry I missed. That was on Friday, July 19th and was called the Bacardi Breezer Giveaway. I bet old Yale Field was rockin' that night!

Seriously, the Ravens sponsor a significant number of promotional nights during the season, although from what I saw I think their "In-Game" Promotions are more fun than their "At-The-Gate" Promotions. The Ravens only sponsored one night of Fireworks, held last year on July 3rd and sponsored by local brewery, Elm City. As for giveaways, look for the Ravens to handout such items as schedule magnets, coffee mugs, Rally dolls (I've got one of those!), baseball caps, mugs, lunch bags, sport bottles, key chains, and souvenir baseballs at the gate. Also, I attended one game on August 11th, where some lucky fans in the stands received free walkmans. I missed the game at the end of the year where one fan was given a brand new car - now, that's a promotion!

The Ravens also were fortunate to have so many local New Haven radio stations sponsoring special events during the week. Monday night home games were sponsored by 101.3 WKCI-FM; Tuesdays were sponsored by 92.5 WWYZ-FM; Wednesdays were 99.9 WEZN-FM; and finally, Thursday nighs were sponsored by 93.7 WZMX-FM.

> Note: Ravens staff tends to favor the First Base side of the field for giveaways. You may have a better chance for a freebie if you're near the Home Team Dugout.

In between innings:

The Ravens have the best In-Game Promotions in the entire Eastern League. During any regular season home game, you will be entertained with over 40 promotions which range from on-field activities, to lucky number drawings from your Raven's Game Program on sale as you enter Yale Field. In fact, there were so many In-Game Activities at Yale Field during the 1996 season, I can only list a few here: Pregame Autograph Corral; Little League Team of the Night; Human Dog Race and the Greyhound Race Track; Sports Haven Horse Race; Elm City Brewing Dizzy Bat Race; A-1 Toyota Potato Sack Race; Mascot Race; and the unique Cuzz-Acres Golf Practice Center Closest to the Pin Contest shot from the first base line out to a pseudo-golf green out in centerfield.

Elm City Dizzy Bat Competition

What song played during 7th inning stretch?   "Take Me Out to the Ballgame"

Radio Station(s) Broadcasting Game:

WAVZ 1300 AM   (Flagship Station -1996)
WMMM 1260 AM; WLIS 1420 AM; WATR 1320 AM (Fridays); TEAMLINE (1(800) 856-4700); WXCT 1220 AM (Spanish).

Eastern League Information:

The Ravens will periodically update Eastern League Scores and Stats on the scoreboards behind the outfield fences during the game. Updated standings are included in the scorecard that comes with the Game Program. (There is also a dry erase board near the main gate which might be used to provide updated stats - when I was there, this board announced the day's honored guest - Hall of Fame Pitcher Bob Feller.)

Team Information

New Haven Ravens (Northern Division)

History:

Yale Field is one of the oldest, operational Minor League parks in the entire country. Built in 1927, it has been the home of Yale baseball for well over sixty years. President George Bush played First Base for the Yale squad as a young Ivy-Leaguer.   Babe Ruth made his last public appearance here, when he donated the original manuscript of his autobiography to the Yale Library in 1948.

As for professional teams in the area, there was a New Haven team in the Eastern League from 1916 through the 1932 season. There was an also another EL team in West Haven for ten years during the 1970's. But there was a long drought of professional play until the major leagues expanded, adding the Colorado Rockies and the Florida Marlins to the National League. By 1994, those organizations had spawned franchise teams in New Haven and Portland respectively. After an expensive and probably overdue renovation, Yale Field became the home of the New Haven Ravens in 1994. Exceeding all expectations, the Ravens not only drew record crowds out to Yale Field, but remarkably, they reached the Eastern League playoffs in both of their first two seasons.

The team quickly has become an integral part of civic life in and around New Haven. Not only participating in the annual Connecticut Cup with Norwich and Hardware City, the New Haven Ravens

have reached out to the community by supporting such important charities as Habitat for Humanity, hosting a Celebrity Softball Blowout for the benefit of the Connecticut Special Olympics (Patrick Ewing, Conan O'Brien, Buck Showalter, Tom Brokaw were scheduled to appear at the 9/21//96 event), sponsoring special literacy programs and the Tommy Fund, which supports pediatric oncology research and care at Yale-New Haven Hospital, and helping to raise money for all sorts of local charities. Truly, the Ravens have become a local favorite, in more ways than one.

Eastern League Championships: None.

1995: New Haven defeats Portland in semifinals (3-1)
Reading defeats New Haven for EL Championship (3-2)

1994: Binghamton defeats New Haven in semifinals (3-0)

AA All Stars:

1998: Yale Field, New Haven to host AA All Star Game (Monday before the 1996 Major League All Star Game)

Ravens' Hall of Fame:

- Angel Echevarria, RF
(1994, '95. 1995 EL All Star, Ravens HR Leader - 29 HR, 132 RBI. 1996 Colorado Rockie.)

- Quinten McCracken, CF
(1994, '95. All time Ravens leader in Hits, AB, Runs Scored, Doubles, Triples and Steals. 1996 Colorado Rockie.)

- Juan Acevedo, Starting P
(1994. '94 AA All Star, '94 EL All Star, '94 EL Pitcher of the Year, '94 EL Co-Rookie of Year, '94 EL ERA Leader, '94 EL Wins Leader. 1995 Colorado Rockie. Traded to NY Mets Organization.)

Rally the Raven

Colorado Rockies Minor League Organization			
Team	**League**	**Level**	**City & Phone**
Colorado Rockies	National League	Major League	Denver, CO (303) ROCKIES
Colorado Springs Sky Sox	Pacific Coast League	AAA	Colorado Springs, CO (719)597-1449
New Haven Ravens	Eastern League	AA	New Haven, CT (203) 782-3140
Salem Avalanche	Carolina League	A	Salem, VA (540) 389-3333
Asheville Tourists	South Atlantic League	A	Asheville, NC (704) 258-0428
Portland Rockies	Northwest League	Short A	Portland, OR (503) 223-2837
Chandler Rockies	Arizona League	Rookie	Chandler, AZ (602) 895-2152

Approximate distance from Yale Field to Coors Field: 1860 miles
(Source: Rand McNally TripMaker Version 1.1 1994; New Haven, CT to Denver, CO)

Mascot:	Rally the Raven
Team Colors:	Teal and black
Visiting Hotel:	Days Hotel, 490 Sawmill Road, West Haven CT 06515 (203) 933-0344
Fan Club:	Fan mail should be addressed to the individual player and sent in care of the Ravens at 252 Derby Ave., West Haven, CT 06516. There is also a Kids Club, and membership includes tickets, instructional baseball camps, membership card, Ravens Baseball, and discounts. Write to the same address for further information.

Directions to stadium:

From I-95:	Eastbound Exit 44 or Westbound Exit 45 to Route 10. Follow Yale Bowl signs. Yale Field is located opposite Yale Bowl on Route 34.
From downtown:	Route 34 west, follow Yale Bowl signs to Yale Field.
From Merritt and Wilbur Cross Pkwys:	Exit 57 for Route 34 East. Follow Route 34 and Yale Bowl signs to Yale Field. Or, take Exit 59 and follow Whalley Ave Yale Bowl signs.
Public Transportation:	Connecticut Transit (203) 624-0151

New Haven

Background

New Haven Green, and the natural "Cathedral of Elms"

New Haven, Connecticut (Pop. 130,474) is geographically defined by the New Haven Harbor, located on Long Island Sound, and by the massive red rock hills of East Rock and West Rock. Originally named Roodenbery by a mariner, Adrian Block of the Dutch East India Company in 1614, the area was colonized in 1638 by English Puritans who changed the name of the area to Quinnipiac, an Indian word which translated as either "long water" or "river place." The settlement was renamed New Haven in 1640 and remained an independent outpost until added to the Connecticut Colony in 1665. From 1701 until 1873, New Haven served as the joint capital of Connecticut with Hartford.

New Haven has a rich colonial history which revolved around at least three aspects: the mercantile trade associated with New Haven Harbor; the religious and community life guided by the three churches on New Haven Green; and the educational standing of the esteemed Yale College (now Yale University). Yale College was founded in 1701, and the permanent siting of the college in New Haven came in 1717. Some of the oldest buildings in town remain on campus, despite the fact that part of the town was burned by British invaders in 1779. (The commander of the British regiment was a 1757 graduate of Yale.)

The town officially incorporated as a city in 1784. New Haven Green since the earliest times has been a focal point for community activities, and continues to fulfill that role today. Charles Dickens, upon the occasion of an 1842 visit to New Haven Green, commented on the "Cathedral of Elms" surrounding its perimeter as "seeming to bring about a kind of compromise between town and country." Perhaps this explains the town's nickname as the "Elm City."

Throughout the 19th century, industry and invention flourished in New Haven. Eli Whitney advanced the theories of interchangeable parts and mass production here, Oliver Winchester made the Winchester rifle famous, Charles Goodyear invented vulcanized rubber, and even A.G. Gilbert created the Erector set, all in New Haven. With the introduction of all these new inventions, New Haven experienced significant growth throughout the period as people of many nationalities and backgrounds immigrated to this Industrial Age manufacturing center.

Today, New Haven, known primarily for its educational, financial, manufacturing, and medical care institutions, is also home to a thriving art culture. Broadway style theaters, acclaimed art and history museums, scholarly library collections, and the fourth oldest symphony orchestra in the country all contribute to the city's cultural life. Along with art, some mention should be made of architecture as there also has been grand architectural achievements in this city. Many of the quality guided tours will introduce you to the renowned 19th century Italian villa-style houses, Victorians, Gothics, as well as other careful restorations and modern creations. One of the most interesting was the exemplary restoration of the 1918 Union Station, which is certainly a fine gateway to this Elm City on the Sound.

Information

Chamber of Commerce/Tourist Bureaus

Greater New Haven Convention & Visitors Bureau
One Long Wharf Drive
New Haven, CT. 06511
(203) 777-8550 or (800) 332-STAY

Greater New Haven Chamber of Commerce
195 Church Street, 15th Floor
New Haven, CT
(203) 787-6735

Yale Visitor Information Center
149 Elm Street
New Haven, CT 06510
(203) 432-2300

Web Site(s):

New Haven On Line:	http://statlab.stat.yale.edu/nhol/
New Haven Chamber of Commerce:	http://newhavenchamber.com
Virtual Tours of Yale University:	http://video.cs.yale.edu/images/ New_Haven_area/Yale/ Tour.html

Daytime Entertainment

Scenic tours

New Haven First
New Haven First Committee
Yale Visitor Information Center
149 Elm Street
New Haven, CT 06510
(203) 432-2300

Every Thursday at 12:00 Noon, a guided tour of life around New Haven Green. You can also arrange guided, group, and/or self-guided tours of Yale University from the Yale Visitor Information Center. (This informative tour should be one of the first things on your agenda while visiting New Haven!)

Walking Tour (Self-Guided)
New Haven Colony Historical Society
114 Whitney Avenue
New Haven, CT 06510
(203) 562-4183

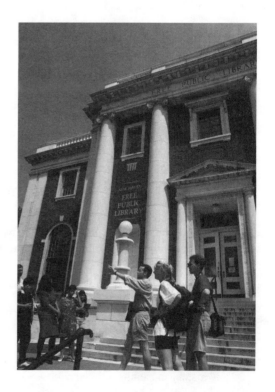

Museums

Tours of Yale University

Yale Center for British Art
1080 Chapel Street
New Haven, CT
(203) 432-2800, or (203) 432-2850

The largest collection of British Art outside of the U.K. Works dating from the 16th century, including Hogarth, Gainsborough, Reynolds, Stubbs, Constable, Turner, and William Blake. Exhibitions change four to six times a year.

Hours: Open Tuesday through Saturday 10 a.m. to 5 p.m.; Sunday Noon to 5 p.m.

Peabody Museum of Natural History
170 Whitney Avenue
New Haven, CT 06520
(203) 432-5050

One of the oldest natural history museums, includes the Pulitzer Prize winning mural, *The Age of Reptiles*. Permanent exhibits on dinosaur fossils, mammals, minerals, Native Americans, local wildlife.

Hours: Open Monday through Saturday 10 a.m. to 5 p.m.; Sunday Noon to 5 p.m.

Yale University Art Gallery
1111 Chapel Street
New Haven, CT
(203) 432-0600

The oldest university sponsored art museum in the country, the gallery founded in 1832 now houses over 100,000 works dating from ancient Egypt to the present. Includes paintings by Van Gogh, Manet, Monet, Picasso, Homer, and Eakins; Greek vases; early Italian and Chinese paintings; ceramics, bronzes, textiles; large collection of American works.

Hours: Open Tuesday through Saturday 10 a.m. to 5 p.m.; Sunday 2 p.m. to 5 p.m.

New Haven Colony Historical Society
114 Whitney Avenue
New Haven, CT. 06514
(203) 562-4183

Museum includes local fine and decorative arts, maritime history and lore, working version of Whitney's cotton gin, milling machine from Whitney Armory, early Morse code receiver, educational library.

Hours: Tuesday through Friday 10 a.m. to 5 p.m.; Sat. & Sun. 2 p.m. to 5 p.m.

Connecticut Children's Museum
22 Wall Street
New Haven, CT 06511
(203) 562-KIDS

For children under seven years old, a "Please Touch" museum.

Summer Hours: Tuesday through Saturday from 10 a.m. to 2 p.m.

Eli Whitney Museum
915 Whitney Ave.
Hamden, CT 06517
(203) 777-1833

Hands on educational center located in Whitney's restored factory north of downtown. Includes fascinating outdoor water learning lab where children can explore the dynamic powers of water, a barn from 1816, and a charming old-fashioned covered bridge. The museum also conducts summer concerts, dances, picnics and storytelling.

Open Sunday, Wed. through Friday Noon to 5 p.m.; Saturday 10 a.m. to 3 p.m.

Shoreline Trolley Museum
17 River Street
East Haven, CT 06512
(203) 467-6927

Three mile trolley ride through scenic woodlands and marsh area. 100 street cars in collection, approximately a dozen on display. Follow signs from I-95.

Summer Hours: 11 a.m. to 5 p.m. every day.

Parks and Gardens

East Rock Park
East Rock Road, New Haven, CT
Davis Street, Hamden, CT
(203) 946-6086 (Ranger station)

Road and walking trails to the summit where you can see all of New Haven; Sailors & Soldiers Monument; Giant Steps; playing fields; rose garden. Ranger Station located at College Woods, near Orange and Cold Spring Streets. Note that entering the park can be confusing. Both listed entrances are on the west side of the park, but you'll need a map ahead of time.

Shoreline Trolley Museum, East Haven, Connecticut

New Haven Green

College, Chapel, Church and Elm Streets
New Haven, CT
(203) 946-8025

Historic site, includes three churches built in early 19th century. Popular lunchtime gathering spot, great for walking. Located right in the center of town.

West Rock Ridge State Park

Wintergreen Avenue
New Haven, CT
(203) 789-7498

Lake Wintergreen, Judge's Cave, hiking, picnicking, scenic views of downtown, West Rock Nature Center (Open Mon.-Fri. 10 a.m. - 4 p.m. Call 946-8016). Follow Whalley Ave. to Fitch St. to Wintergreen Ave.

First Church of Christ, on New Haven Green (1815)

Cruises/Charters

M/V Liberty Belle

P.O. Box 9661
Long Wharf Pier
New Haven, CT 06536
(800) 745-BOAT

Harbor & Sound Cruises, Brunch Buffet & Cruise, Oldies Cruise and Dance, Moonlight Cruise.

Canoe New Haven

(203) 432-6570, (203) 389-1037

Canoe excursions, river cleanup, nature outings. West River Ranger 946-8028; Mill River Ranger 946-6086; Quinnipiac River Ranger 946-8790.

Schooner, Inc.

60 South Water Street
New Haven, CT 06519
(203) 865-1737

Educational sea adventure cruise, sunset cruise

Charter Referrals

Master Bait & Tackle Co.
(203) 469-6525

Public Beaches

Lighthouse Point Park, Carousel, & Beach

End of Townsend Avenue
I-95 Exit 50
East Haven, CT
(203) 946-8790, (203) 787-8790

A large public beach located near the end of the east side of New Haven Harbor, plenty of room to sunbathe, swim, run, picnic and play. Lifeguards, lighthouse, restored carousel, playground, fishing, biking, rollerblading, restrooms. Parking Fees during summer months. No concessions onsite, but there is a convenience store at the corner of Lighthouse and Townsend, about a half mile or so before the entrance.

West Haven Beach
Capt. Thomas Boulevard and
Ocean Ave
West Haven, CT
(203) 937-3651

Three miles of beach on Long
Island Sound. Fees charged.
(There are a number of beaches in
West Haven, including Bradley
Point, Morse, Oak Street, and
Sandy Point. The phone number
listed is for the West Haven Parks
& Recreation Department. Call
for more information.)

Micro-Breweries

New Haven Brewing Company
458 Grand Avenue
New Haven, CT
(203) 772-2739

Saturday tours begin at 11 a.m. Sample Blackbird Ale or the Elm City Connecticut Ale, both special brews served at Yale Field. Call ahead for directions and reservations.

Public Golf course/Sports Related Entertainment

Alling Memorial Golf Course
35 Eastern Street
New Haven, CT 06513
(203) 946-8013

18 hole municipal course designed by Robert D. Pryde, and built in 1930. Crowded, you should call in advance, tee times are accepted 3 days in advance. Pro Shop opens at 7 a.m., takes calls beginning at 6:30 a.m. Locker rooms, Lessons, Practice green, 19th hole. Recommend call for directions. Statistics:

>
> Blue Yardage 6241, Rating 69.5, Slope 123, Par 72
> White Yardage 5884, Rating 68.0, Slope 119, Par 72
> Red Yardage 5071, Rating 68.0, Slope 121, Par 72

Sports Haven
600 Long Wharf Drive
New Haven, CT 06511-5972
(203) 821-3100

Four-story indoor sports entertainment facility includes racebook for thoroughbred, harness and greyhound racing, restaurant, Shark Bar, food court, billiards and game room. Open at 11 a.m, wagering begins at Noon.

Milford Jai-Alai
311 Old Gate Lane
Milford, CT 06460
(203) 877-4211 or (800) 972-9650

Pilot Pen International Tennis Tournament
555 Long Wharf Drive
New Haven, CT 06511
(888) 99-PILOT

Seasonal tournament in August, scheduled in between Wimbledon and the U.S. Open, draws internationally renowned professional players.

Milford Amusement Center
1607 Boston Post Road
Milford, CT
(203) 877-3229

Miniature golf, arcade, batting cages, kiddie rides. Indoors open from 10 a.m. to midnight, outdoor areas in season open Noon to midnight.

Shopping Malls

Connecticut Post Mall
1201 Boston Post Road
Milford, CT
(203) 878-6837

Sports Haven

Caldor, Filene's, JC Penney, the Wiz, Theaters, Food Court, and over 130 specialty stores. Exit 39B off I-95.

Hours: Monday through Saturday 10 a.m. to 9 p.m.; Sunday 11 a.m. to 6 p.m.

Seasonal Events

Dates are approximate, contact regional tourism offices listed above for updated schedule information.

June: Fun-Fest; St. Francis Strawberry Festival; Trumbull Day; St. Andrew Annual Italian Feast; Country Strawberry Festival; Festival East; CT Irish Festival & Fair; Art on the Edge.

July: New Haven Harborfest; New England Arts & Crafts Festival; Summer Food Festival; St. Maria Maddalena Festival.

August: Pilot Pen International Tennis Tournament; Sunfish Regatta; Blueberry & Craft Festival;

Summertime Street Festival; Holy Rosary Parish Italian Festival; Milford Oyster Festival

Summer: Jazz on the Green; Greater New Haven Acoustic Music Society Concerts; Picnic on the River.

Accommodations/Other

Hotels and Motels

Visiting Hotel for the New Haven Ravens:

Days Hotel West Haven
490 Saw Mill Road
West Haven, CT 06516
(203) 933-0344
Lounge, indoor pool, fitness center, shuttle service. (No breakfast, but near a Dunkin Donuts & Denny's)

New Haven

Marriott Residence Inn
3 Long Wharf Drive
New Haven, CT 06511
(203) 777-5337 or
(800) 331-3131
http://www.resinn.com
Complimentary breakfast, Kitchens, Fireplaces, outdoor pool, whirlpool spa, shuttle service. (Near waterfront.)

Howard Johnson
Long Wharf
400 Sargent Drive
New Haven, CT 06511
(203) 562-1111 or
(800) 243-0059
Restaurant & Lounge, pool, laundry, AAA & Entertainment discounts. (Near waterfront.)

Holiday Inn New Haven
30 Whalley Road
New Haven, CT 06511-3288
(203) 777-6221 or
(800) HOLIDAY
Restaurant & Lounge, outdoor pool, fitness center, room service, AAA discount (Downtown.)

Colony Inn New Haven
1157 Chapel Street
New Haven, CT 06511
(203) 776-1234 or
(800) 458-8810
Restaurant & Lounge, room service, courtesy van. (Downtown.)

New Haven Hotel
229 George Street
New Haven, CT 06510
(203) 498-3100
Restaurant & Lounge, room service, lap pool, connected to Downtown Health & Racquet Club. (Downtown)

Milford

Hampton Inn
129 Plains Road
Milford, CT 06460
(203) 874-4400 or
(800) HAMPTON
Continental Breakfast Buffet, free local calls, AAA discount.

Bed and Breakfast

Call Bed & Breakfast, Ltd., at (203) 469-3260 for recommendations.

Campgrounds

Call Connecticut Campground Owners Association at (860) 521-4704.

Hospitals

Yale-New Haven Hospital
20 York Street
New Haven, CT
(203) 785-4242 or (203) 785-2000

Hospital of St. Raphael
1450 Chapel Street
New Haven, CT
(203) 789-3000 or (203) 789-4304

Transportation

Lighthouse Point Park

Tweed-New Haven Airport: (203) 946-8283
AMTRAK: (800) USA-RAIL
(800) 523-8760
(Metroliner)
METRO-North: (800) METRO-INFO
**Bridgeport & Port Jefferson
Steamboat Co.**: (203) 367-3043 or (516) 473-0286
CT Transit: (203) 624-0151
Greyhound: (203) 772-2470
CT Limousine: (800) 472-LIMO
Metro Taxi: (203) 777-7777
New Haven Taxi: (203) 777-0000
Yellow Cab: (203) 777-5555

Norwich Navigators

Team: **Norwich Navigators** (Northern Division)

Stadium: **Senator Thomas J. Dodd Memorial Stadium**

Office Address: 14 Stott Road, Norwich, CT. 06360
Mailing Address: P.O. Box 6003, Yantic, CT. 06389
Phone: (860) 887-7962
Fax: (860) 886-5996
Web Site(s): http://www.gators.com (official);
http://www.minorleaguebaseball.com/teams/norwich/

Team Ownership:

Operated by: Minor League Sports Enterprises, LP
Principals: Barry Gordon (Chairman & CEO), Hank Smith (President), Mark Klee (V.P.), Robert Friedman (V.P.), Neil Goldman (V.P. and General Counsel)
General Manager: Brian Mahoney

Affiliation: New York Yankees

Years in Eastern League: 1995-Present

Stadium Physical Characteristics
Age, Built in: 1995
Stadium Owner: City of Norwich

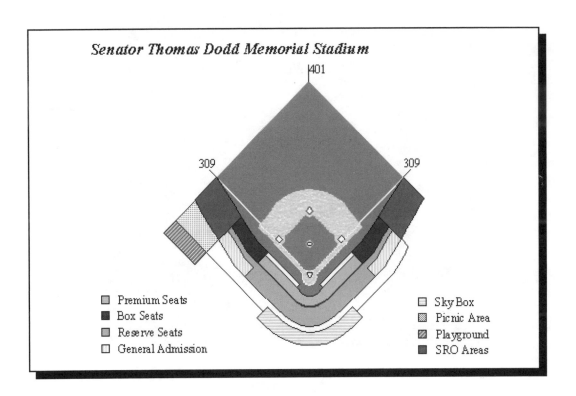

Senator Thomas Dodd Memorial Stadium

401

309   309

☐ Premium Seats
■ Box Seats
■ Reserve Seats
☐ General Admission

☐ Sky Box
▨ Picnic Area
▨ Playground
■ SRO Areas

Bullpens: Inside the fence, in foul territory

Playing Surface: Natural grass

Characteristics:

Senator Thomas J. Dodd Memorial Stadium is another one of the open stadiums in the Eastern League built at ground level. These types of parks include a wide concession concourse extending all the way around from foul pole to foul pole. The closest cousin to Dodd Memorial has to be Prince George's Stadium in Bowie, and indeed, they are remarkably similar. Not only in the design and construction, but also in the layout. Both are concrete stadiums with an open grassy lawn area at the end of right field; both have playgrounds for the kids, (although Norwich's is much larger); and, both have plenty of room for SRO viewing.

As for the design of the field itself, foul territory here is of a standard size out until about first and third base

Tater the Gator welcomes you to Dodd Memorial Stadium

where the stands start to curve back in on the field. The foul territory directly behind home plate is actually pretty small, with on-deck circles closer to the batter's box than any others I've seen. Also, the dugouts have a protective screen in front of them, perhaps to deflect those hot, lined-fouls you'll often see coming off the plate. As far as I know, this is the only stadium which offers such protection.

Speaking of foul balls, you definitely have a good chance of catching one or two here. Not only is there no netting over top the seats behind home plate, but the roof of the second level is angled such that many foul balls hit up there will roll back into the stands.

The only serious complaint about the layout of Dodd Memorial Stadium is that there is no cross-aisle in the stands, so there is very little walking room between rows. You won't have anyone walking in front of you during the game, which is nice, but I saw a lot of people cutting through the rows anyway, almost oblivious to the people they were stepping on. (That was especially true of the waitresses. In fact, I saw a lot of people on a crowded night casually walking on top of the dugouts in order to get around between innings.)

Capacity: 6,200 +

	1995	1996
Attendance	281,473	269,022

1996 Average Attendance:

No. of Openings: 70
1996 Daily Average: 3,843

All Time Attendance Records:

Daily: 7,056 on August 21, 1996
             (David Cone appearance)

Seasonal: 281,473 in 1995

Navigators' Seasonal Attendance

285000
280000
275000
270000
265000
260000
255000
250000

1995   1996

☐ Attendance

Skyboxes: Yes

Type of Seating: The coolest thing about the seats at Dodd Stadium has to be the waitress service. I was fortunate enough to have Premium Seats. These were comfortable, with plenty of room, and included armrests and cupholders. When you arrived, there was a menu in your cupholder for waitress service. (More on that later.) The Box Seats also seemed similar to Premium, only further away from the field. Reserved seats also were individual seats with armrests, while General Admission was made up of aluminum bleachers.

Covered Seating: Very limited, in the last two or three rows underneath the skybox level behind home plate. (There is a covered concession concourse for SRO, but you can still see the game from this location.)

Restrooms: Ladies: 2
Men: 2
Changing tables: Two family restrooms on the Carberry Concourse behind home plate.

Customer Service Window: Located behind home plate near the Beacon Baseball Store.

Smoking Policy: Not permitted in any seating areas, however, you may smoke at the very far ends of the Carberry Concourse.

First Aid: Station located behind home plate next to the Information Window.

Wheelchair
& Handicapped Seating: Entrance to Dodd Stadium is at ground level, so there is no need for ramps. Plenty of room for Wheelchairs and companions around the Carberry Concourse. In addition, call ahead, or ask the ushers about Dodd Stadium's Safe Seat Service - three wheelchairs available for those in need of special assistance.

Telephones: Four (4)

ATM: Yes, outside the Main Entrance, before you enter the Stadium.

Scoreboard: An excellent quality scoreboard is located just over the fence in right center field. Dodd Stadium has about three cameras tuned into the action, and this is the only Eastern League stadium that I know of that actually broadcasts live action replays on their scoreboard's multicolor graphic display. (I wonder how the EL umpires like working at Dodd?)

Game Clock: Right center field, on the scoreboard.

Sound: Excellent high quality sound from directly overhead.

Sunsets? On the first base side.

Autographs:

Yes, you can find Navigator players at the special autograph table set up on the Carberry Concourse behind home plate, or you can sometimes find them willing to sign for you over on the first base side.

Concessions and Souvenirs

Before I discuss the stadium food at Dodd Stadium, I must give a nod to the excellent waitress service. Now, don't get me wrong, there's nothing amiss about standing in a long concession line to get a dog and a beer during the middle of a riveting evening of Eastern League baseball. (And when it's crowded at Dodd Stadium, you <u>will</u> stand in a long line.) However, it's much nicer to be able to remain in your seat and not miss a single moment of the action. Other stadiums have waitress service, Yale Field comes to mind, but often that's limited to either the really expensive seats or to the luxury skyboxes. Here, at Dodd, the waitresses treat everyone in Premium and Box Seats like an owner of the club. (Okay, maybe not that great, but they do treat you special.) When you arrive at your seat, you'll find a Box Seat Menu in the cupholder in front of you. Listed on the back is practically the entire concession menu, ranging from Dugout Dogs, Sausages, Pizza Hut Pizzas, and Soup, all the way to 20 ounce Draft Beers, sodas, and Hot Chocolate. All you do is fill out the form, indicate the quantity desired (better to get what everyone in your group wants at once) and then signal your attendant. Your waiter or waitress will be right back with your order, and you won't have to get out of your seat until the 7th inning stretch! (That's when Box Seat service ends.) Oh, and one last thing, since these young men and women work for tips, you'll find gratuities are deeply appreciated.

Best stadium food:

I have four recommendations. First, my favorite item at Dodd Stadium was the New England Clam Chowder. Soup? At a baseball game? Are you nuts? That was my first reaction as well, but this was great! I'm sure there are other restaurants in Norwich, New London and Mystic where you'll find a better cup of chowder, I'm almost 100% positive of that fact, however on a chilly night, when you're sitting on a cold aluminum bench watching three hours of Minor League Baseball,

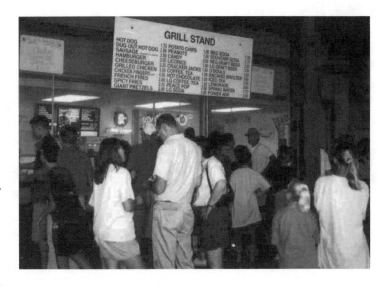

there's nothing like a hot cup of soup to warm you up inside. (Or chili, ...that's on the menu, too.) I think Norwich has hit on a nice concession, and I wouldn't be too surprised to find it on future menus at some of the other stadiums in the Northern Division.

Second came the Grilled Sausage. This was served, of course, with peppers and onions, the only real way to enjoy grilled sausage. The size was decent, and it was juicy, spicy and hot on the inside, with just the right amount of grilled crunch on the outside to let you know this baby wasn't boiled. Easy to recommend. Third, I really liked the Spicy Fries. They were hot but not too spicy, and you could really taste the flavor. My only complaint was that these fries would be a better buy if they gave you more.

Finally, in addition to the regular concession menu, you'll find that Dodd Stadium also offers dining specials. No, you're not going to find Lobster Ravioli or fancy-schmancy Seafood Primavera here, but you will find some nice periodic changes in the menu in case you get bored with hot dogs after 71 games. (I assume the specials change from homestand to homestand.) For the games I attended, the special of the night was the Chicken Parmesan Sandwich. Basically, it was the Chicken Sandwich that's on the regular concession menu, but topped with parmesan cheese and tomato sauce. Not too difficult for the staff to make, I imagine, but it was quite tangy, and most definitely a nice change. The Stadium Announcer should let you know what the night's special is before the game, so listen up, or just ask when you get up to the concession window if you're not sure.

Concessions

in stands: In addition to the special Waitress Service, vendors sell Hot Dogs, Peanuts, Candy, and Ice Cream in the stands.

Hot Dog: The Dugout Dog was a full quarter pound of meat! I don't think there's much else to add to that recommendation. At only $2.50, this was an exceptional value.

Peanuts: $1.50

Beer:

Beer Sales end at the end of the 7th inning. Proof of age is required.

On tap:	Budweiser, Bud Light, Coors, Coors Light, Miller, Miller Lite, Red Dog
In stands:	Only through the Waitress Service.
Microbrews:	Navigator Ale, Honey Brown, Sam Adam's, Pete's Wicked
Non-alcoholic:	O'Douls
Wine:	Bacardi Breezers (assorted flavors)

Desserts: Ben & Jerry's Ice Cream, Italian Ice, Sno-Cones, Slush Puppy

Other: Two other things I want to mention. First, there is a special Kid's Club Concession window along the 3rd base side of the Carberry Concourse. If you want to avoid the lines, try a Gator Value Meal which includes a Hot Dog, Soda, and Fries, all for one low price. Secondly, Dodd Stadium sells what had to be the largest tub of popcorn I've ever seen! At 85 ounces, you are definitely going to have leftovers!

View of Field from Concession Stands:

Yes, the Carberry Concourse is a large and open standing room only walkway from which you can view the entire playing field. If the concession lines aren't too long, then you can quickly turn your head in case some Navigator knocks one out over the shortened outfield fences. My only complaint is that when the concession lines are long, you won't be able to see the field while you're waiting. With the ability to show instant replays on the scoreboard, and with all the camera coverage around the

stadium, you'd think Norwich might be able to install some monitors near the concession windows like Portland and Trenton, for example.

Gift Shop:

The Beacon Baseball Shop showcases the most colorful merchandise in the Eastern League, and apparently the most popular. New Era Cap Company reported in late 1995 that the Navigators had the best selling baseball cap in all of the Minor Leagues! With over seventy different items for sale in the main gift

shop near the entrance, and the smaller souvenir booth down the 3rd base side of the Carberry Concourse, you're guaranteed to find great ways to show off your Navigators spirit. Some memorabilia you'll find includes the popular baseball caps like the best selling Road Cap and the New York Yankees Farm System Cap; t-shirts; golf shirts; dress denim shirts; windbreakers; sweatshirts; souvenir bats, balls, and other collectibles; and of course, the Totally Tater line of kid's wear.

(And finally, don't forget that you can drop off those great Navigator photos you took during the game at the Film Drop Box located next to the Information Window. Film dropped off here was developed by Cooper's Photo during 1996, and was available for pick up after noon the following day.)

Admission*:

Regular Ticket Prices	
Premium	$8.00
Box	$7.50
Reserve	$6.00
General Admission Adult Child/Senior	$5.00 $3.50

Kids and Seniors:

General Admission discounts are available for children 15 and under, and seniors 60 and over.

Navigators Special Ticket Line Up			
	Premium	Box	Reserve
Full Season (71 games)	$560.00	$525.00	$420.00
Half Season (35 games)	$280.00	$262.50	$210.00
Weekend Packages (21 games) Every Friday & Saturday or Every Saturday & Sunday	Not Available	$157.50	$126.00
Gator Packages (7 games)	Not Available	$52.50	$42.00

Group Ticket Prices				
	Regular	**25-99**	**100-499**	**500 +**
Premium	$8.00	$8.00	$8.00	$8.00
Box	$7.50	$7.50	$7.50	$7.50
Reserve	$6.00	$5.00	$4.75	$4.50
General Admission Adult	$5.00	$4.00	$3.75	$3.50
Child/Senior	$3.50	$2.50	$2.25	$2.00

You have a number of different ways to entertain your group at Senator Thomas J. Dodd Memorial Stadium. The discounted ticket prices for group admissions (per person) are listed here. Groups are guaranteed block seating together, and each group receives recognition over the P.A. system, as well as the scoreboard display in right center field. Plus, the group leader receives a special gift from the Navigators. Below are a few extra ways to customize your group outing:

Group Package Additions		
Single	Norwich Navigators Pennant	$2.00 per person
Double	Food Coupon good for Hot Dog, Chips, and a Soft Drink	$3.75 per person
Triple	Navigators Pennant and a Food Coupon	$5.75 per person

1. **Gator Garden Barbeque**:

Located in the Mashantucket Pequot Picnic Area down the left field line, your group can enjoy an all-you-can-eat barbeque before the game, and then watch some great Navigators baseball. Listed below are two menu packages to choose from, and the ticket price includes your price of admission. The picnic lasts for 1 ½ hours, and you can choose what time you'd like to begin, either before or during the game. Then, during the game your group will be announced over the Navigators P.A. system, and on the scoreboard in right center field. The minimum group size is 25 persons, and a $100.00 non-refundable deposit is required to reserve your outing. Choose from either of these menus:

The Home Run	Hamburgers, Hot Dogs, Potato Salad, Watermelon, Pretzels, and Soda	$15.75 per person
The Grand Slam	BBQ Chicken, Hot Dogs, Potato Salad, Watermelon, Pretzels, and Soda	$17.75 per person

2. **SkyBox Rentals**:

Senator Thomas J. Dodd Memorial Stadium offers another great way to watch a game, through their deluxe SkyBox accommodations. Your group can enjoy the game from an air conditioned/heated box on the second level above the diamond. Each furnished SkyBox has twelve outdoor seats, popcorn, scorecards, and the famous Navigators Waitress Service offering the full catering menu, plus beer, wine, and liquor at your request. The price is just $385.00 per

night for twelve tickets, and then only another $8.00 per person for additional tickets up to twenty.

3.   **Birthday Parties with "Tater the Gator"**:

Dodd Stadium is the perfect place for a birthday outing. Groups of 8 or more (with at least 1 adult) receive first class treatment on that special day. For only $12.00 per person, every member of the party gets an admission ticket, a food coupon good for a hot dog, chips, and a soda, some birthday cake, a Navigators pennant, and a wristband good for unlimited rides in the Navigator Playground (the biggest playground in all of the Eastern League!). In addition, the special birthday boy or girl receives a free Navigator logo baseball, free rounds at the batting cage and speed pitch, a special visit by Tater, and their name in lights on the scoreboard and announced over the P.A. system.

4.   **Future Navigator Team Nights**:

Little League teams can take the field at Dodd Memorial Stadium with the Navigators during the singing of the Star Spangled Banner. The name of the team will also get announced on the P.A. system and broadcast in lights on the scoreboard display. General Admission is $3.00, Reserve is $5.00, and a minimum team size of 15 people required. Call ahead, because this special treatment goes on a first come, first served basis.

5.   **50/50 Fundraisers**:

Working with non-profit or charity organizations, the Navigators will donate upto 50% of each ticket sold to that organization. You must call for arrangements.

There are also a number of rules to keep in mind when organizing a group outing. You can reserve your date with a credit card, but full payment must be made at least 48 hours in advance, no will call payments allowed, nor are there any exchanges or refunds. If there is a cancellation or rain out, tickets may be exchanged to a future game subject to availability. Unused tickets can be exchanged for General Admission tickets to future Sunday through Thursday games, subject to availability. Any game or promotional dates are subject to change without notice.

[*1996 Data: Prices subject to change. Call (860) 887-7962 for updated information.]

Ticket Sales:

Address: Norwich Navigators, c/o Tickets, P.O. Box 6003, Yantic, CT., 06389 (Add $1.75 for postage and handling)

Phone: (860) 892-2030; 1 (800) 64GATOR

Credit Cards: Visa, MasterCard, Discover, American Express

Hours Ticket Window Open:

Non-Game Days:	Monday through Friday 10:00 a.m. to 5:00 p.m.
	Saturday 10:00 a.m to 4:00 p.m.
Game Days:	10:00 a.m. until the end of the game.

Rain Check Policy: Tickets to any game that is postponed before that game becomes official may be exchanged for a future regular season home game, depending upon availability. No refunds.

Game Times	
Weekdays: April & May June through September	 6:35 p.m. 7:05 p.m.
Saturday	7:05 p.m.
Sunday	2:05 p.m.

(See schedule for day games. All game times subject to change.)

Time Gates open: 1 ½ hours before game time.

Parking: $2.00

There is space for 2,000 cars at Dodd Stadium, and even on the night that David Cone pitched for Norwich, I had no trouble finding a space since I arrived early for the game. That being said, Dodd Stadium has experienced significant traffic flow problems (It's the only park in the league that distributes Traffic Flow Pattern Charts.) If you are unsure at all about Traffic flow into and out of Dodd Stadium, my recommendation is you call the club and ask them nicely to fax you a copy of their Flow Pattern Charts. I'm sure they'd be happy to oblige. Or, better yet, take advantage of the Navigators fantastic web page, at http://www.gators.com for more information.

Other

For the kids:

The Navigators have the best facilities for kids in the Eastern League. That wasn't easy to admit with this great marketing competition. Bowie has a Carousel and a Playground, Portland has a Basketball game, Harrisburg has City Island, and almost all the stadiums have a Speed Pitch of some sort, but only Norwich has Tater's Playground with three rides and a Speed Pitch, in addition to Tater's Playhouse,

an Indoor Arcade with over a dozen up to date video games, plus a Ben & Jerry's Ice Cream cart! (Not to mention, Tater is one of the fan friendliest of mascots in the league.)

Tater's Playground is the largest one I've seen in the league. I saw some great rides like a moonwalk (the big Giraffe), two children's rides (horsies and cars), a jungle gym, the speed pitch, and a large party tent and picnic tables for birthday outings. There were also attendants on duty to make sure everything was safe and fun.

In addition, in 1996 the Navigators sponsored an Instructional Baseball Camp for youths ages 6 to 16. There were five separate sessions held around the region with the purpose of teaching the fundamentals of the game, provided directly from Navigators staff, players, local college and high school coaches. These classes fill up quickly, so if you're interested, enroll early.

Besides these entertainment amenities at the stadium, Norwich tries to keep your outings fun for all ages by reserving Section 19 of the stadium for families. There is no alcohol nor foul language permitted in this section. Although it's unfortunate this action was necessary, of course, it's still a great idea that other stadiums can learn from.

I don't mean to pick on any one stadium, but it might be a good idea for the P.A. announcer at Dodd Memorial Stadium to remind the audience before each home game that there are a lot of kids in the crowd, and to please watch their language. Most Minor League fans would agree that the Eastern League is all about good, clean family entertainment. Many other stadiums in the Eastern League make this sort of announcement, and for the most part, the vast majority of Minor League fans are very mindful of the children.

Promotions and Giveaways:

Tater meets a Tot

Four nights of Post Game Fireworks; visits from the Blues Brothers, the Famous Chicken, and Sport; Singles Night; Boy Scout Day; Little League Night; Mystick Village Hot Air Balloon Fan Fly Day; and, tons of giveaways are all ways the Norwich Navigators promote the club. In 1996, you could have registered to win a pool, a spa, a gazebo, or an all expenses paid trip to Walt Disney World. If you were early out to the park, you could have received great giveaways like magnet schedules, hats, hot cups, sunglasses, Yankees magazine, frisbees, gym bags, autograph books, bumber stickers, logo baseballs, beach towels, t-shirts, key chains, can coolers, fanny packs, batting gloves, socks, squeeze bottles, wristbands, posters, bats, pennants, batting helmets, wallets, or backpacks. I'm sure there will be even more great giveaways in the future. Call for your Navigators schedule for more information.

There were also a number of ongoing contests that were held at every home game during the 1996 season. In fact, there were so many, I don't have enough room here to list them all. I was originally going to create another chart for your use, but that would have been about three pages long so I'll just mention the highlights.

Some giveaways were based on performance. These included, but weren't limited to, a number of different contests that depended upon the Navigators hitting a home run, such as the Better Val-U Five and Five Contest, where if a Navigator's player hit a home run into a shopping bag on the billboard, the player and one lucky fan received $5,000 each; there was also the Cross Sound Ferry Hi-Speed Stolen Base Contest, which meant whenever a Navigators player steals a base, one fan wins round trip fare on the Cross Sound Ferry's Hi Speed-Sea Jet; and also, there was the Groton Cyclery Hit for the Cycle Contest, which gave away a free cycle to one lucky fan whenever the entire Navigators team hit for the cycle.

Other giveaways included two best seat in the house contests, sponsored by Brandy's Restaurant and GEICO respectively, where lucky fans could get moved up from reserve or general admission to the front row; the Holmgren Subaru Pitch and Win where you had a chance to win a brand new Subaru Outback; the Bob's Stores "Let's Make a Deal" contest (I saw one fan give up a chance to win $1,000.00 in cash); and many other on-field contests like the Balloon Toss, the Mascot Race, Dugout Bowling, Dice Game, the Dizzy Bat Race, Dugout Golf and the ever popular Slingshot tosses.

Finally worth mentioning are the Lucky Number contests. You have to buy a Souvenir Yearbook first, of course. Inside random yearbooks are lucky numbers stamped on over a dozen different merchant's advertisements. If you had a lucky number, you won, but only if you bought a program!

What song played during 7th inning stretch?   "Take Me Out to the Ballgame"

Radio Station Broadcasting Game: WVVE 102.3 FM

- The Navigators post Eastern League Leaders, Standings, and that Game's Lineup on the Carberry Concourse near home plate.

- Also for sale as you enter Dodd Stadium is the "Gator Guide", a weekly publication covering Norwich Navigator Baseball. This is by far the best little weekly periodical I've seen in the league. For only 50 ¢, you get updated Eastern League standings and stats; an Eastern League summary; a Norwich Navigators Alumni Report; a copy of the remaining schedule; box scores for the entire week in review; about three full pages of updated team statistics for all ten teams in the league; feature articles about Navigators baseball specifically, and the Eastern League in general; and finally, color photographs that are at least as good as any national daily big town paper.

Team Information

Norwich Navigators (Northern Division)

History:

Records from Mystic Seaport indicate that around the late 1860's there were at least three amateur baseball clubs playing in southeastern Connecticut. This included a team known as the Oceanic Base Ball Club in Mystic, the Uncas Base Ball Club in Norwich, and New London's Pequot Club. The Uncas Base Ball Club played at Williams Park. Play was governed by the Connecticut Base Ball Players Association after 1867, and there were around 20 organized clubs in the state at that time. In later years, Minor League teams played in the Connecticut State League which was founded in the early 1880's. There are reports of a Norwich team playing in the Connecticut League from around 1902 to 1907. Norwich also apparently had a club listed under the Connecticut Association around 1910.

The return of professional baseball to Norwich was a long time coming. Senator Christopher Dodd's lobbying efforts were instrumental in moving the Yankee's AA affiliate from Albany to Norwich. Albany had been members of the Eastern League at least as far back as 1945 when they won the Eastern

League Championship (Albany teams won in 1945, 1954, 1988, 1989, and 1991), so the effort couldn't have been insignificant. The Albany Yankees also produced such great players as Bernie Williams, Doug Drabek, Deion Sanders, Jim Leyritz, Sterling Hitchock, Pat Kelly, Mark Hutton, and Buck Showalter.

Dozens of people and organizations also had a hand in moving the club to Norwich, including the U.S. Senator, the state of Connecticut, the City of Norwich, the Stadium Authority, the owners of the team, the advisory board, and most importantly, the citizens of the surrounding communities who demonstrated that professional baseball could be viable in this region once again. Opening Day came on April 17, 1995 and Norwich Navigators baseball has been exciting ever since. Whether that enthusiasm is expressed by standing and clapping until the Navigators throw the first strike of the game, or by fans executing the only double "Wave" I've ever seen, baseball has come to town big time.

Not that there hasn't been a period of adjustment. 1995 was a learning experience for everyone, and that doesn't start and end with the traffic flow problems. There were other adjustments to be made, including moving the fences in about five feet and reducing their height to eight feet, increasing the size of the picnic area, and providing more entertainment opportunities for the youngsters during those long drawn out pitcher's duels.

Norwich also plays in the Connecticut Cup competition against rival Connecticut teams Hardware City and New Haven, where the team with the best record matched against the other two Connecticut teams takes the prize. Norwich won the Cup in 1995.

Eastern League Championships: None.

Players who went on to the Major Leagues:

Ramiro Mendoza (1995); Ruben Rivera (1995); Andy Fox (1995); Marty Janzen (1995); David Cone (1996 - rehab assignment).

New York Yankees Minor League Organization			
Team	**League**	**Level**	**City & Phone**
New York Yankees	American League	Major League	New York, NY (718) 293-4300
Columbus Clippers	International League	AAA	Columbus, OH (614) 462-5250
Norwich Navigators	Eastern League	AA	Norwich, CT (860) 887-7962
Tampa Yankees	Florida State League	A	Tampa, FL (813) 632-9855
Greensboro Bats	South Atlantic League	A	Greensboro, NC (910) 333-2287
Oneonta Yankees	New York-Penn League	Short A	Oneonta, NY (607) 432-6326
Gulf Coast Yankees	Gulf Coast League	Rookie	Tampa, FL (813) 875-7753

Approximate distance from Dodd Stadium to Yankee Stadium: 136 miles.
(Source: Rand McNally TripMaker Version 1.1 1994; Norwich, CT to New York, NY)

THOMAS J. DODD
May 15, 1907 - May 24, 1971

Special Dedications	
Senator Thomas J. Dodd Memorial Stadium	U.S. Senator for Connecticut from 1959 to 1971. Prosecutor at Nuremburg Father of Senator Christopher Dodd (D-Ct)
Lefty Dugas Drive	Major League Ballplayer
Milton's Way	Milton Jacobson - Norwich attorney and volunteer
The Burchard Marshall Skyboxes	Former Player - Negro Leagues
Glenn Carberry Concourse	Norwich attorney helped acquire the Navigators
Thomas Winters Press Box	Editor of Norwich Bulletin 1929 - 1988
Mashantucket Pequot Picnic Area	Donated Funds for Construction

Mascot:	Tater the Gator
Team Colors:	Purple, green, yellow, brown, black and red
Visiting	
Hotel:	Radisson Hotel - New London, 35 Governor Winthrop Blvd., New London, CT. 06320. (860) 443-7000
Fan Club:	Navigators Booster Club/Hank Fredella, 16 Bestview Road, Quaker Hill, CT. 06375 (Single $10.00; Couples $15.00; Family $20.00)
Other:	Dodd Memorial Stadium will host the Big East Baseball Tournament through 1998. The event usually takes place in May, with the winner moving on to the NCAA Tournament. Call 1 (800) 64GATOR for more information.

Directions to stadium:

Dodd Stadium is located in the middle of Norwich Industrial Park, and there are plenty of signs to help guide you to the game. (Or you can do what I did, and just follow all the cars.)

From the South: I-395 North to 81 West (Hartford). Follow the Route 2 connector, then bear right at Route 32. Take a right at the light near the Holmgren Subaru onto New Park Ave. Follow the signs from this point by proceeding up the hill, then take a left on Wisconsin Ave. Continue until you reach the T, take a right on Stott Avenue and follow to Dodd Stadium.

From Willimantic: Route 32S to the Franklin/Norwich border. At the light near Holmgren Subaru, take left onto New Park Ave. Follow the signs and the above directions.

From North: I-395 South to 82. Take a right onto West Town St, then right at the first stoplight onto Connecticut Ave. Continue up the hill, then a left onto Wisconsin Ave. Follow Wisconsin to the T, then take a right onto Stott Ave. Stott takes you to Dodd.

From Hartford: Take Route 2 E to Exit 27. Proceed off the exit ramp through the yield sign and then through the first light. At the second light, take a left into Norwich Industrial Park. Follow the signs and the above directions.

Norwich/Mystic/New London

Background

Norwich, also known as the "Rose of New England", is an industrial town of approximately 37,391 people, located in southeastern Connecticut. The area which is today Norwich was originally inhabited by the Pequots, and then the Mohegans, two revered Indian tribes whose presence is still felt in the region. Approximately nine square miles of the land at the head of the Yantic was purchased from Uncas, the chief of the Mohegans for about $350, and then settled in the mid-17th century. That area became Norwichtown in 1659, and today remains a village where you'll find historic structures like the Leffingwell House Museum, the Governor Samuel Huntington House (a signer of the

Declaration of Independence), the Meeting House Rocks, and the First Congregational Church Norwichtown close around the Norwichtown Green.

The city of Norwich was incorporated in 1784 and developed quickly as a major shipbuilding center located at the headwaters of the Thames River, where the Yantic and Shetucket rivers meet. The confluence of these rivers was an ideal location for the burgeoning trade markets in the New World, and Norwich became one of the first major manufacturing areas in the colony. Mills sprang up in the area before and after the Revolutionary War, and demand for manufactured goods from Norwich continued through the Civil War, and well through the end of the 19th century. For a time, Norwich boasted more millionaires per capita than anywhere else in the United States.

Today, Norwich is undergoing an economic revitalization, and the downtown Norwich business district has been listed on the National Register of Historic Places. There are twelve communities in the area served by the Norwich Area Chamber of Commerce, and the Greater Norwich region is home to well over 108,500 people. These twelve towns are on their way to once again becoming an important

A view of downtown Norwich, looking across the Marina at American Wharf

manufacturing center, producing such commodities as textiles, furniture, metal and paper goods, medical supplies, and electronics. Why, even Senator Thomas Dodd Memorial Stadium is located in the middle of Norwich Industrial Park, a large, new corporate area developed west of the main town center.

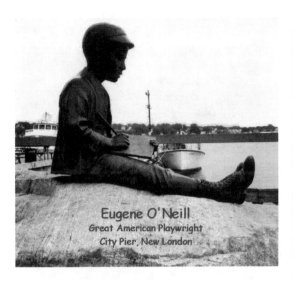

Eugene O'Neill
Great American Playwright
City Pier, New London

Further down the Thames lies the town of New London, Connecticut, incorporated also in 1784, with a population today of approximately 28,540. This area, along with nearby Groton, is still a significant deepwater port on Long Island Sound, and is perhaps more famous for its nuclear submarines rather than its historic whaling industry. In addition, New London is the home of the United States Coast Guard Academy and Connecticut College. As for a curious historical link between Norwich and New London, General Benedict Arnold was born in Norwich in 1741, and was once a decorated soldier during the American Revolution until he became a traitor to the colonial cause. After betraying his former army, Arnold led an attack of the British on New London in 1781, burning more than 150 buildings, and decimating the colonial army at Fort Griswold.

Also nearby to Norwich is Mystic, a smaller village only around population 2,618, located at the mouth of the Mystic River near Fishers Island Sound. Once an important whaling and shipbuilding center, Mystic, from the Algonquin word meaning "great tidal river", remains a picturesque setting and a very popular tourist destination. The Mystic Seaport is home today to historic tall ships and a replica 19th century village.

Information

Chamber of Commerce/Tourist Bureaus

Norwich Tourism Commission
69 Main Street
Norwich, CT. 06360
(860) 886-4683

Norwich Area Chamber of Commerce
35 Main Street
Norwich, CT 06360
(860) 887-1647

Southeastern Connecticut Tourism District
P.O. Box 89
470 Bank Street
New London, CT 06320
(860) 444-2206 or (800) TO-ENJOY

Mystic Chamber of Commerce
16 Cottrell Street
Mystic, CT
(860) 572-9578

Downtown New London Association
(860) 444-1789

Office of Development & Planning
111 Union Street
New London, CT 06320
(860) 447-5203

Web Site (s):   http://www.mysticmore.com; http://www.visitorguides.com

Daytime Entertainment

First Congregational Church, Norwichtown

Guided tours

Three Self-Guided Walking Tour Maps are available from the Norwich Tourism Office:

- ### Historic Broadway & Union Street

    St. Patrick Cathedral, Park Congregational Church, Norwich Free Academy, and Slater Memorial Museum

- ### Historic Washington & Broad Street

    Masonic Temple, Congregation Brothers of Joseph, Chelsea Parade and war memorials such as U.S.S. Maine Monument

- ### Historic Norwichtown

    Leffingwell House, Huntington House, Norwichtown Green, First Congregational Church

Museums

Mystic Seaport, The Museum of America and the Sea

75 Greenmanville Ave., P.O. Box 6000
Mystic, CT 06355-0990
(860) 572-5315

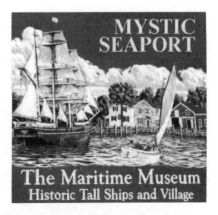

One of the best daytime attractions in the region, Mystic Seaport is more than just a fascinating maritime museum. The setting along the scenic Mystic River also includes a replica 19th century seaport village where you can experience and imagine New England life from over a hundred years ago; historic tall ships like the Charles W. Morgan, a National Historical Landmark; a planetarium; a children's museum, with an abundance of hands on activities; stores, including America's largest Maritime Bookstore; dining at the Seamen's Inne, and street vendors serving authentic Yankee Fare. During the summer, you can also

take a cruise on the Mystic aboard the *Sabino*, a classic coal-fired steamboat. There are also a number of seasonal events at the Seaport, including, during the summer months, Lobsterfest, Small Craft Weekend, Sea Music Festival, Independence Weekend, Project Oceanology Cruises, the Antique Marine Engine Exposition, and A Taste of History.

Exit 90 off I-95, 1 mile south on Route 27. Ample free parking. Open every day but Christmas. Call for exact hours, or visit the Mystic Seaport Web site at http://www.mystic.org

Families stroll by the Charles W. Morgan at Mystic Seaport

U.S.S. Nautilus Memorial, Submarine Force Library & Museum
NAVSUBASE
P.O. Box 571B
Groton, CT 06349-5000
(860) 449-3174; (800) 343-0079

Walk through submarine exhibit to discover the world's first nuclear-powered vessel; first ship to explore the North Pole; first submarine to journey 20,000 leagues under the sea. Museum includes exhibits on history of the submarine; three operating periscopes; recreated submarine attack center; control room; two mini-theaters; and, models of submarines from the Revolutionary War, through World War II, up to the present.

I-95 Exit 86, follow USS Nautilus signs. Open year round, Summer Hours: 9:00 a.m. to 5:00 p.m, Tuesdays 1:00 p.m. to 5:00 p.m. Closed first full week of May.

The Slater Memorial Museum
108 Crescent Street, Norwich, CT 06360
(860) 887-2506

Dedicated on November 4, 1886, this three story Romanesque structure includes a wide collection of Greek, Roman, and Renaissance casts; American and European art and furniture dating between the 17th and 20th centuries, American Indian artifacts, Vanderpoel Collection of Oriental art, African art, gun collection, Egyptian art objects and textiles.

Hours: Tues-Fri 9:00 a.m. to 4:00 p.m.; Sat, Sun 1:00 p.m. to 4:00 p.m. July-August , open Tues-Sun 1:00 p.m. to 4:00 p.m.

Leffingwell House Museum
348 Washington Street
Norwich, CT
(860) 889-9440

Restored example of New England colonial architecture. Built in 1675 by Stephen Backus, acquired in 1700 by Thomas Leffingwell who turned the house into an inn. Christopher Leffingwell, Thomas' grandson and an early merchant/industrialist in the region, played significant roles in the American Revolution. When threatened with demolishment of the house in 1956 in order to construct Route 2, the Society of Founders acquired the property and moved the house and began the restoration.

Open during the Summer, and by appointment.

United States Coast Guard Museum
Waesche Hall
United States Coast Guard Academy
New London, CT
(860) 444-8511

Museum displays over 6,000 artifacts, including a 13-foot, first order lighthouse lens from the Cape Ann Lighthouse, and over 200 ship models. The Coast Guard Academy is an open installation, and visitors are encourage to take self guided tours. There is in addition to the museum, a Visitor's Center, gift shop, snack bar, and the U.S.C.G. *Barque Eagle*, the largest classic Tall Ship flying the American Flag. (Call the ship at 444-8595 for visiting hours.)

I-95 North, Exit 82A; I-95 South, Exit 83, follow signs to Academy. Visitor Center Hours May-Oct. 9:00 a.m. to 5:00 p.m., open weekends in April 10:00 a.m. to 5:00 p.m. (Vis.Cent.# 444-8611)

Nathan Hale Schoolhouse
The Parade
New London, CT.
(860) 443-7949

One of the two one-room schoolhouses American Revolutionary and Patriot Nathan Hale taught in is open to the public, free of charge courtesy of the Sons of the American Revolution. Also honoring the man whose famous last words, "I only regret that I have but one life to lose for my country," inspired a nation, there are two statues of Hale in New London, one at Mitchell College, and the other as shown here at Williams Park.

Parks and Gardens

Mohegan Park

Located in the geographic center of Norwich, Mohegan Park is the largest park in the city. At 385 acres, this park includes Spaulding Pond (which allows swimming), the Mohegan Park Zoo and Monkey House, and the Norwich Memorial Rose Garden (over 120 varieties of roses, in season). Mohegan Park, if you're adept enough to find it, also offers shaded picnic areas and pavilions, a playground for children, walking and jogging areas, a concession booth, and restrooms. No wheeled activities are allowed (that means no skateboards or rollerblades), and no dogs.
From Broadway, turn on Rockwell Street and follow the road signs to the Park and Rose Garden. Call (860) 886-2381 x. 259, or the Norwich Tourism Office.

Howard T. Brown Memorial Park

Looking north from Howard Brown Memorial Park

Located near the deepest point of the Thames harbor, Howard T. Brown Memorial Park is an excellent green location to just sit and watch the boats go by on a lazy summer afternoon before baseball. Watch for seasonal events to take place here, including the Gazebo Summer Music Series and Harbor Day Festival.

Call (860) 886-2381 x. 259 for more info, or contact the Norwich Tourism Office.

Aquariums

Mystic Marinelife Aquarium
55 Coogan Boulevard
Mystic, CT 06355-1997
(860) 572-5955

This nonprofit marine science center is home to all sorts of fascinating aquatic creatures. There are more than 3,500 marine animals in over 40 exhibits, and these include performing beluga whales and dolphins at the Marine Theater, seals and Stellar's sea lions at Seal Island, and penguins at the unique Penguin Pavilion. There are hands on exhibits for children of all ages, and special exhibits that will teach the importance of wise marine conservation.

Exit 90 off I-95, free parking, restaurants, hotels, group rates.

Open 9:00 a.m. to 5:00 p.m from September through June, 9:00 a.m. to 6:00 p.m. July through Labor Day.

Casinos

Foxwoods Resort Casino

Route 2, P.O. Box 410, Ledyard, CT 06339
(860) 885-3000; 1 (800) PLAY-BIG

Operated by the Mashantucket Pequot Tribe, Foxwoods offers a world of entertainment possibilities in one location in southeastern Connecticut. Blackjack, Craps, Roulette, Baccarat, Big Six Wheel, Poker, Race Book, Keno, Bingo, live entertainment, and fine restaurants. Future expansion plans call for a 302 room hotel, two golf courses, campgrounds with walking and horseback trails, Native American Museum Research Center, heliport, lakeside facilities, shopping mall, three theaters, health club, and more.

Mohegan Sun Casino

Mohegan Sun Boulevard, P.O. Box 548, Uncasville, CT. 06382
(860) 204-8000; 1 (888) 226-7711

The newest casino in the region, Mohegan Sun opened during the 1996 Indian Summer. Year round seasonal entertainment awaits at this 150,000 square foot gaming center close to the heart of Norwich. Blackjack, Craps, Roulette, Poker, Pai Gow, Caribbean Stud, Baccarat, High Stakes Bingo, nearly 3,000 Slot Machines. Restaurants, Food Court, Sports Bar, live entertainment, childcare complex.

Cruises/Charters

Windjammer Mystic Whaler

P.O. Box 189
Mystic, CT. 06355
(860) 536-4218, (800) 697-8420

Twilight Cruise, Lobster Dinner Cruise, Daysail, Multi-Day Cruises aboard rebuilt classic schooner *Mystic Whaler*.

Voyager Cruises

Steamboat Wharf
Mystic, CT. 06355
(860) 536-0416

Half-Day Sail, Sunset Cruise aboard schooner *Argia*

Sunbeam Fleet

Captain John's Sport Fishing Center
15 First Street
Waterford, CT. 06385
(860) 443-7259

Deep Sea Fishing Charters and Party Boats,
July&August Whale Watches

Hel-Cat II

Hel-Cat Dock on the Thames River
181 Thames St
Groton, CT 06340
(860) 535-2066

Party Fishing Boats, Deep Sea Fishing,
Night Fishing, After Hours Charters

Thames River Cruises

City Pier, P.O. Box 1673
New London, CT 06320
(860) 444-SUBS

Sightseeing River Cruises

Public Beaches

Ocean Beach Park

End of Ocean Avenue
New London, CT 06320
(860) 447-3031; (800) 510-SAND

Half-mile boardwalk, giant triple waterslide, beach volleyball, miniature golf, indoor family fun center and arcade, playground, picnic areas, lounge & deck, concessions, gift shop, restrooms, first aid, lockers, telephones, showers.

Public Golf course, driving range, and miniature golf

Norwich Golf Course

685 New London Turnpike
Norwich, CT
(860) 889-6973

18 holes. Designed by Donald Ross, and built in 1920. Tee times accepted 3 days in advance, Pro Shop opens 7:00 a.m. Gas golf carts, pull carts available. Pro Shop, Lessons, Locker Rooms, Caddy Shack Restaurant & Lounge (887-8231). No driving range, but Malerba's is just across the street, see below. Statistics:

> Blue Yardage 6183, Rating 69.6, Slope 123, Par 71
> White Yardage 5872, Rating 68.2, Slope 120, Par 71
> Red Yardage 5104, Rating 70.2, Slope 118, Par 71

Shennecossett Golf Club

Plant St.
Groton, CT 06340
(860) 445-0262

18 holes. Scottish/traditional design course designed by Donald Ross, and built in 1898. Tee times accepted 3 days in advance, pro shop opens 7:00 a.m. Gas golf carts, pull carts available. No driving range. Statistics:

Blue Yardage 6491, Rating 71.1, Slope 122, Par 72
White Yardage 6142, Rating 69.5, Slope 118, Par 72
Red Yardage 5796, Rating 73.2, Slope 121, Par 76

Malerba's Golf Driving Range
650 New London Turnpike
Norwich, CT
(860) 889-5770

Putts Up Dock Miniature Gold & Bumper Boats
One Chelsea Harbor Drive, Norwich, CT 06360
(860) 886-PUTT

Located on the waterfront, this is a major attraction in downtown Norwich. Volcanoes, waterfalls, bumper boats, miniature golf.

Shopping Malls/Outlets

Crystal Mall
850 Hartford Turnpike
Waterford, CT 06385
(860) 442-8500

Sear's, Macy's, Filene's, JC Penney, Crystal Pushcart Market, Food Court, over 150 other specialty stores. Customer Service Booth, Restrooms, ATM.

Hours: Mon-Sat 9:30 a.m. to 9:30 p.m; Sunday 11 a.m. to 6 p.m. Directions: I-95 exit 82 to Route 85; I-395 exit 77 to Route 85.

Mystic Factory Outlets: I & II
Coogan Boulevard
Mystic, CT 06355
(860) 443-4788

Twenty four outlet stores located next to Mystic Aquarium and Olde Mistick Village.

Hours April-Dec Mon-Fri 10 a.m. to 9 p.m., Sat 10 a.m. to 7 p.m.; Sun. 11 a.m to 6 p.m.

I-95, Exit 90, Route 27, then left onto Coogan Boulevard

Olde Mistick Village
Route 27 and Coogan Boulevard, P.O. Box 176
Mystic, CT 06355
(860) 536-4941

Stores, Restaurants, Crafts located near Aquarium and Outlets.

Seasonal Events

Dates are approximate, contact regional tourism offices listed above for updated schedule information.

Norwich
April: Annual Spring Fair. May: Spring Craft Fair; Norwich A'Bloom; Eastern Connecticut Chamber of Commerce Annual Golf Tournament; Chelsea Street Festival. July: Fireworks at Norwich Harbor; Eastern Connecticut Antique Auto Exchange and Show. August: Harbor Day. September: Historic Norwichtown Days.

Mystic
April: Garden Series. May: Lobsterfest; Decoration Day. June: Small Craft Weekend; Sea Music Festival; Wooden Boat Show. July: Independence Weekend; Antique & Classic Boat Rendezvous; Project Oceanology Cruises. August: A Taste of History; Antique Marine Engine Exposition. September: Schooner Days.

New London
June: Connecticut Early Music Festival. July: Sailfest. August: Festival Italiano

Groton
July: SUBFEST

Upper Yantic Falls, Norwich

Accommodations/Other

Visiting Hotel for the Norwich Navigators:
Radisson Hotel
35 Governor Winthrop Blvd
New London, CT 06320
(860) 443-7000
Restaurant & Lounge, Swimming Pool, Room Service, Entertainment & AAA Discounts may be available

Norwich

Norwich Inn & Spa
607 West Thames Street, Route 32
Norwich, CT 06360
1 (800) ASK-4-SPA; (860) 886-2401
Restaurant, Full Spa facilities, Fitness
Center, Swimming Pool, Hiking, Golf,
Tennis, Entertainment Discount
(Sunday through Thursday, depending
upon availability)

Ramada Hotel
10 Laura Blvd
Norwich, CT 06360
(860) 889-5201
Restaurant & Lounge, Swimming Pool,
Room Service, AAA Discounts

Mystic

Marriott Residence Inn
42 Whitehall Ave
Mystic, CT 06355
(860) 536-5150
Complimentary Deluxe Continental
Breakfast, Weekday Social Hours,
Swimming Pool, Tennis, Exercise
Facility, Kitchen Facilities & Grocery
Shopping Service, AAA Discounts

Mystic Hilton
20 Coogan Boulevard
Mystic, CT 06355
(860) 572-0731
1 (800) HILTONS
Restaurant & Lounge, Swimming Pool,
Exercise Room, Game Room, Kitchen
Facilities, Room Service,
Entertainment Discounts (through mid-
June)

Best Western Mystic Sovereign Hotel
9 Whitehall Ave
Mystic, CT 06355
(860) 536-4281
Restaurant & Lounge, Swimming Pool,
Game Room & Playground, AAA,
AARP, Entertainment Discounts

Comfort Inn
48 Whitehall Ave
Mystic, CT 06355
(860) 572-8531 or (800) 228-5150
Complimentary Continental Breakfast,
shuttle to Foxwoods, Swimming Pool,
Exercise Facility, AAA Discounts

Days Inn
55 Whitehall Ave
Mystic, CT 06355
(860) 572-0574 or (800) DAYS-INN
Restaurant, shuttle to Foxwoods,
Swimming Pool, Exercise Facility,
Room Service, AAA Discounts

New London

Holiday Inn
I-95 and Frontage Road
New London, CT 06320
(860) 442-0631 or (800) HOLIDAY
Restaurant & Lounge, Swimming Pool,
Exercise Facility, Kitchen Facilities,
Game Room, Room Service, AAA &
Entertainment Discounts based upon
availability

Red Roof Inn
707 Colman Street
New London, CT 06320
(860) 444-0001 or (800) THE-ROOF

Groton

Best Western Olympic Inn
360 Route 12
Groton, CT 06340
(860) 445-8000
Restaurant & Lounge, Game Room,
Room Service, shuttle to Foxwoods,
AAA & Entertainment Discounts

Ledyard

Foxwoods Resort Casino
Route 2, P.O. Box 410
Ledyard, CT 06339
(860) 885-3000 or (800) PLAY-BIG
Casino, Restaurant & Lounge,
Swimming Pool, Exercise Room, Game
Room, Room Service

Inns/Bed and Breakfast

Steamboat Inn
73 Steamboat Wharf
Mystic, CT 06355
(860) 536-8300
Continental Plus Breakfast, whirlpool
baths, AC, TV, downtown Mystic, river
views available

The Whaler's Inn
20 East Main Street
Mystic, CT 06355
(860) 536-1506 or (800) 243-2588
Located in Downtown Mystic

Marinas

The Marina at American Wharf
One American Wharf
Norwich, CT 06360
(860) 886-6363

Full service 200 slip marina, cable tv, telephone, elec. & wtr, dockside service, restaurant, mail service,
pump-out station, gas, Chelsea Harbor Park, shower and locker facilities, swimming pool

Hospitals

William W. Backus Hospital
326 Washington Street
Norwich, CT
(860) 889-8331

Lawrence & Memorial Hospital
365 Montauk Ave
New London, CT
(860) 442-0711

Transportation

AMTRAK
(800) USA-RAIL

Groton/New London Airport
155 Tower Ave.
Groton, CT
(860) 445-8549

Greyhound Bus Lines
New London, CT
(860) 447-3841;
(800) 231-2222

SEAT/Southeastern Area Transit
(860) 886-2631

Block Island Ferry
New London, CT to
Block Island, RI
(860) 442-7891

Cross Sound Ferry
New London, CT to
Long Island
(860) 443-7394

Fishers Island Ferry
New London, CT to Fishers
Island
(860) 442-0165

Viking Passenger Ferry
New London, CT to
Montauk, N.Y.
(800) MONTAUK

Portland Sea Dogs

Team: **Portland Sea Dogs** (Northern Division)

Stadium: **Hadlock Field**

Office Address: 271 Park Avenue, Portland ME 04102
Mailing Address: P.O. Box 636, Portland, ME 04104
Phone: (207) 874-9300
Fax: (207) 780-0317
Web Site(s): http://www.ime.net/seadogs;
http://www.fanlink.com/PORTLAND_SEADOGS;
http://minorleaguebaseball.com/teams/portland-me/; email: seadogs@ime.net

Team Ownership:

Operated by: Portland Maine Baseball, Inc.
Principals: Dan Burke, Owner; Charles Eshbach,
President & GM

Affiliation: Florida Marlins

Years in Eastern League: 1994-Present

Stadium Physical Characteristics

Age, Built in: 1994

Stadium Owner: City of Portland

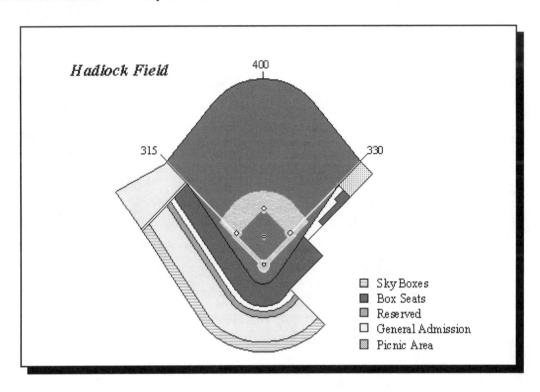

Hadlock Field

400

315

330

☐ Sky Boxes
■ Box Seats
▨ Reserved
☐ General Admission
▨ Picnic Area

Bullpens: Behind the fences, outside of foul territory. The Visiting Bullpen near Left Field is the easier of the two to see from the stands. Home Bullpen is beyond the outfield wall.

Playing Surface: Natural grass

Characteristics:

Probably the most distinctive stadium in all of the Eastern League, Hadlock Field captures the aura of back-to-the-future ballparks with the inclusion of the historic Portland Exposition Building, a local

landmark for over eighty years, in the stadium layout. Although some may say that the location of the Expo Building along the right field line limits the number of bleachers at Hadlock Field, most will say it is a vital part of the character and the framework of a magnificent, urban ballpark.

But, don't let the historic old brick facade fool you, Hadlock Field is a modern facility providing all the amenities Minor League Baseball fans expect. This includes a high tech scoreboard out in left center field, a well-stocked souvenir shoppe, concession areas second to none, and especially, a great venue to catch a game. There are no impeded views whatsoever at the stadium since the stands are all open to the elements. (That also means that the stands are quite open to foul balls. In fact, of all the stadiums I visited, I think Hadlock Field affords one of the best opportunities to walk away with a souvenir. Of course, the Sea Dogs encourage you to "Stay Alert!" at all times.)

As for the stands, although access to the higher General Admission areas is on a rather steep incline, the friendly confines of Hadlock Field insure that every seat is a good one. Plan to arrive early, no later than ½ hour before the first pitch, because loyal Sea Dogs' fans know that at some point the public address announcer will be pleading with the faithful to "squish-in" for the latecomers. This is due to the popularity of all the home games. In fact, I spoke with some very friendly ushers who told me every year since the inaugural season in 1994, the Sea Dogs have had to add more seating at Hadlock Field because of the high demand. This includes the bleachers in left field, and the smaller ones out in right. (I've even been told the Sea Dogs are considering cutting back on the picnic area so they can squish in even more fans.) Oh, and don't forget to dress warm. We are talking Maine here, and unless you've had a bright afternoon sun warming the first base side seats, it can get chilly during the night games. (In 1996, Portland hosted what appears to be the greatest number of day games during the week, probably for this very reason.)

One final characteristic, Hadlock Field is half concrete and half metal. Metal stands, for some reason, encourage foot stomping, hand clapping behavior amongst the fans when things are going well for the team. Although not as loud as some all-metal stadiums, like, say, Yale Field, there's still a check-your-beer-or-soda type vibration running through the stands. Just thought you should know ahead of time.

Capacity: 6,860

	1994	1995	1996
Attendance	375,197	429,763	408,503

1996 Average Attendance:

No. Of Openings: 68
1996 Daily Average: 6,007

(24,723 attended in the 1996 postseason)

All Time Attendance Records:

Daily: 6,864 on July 3, 1995, and
on July 25, 1996

Seasonal: 429,763 in 1995

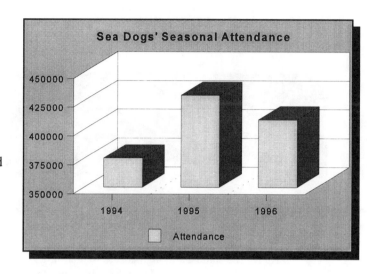

Skyboxes: 12 (Named after
Hall of Fame players, from Aaron to Yaztremski)

Type of Seating: The Box and Reserved Seating areas at Hadlock Field have comfortable armrests for your convenience. General Admission seating is comprised of plastic-like bleachers, which are generally more comfortable than the aluminum bleachers you find at most stadiums.

Covered Seating:

No, however, the concession concourse is underneath the stands if you need to wait out a rain delay, or otherwise just want to get out of the sun for a bit.

Restrooms:

Ladies: 3
Men: 2
Changing tables: Yes

Customer Service
Window: Yes, located behind home plate near the main entrance.

Smoking Policy: Not permitted in the stands. There is a smoking area behind the left field stands.

First Aid: Located on the third base side of the concourse, opposite security.

Wheelchair & Handicapped Seating: Yes, in the last row behind the Box Seats. Ramps at both ends of the stadium.

Telephones: Four.

ATM: No.

You can purchase space for announcements on the Hadlock Field scoreboard for just $25.00 per message. These messages can be submitted anytime before the game day, or even prior to the start of the third inning, subject to any necessary editing of course. Call 879-9500, or fax your announcement to (207) 780-0317.

Scoreboard:

There is a large scoreboard behind the left center field wall. It has both a graphical and an electronic display providing all the information you'll need to follow the game. The graphical display here is exceptional.

Game Clock:

Yes, over the scoreboard. There is also a digital clock in right.

Sound: Adequate. (The Sea Dogs like to pipe golden oldies through the speakers in between innings.)

Sunsets? Third Base Side.

Autographs:

There is an autograph table set up on the third base side of the concourse where you can collect Sea Dogs signatures for approximately fifteen minutes, beginning forty-five minutes before game time.

Concessions and Souvenirs

The Sea Dogs provide a wide variety of concessions to please any palate. In fact, there were so many, this is one stadium where I didn't get a chance to sample some of the items I would've liked (e.g. the Short Stop Sub Shop - only stadium where you can get a nice deli sandwich for a reasonable price). As for a general comment, you should know ahead of time that Hadlock Field has the most conservative beer policy of any stadium in the Eastern League. There are only two locations to buy draft beer, and you are required to produce a photo ID every time you buy a beer (only ONE per customer), no matter whether you're 21 or 121 years old. In addition, when the Sea Dogs call last call, you better believe it. Beer sales end promptly as soon as the 7th inning stretch begins, and I do mean Promptly! (I tried to purchase one last beer without knowing this policy, and I almost lost a couple fingers when they slammed the window shut.)

Best stadium food:

I found my grilled food out at the Specialty Sandwich area near right field. The Steak Sandwich was good, but a little too chewy for my liking. There was also a grilled chicken sandwich if I'm not mistaken, but my favorite was the Grilled Sausage. The Sausage had a real nice smoky flavor, which was complemented by the fresh peppers and onions served up on a soft, warm bun. Surprisingly, the lines weren't too long out here, which I guess can be interpreted as a bad sign by some, but I thought all the Specialty items were a good value and well worth recommending.

The other concession which ranks right up there with the best are the french fries. These are the good, crinkle-cut style fries which everyone is willing to wait for, even if that means missing a inning or so of the action.

Local cuisine:

The Sea Dogs serve up a fish sandwich at the Fried Food windows, and I guess this can be called a local item, but I noticed there weren't too many locals ordering it. Served more like a Fish Hot Dog rather than a sandwich, there was more filler than fish inside. Try a regular hot dog instead.

Concessions in stands:

Hot Dogs, Soda, Popcorn, Candy, and Ice Cream.

Hot Dog:

The Hot Dogs at Hadlock Field are actually quite good. They're nice and juicy, and at between seven and eight inches in length, a real bargain at only $1.50. For another buck twenty five, you can turn your hot dog into a gourmet by topping it with chili, cheese and/or sauerkraut. These options are, for want of no better words, simply excellent! Everyone knows you just can't go wrong with a regular dog, and that's why the Ballpark Fare windows (which also serve pizza and stuffed bread) are the longest concession lines in the park.

Peanuts:
$1.25

Beer:

On tap:	Bud, Bud Light
In stands:	none
Microbrews:	Geary's
Non-alcoholic:	O'Douls
Wine:	none

Desserts: Candy, Ice Cream, Sea Dog Biscuit, Milk and Cookies

View of Field from Concession Stands: No. However, there are televisions everywhere which show Live Action footage while you're waiting in line. It's not the same, but at least you won't miss a moment of the game.

Gift Shop:

The Sea Dog Souvenir Shoppe is located near the main entrance on the left as you walk in. Selling items containing the hottest logo in The Minor Leagues, the Souvenir Shoppe stocks merchandise ranging from souvenir bats and balls, to underwear, shirts, sweaters and jackets. They even sell already worn game jerseys, if that's the type of souvenir you're after. Not only is the Shoppe open before, during, and after every Sea Dog home game, it is open all year, Monday through Friday 9 a.m. to 5 p.m., and Saturdays from 11 a.m. to 4 p.m. Call 1 (800) 936-DOGS for a free brochure.

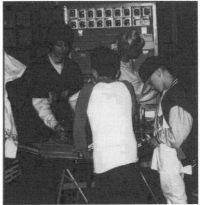

Fans check out some merchandise at a Souvenir Booth set up just outside the main gift shop.

Admission*:

Individual Game Prices		
	Adult	Child (16 and under) Senior (62 and over)
Box (Sold Out)	$6.00	$5.00
Reserved	$5.00	$4.00
General Admission	$4.00	$2.00

Season Ticket Prices (71 Games)	
All-Star Plan (One Year)	$350.00 per seat
Hall of Fame Plan (Three Years)	Discounted. Call 879-9500 for info.

Discounted Group Rates		
Adults	General Admission	Reserved
20-999	$3.50	$4.50
1000+	$3.00	N/A
Child/Senior	General Admission	Reserved
20-999	$1.50	$3.50
1000+	$1.00	N/A

Restrictions apply to Weekend Group Rates

Group Functions:

Picnic Area:

The Sea Dogs in 1996 could accommodate groups of 75 to 128 people in their picnic grove near the Expo Building in right field. The per person price includes a Box Seat, and you have four different menus to choose from when you make your arrangements. To reserve an available date, you will need to provide a $375.00 non refundable deposit. Then at least two weeks prior, you need to have a final head count, and also, you must pay the remaining balance. Call 879-9500 for more information.

The following menus were available in the picnic area during 1996:

Hamburger and Hot Dogs	$15.00 per person
Chicken Barbecue	$16.00 per person
Sparerib Barbecue	$17.00 per person
Steak Barbecue	$19.00 per person

All menus include baked beans, cole slaw, iced tea/lemonade, watermelon and a Sea Dogs Ice Cream Biscuit.

Skybox:

Groups up to 22 people can rent one of the dozen skyboxes for $400.00 per game. Each skybox is heated and air conditioned, includes a color television, and provides both indoor and outdoor seating. Catering options are available, as well as waiter and waitress service should you decide.

Portland Room:

The Portland Room is available for meetings and other private functions at Hadlock Field. Located on the main concourse level, the Portland Room can accommodate groups of 25 to 45 people, and includes reserved seats for the game, and a variety of catering arrangements for your convenience. The Portland Room can be reserved both on game days, and on non-game days as well.

Birthday Parties:

Children 12 and under can have a special birthday party at regular Sea Dogs home games for only $12.00 per person. Your child will be treated like a star at Hadlock Field with their name in lights on the Sea Dogs Scoreboard plus a special announcement over the public address system. In addition, every birthday child gets the chance to have a picture taken with one of the Sea Dogs players. The Sea Dogs Birthday Party includes:

Slugger, The Sea Dog, one of the coolest team mascots in the League.

PORTLAND
Sea Dogs™

One General Admission ticket ($2.00 upgrade to Reserved Seats available)
Hot Dog and Regular Soda (Pizza is 50¢ more per slice.)
Large Bowl of Popcorn
Sea Dogs Birthday Cake
Sea Dogs Birthday Goody Bag of Surprises

Make your reservations for a birthday party early. The Sea Dogs can accommodate birthday groups of 8 to 15 people, and there is a $25.00 non-refundable deposit required.

[***1996 Data: Prices subject to change. Call (207) 879-9500 for more information.**]

Ticket Sales: Portland, Maine Baseball, Inc.

    Address: P.O. Box 636, Portland, Maine 04104
    Phone: (207) 879-9500
    Credit Cards: MasterCard, Visa, American Express
    Hours Ticket Window Open: Monday through Friday 9:00 a.m. to 5:00 p.m.
        Saturday 11:00 a.m. to 4:00 p.m.

Rain Check Policy: If a game is canceled before 5 innings are played (4 ½ if the home team is ahead), your ticket may be exchanged at the Box Office for another ticket of equal value to a future regular season game, depending upon availability. No Cash Refunds.

Upgrade Policy: General Admission tickets may be upgraded to Reserved, depending on availability, to the same game at the Box Office window by paying the price differential. Child/Senior tickets may also be upgraded to Adult tickets.

Game times:

April to Mid-May:

Weekdays:	Most 6:00 p.m.; some are 1:00 p.m. or Noon.
Saturday:	1:00 p.m.
Sunday:	1:00 p.m.

Mid-May to September:

Weekdays:	7:00 p.m.
Saturday:	1:00 p.m. until Mid-July, 7:00 p.m. thereafter.
Sunday:	1:00 p.m. until Mid-July, 4:00 p.m. thereafter.

(See schedule for updated information. All game times subject to change.)

Time Gates open:

1 ½ hours before game begins.

Parking:

1. Ramada Inn Shuttle Lot, located at the Ramada on Congress St. Shuttle bus is $1.00 per person, two kids under 12 are free. Buses run from 1 hour before game, to after game. Call (207) 774-0351

2. USM Parking, located on Bedford Street, short walk away. Call (207) 879-0945.

Other

Must be a Knuckleball Pitcher....

For the kids:

The Four Seasons Baseball Speedpitch is located over near left field, where the kids can test their baseball pitching skills. There is also a basketball shoot out located in this open area under the left field stands if you prefer. Also, when a Sea Dog hits a home run, look behind the centerfield wall for a replica of the Portland Head Light to emerge, with sirens blaring, and fireworks blasting to celebrate the run.

Like most of the teams in the EL, Portland has a great mascot, Slugger the Sea Dog who always puts on a good show for the fans, and especially for the kids. Don't be surprised to hear a young voice behind you ask, at least two or three times a game, "When's Slugger coming out to play?" Portland fans of all ages love their mascot, and I'd have to say, he's one of the fan-friendliest puppies in town.

Promotions and Giveaways:

The Sea Dogs put on some great promotions, but given the level of fan loyalty in the Portland area, this is one club that probably would still have great attendance figures even if there wasn't a single promotion or giveaway the entire season. There were over forty special promotional nights at Hadlock Field, including a visit by the Colorado Silver Bullets Woman's Professional Baseball Team; two special

Fireworks Nights; a number of home games sponsored by WPOR, WMTW, WZAN, and WHOM; special outings to benefit local charities and organizations; and also, a number of giveaways like schedule magnets, poster schedules, and baseball cards.

Further, every Tuesday night home game in 1996 was special C.N. Brown/Citgo family night, where the whole family could be admitted in general admission for only $9.00 with a special Family Night coupon. Every Wednesday home game was Shop 'n Save $1.00 off night in 1996, where a valid coupon would be good for a dollar off admission to that night's game.

In between innings:

A young fan waits for Slugger to race around the bases.

The big promotion at Hadlock Field in 1996 was the Payoff Pitch. Each game during the middle of the sixth inning, one lucky fan was chosen at random to compete on the field for the chance to win, among other things, a new car! If your lucky number was called, then you'd be escorted on the field to try to throw a baseball through a hole in a special sign. If you made it on the first try, you could have won a brand new Dodge Neon. Other prizes for the Payoff included a $500.00 savings bond from Key Bank, a $25 gift certificate for service at a local Dodge dealer, a 3 foot sub from Subway, or some other consolation prize (just in case you couldn't hit the side of a barn if your life depended on it.)

There were also chances to win all sorts of Lucky Number prizes throughout the game. You need to buy a souvenir program as you enter the stadium, and then listen over the P.A. system to see if your number is up. (If you miss the announcement, the Sea Dogs post all Lucky Numbers by the information window behind home plate, a great feature that should be picked up by the other clubs.)

And, of course, the most entertaining aspect between innings was provided by Slugger during those races around the field. Slugger is a loyal friend to fans and players alike, but when it comes to racing children around the field, he's the slowest dog I've ever seen. He's so slow, the Sea Dogs give him an ATV for the race, and even then he still can't beat anybody. But, it's all good, clean fun anyway.

What song played during 7th inning stretch?

"Take Me Out to the Ballgame" (Sung enthusiastically by the entire home crowd.)

Radio Station Broadcasting Game:

WPOR 1490 AM (Flagship); WTME 1240 AM; WKTQ 1450 AM; WOXO 92.7 FM; WTBM 100.7 FM; WQEZ 104.7 FM. (Note also, WMTW-TV, Channel 8 broadcast at least four home games during the 1996 season. Check schedule for listings.)

Eastern League Information: Current EL standings posted near the main entrance.

Speaker's Bureau: You can schedule a representative of the Portland Sea Dogs Front Office to speak at functions by calling (207) 874-9300. (You can also arrange an appearance by Slugger the Sea Dog at either public or private events by calling (207) 879-9500.)

Team Information

Portland Sea Dogs (Northern Division)

History:

      Maine's love affair with professional baseball has been an on-again, off-again affair since the beginning of this century. There have been a number of different franchises in the Portland region since that time, including Hugh Duffy's Portland Duffs from 1913-1916; John "Magnate" Haley's New England League Portland Gulls from approximately 1946-1948; the Portland Pilots, who won the New England League title in 1949 while playing in a renovated high school football stadium; the Old Orchard Beach Maine Guides from 1984-1988; and finally, and most successfully so far, the Portland Sea Dogs, 1994 to the present.

      When rumors first started floating around about the possibility of professional baseball coming back to Portland around 1992, the Portland community mobilized quickly around the idea, and a volunteer civic group called Citizens for Portland Baseball was formed to activate local support. Citizens for Portland Baseball was founded and directed by Mr. Bill Troubh, the former Mayor of Portland, and currently the new 1996 Eastern League President. Working in cooperation with owner Dan Burke, Citizens for Portland Baseball assisted in taking season ticket deposits, helped sponsor a "Name-the-Team" contest, rented a store to promote Portland baseball, and raised $200,000 to renovate Hadlock Field.

      The Portland Sea Dogs came into the Eastern League at the same time as the New Haven Ravens, when expansion created two new major league teams in Florida and Colorado respectively. Obviously, Portland fans were starved for professional baseball as the new affiliate of the Florida Marlins immediately eclipsed Eastern League attendance records in their inaugural season, and easily surpassed one million fans in just their third full season of play at Hadlock Field.

      By the way, in case you were wondering how the stadium got its name, Hadlock Field is named after Edson B. Hadlock, Jr., the dedicated coach of the Portland High School Baseball Team for 29 years from 1956 to 1978.

Eastern League Championships: None.

1996:   Portland defeats Binghamton in Semifinals (3-2)

Harrisburg defeats Portland for EL Championship (3-1)

1995:   New Haven defeats Portland in Semifinals (3-1)

Players who went on to the Major Leagues:

Charles Johnson (1994); Jesus Tavarez (1994); Jay Powell (1995); Ralph Milliard (1995); Edgar Renteria (1995); Billy McMillon (1995); Luis Castillo (1996);

Florida Marlins Minor League Organization			
Team	**League**	**Level**	**City & Phone**
Florida Marlins	National League	Major League	Miami, Florida (305) 626-7400
Charlotte Knights	International League	AAA	Fort Mill, SC (803) 548-8050
Portland Sea Dogs	Eastern League	AA	Portland, ME (207) 874-9300
Brevard County Manatees	Florida State League	A	Melbourne, FL (407) 633-9200
Kane County Cougars	Midwest League	A	Geneva, IL (708) 232-8811
Oneida County Blue Marlins	New York-Penn League	Short A	Utica, NY (315) 738-0999
Gulf Coast Marlins	Gulf Coast League	Rookie	Melbourne, FL (407) 633-8119
Dominican Summer League Marlins	Dominican Summer League	Rookie	Santo Domingo, Dominican Republic (809) 537-4227

Approximate distance from Hadlock Field to Pro Player Stadium: 1584 miles
(Source: Rand McNally TripMaker Version 1.1 1994; Portland, ME to Miami, FL)

Mascot: Slugger the Sea Dog
Team Colors: Teal, black and white
**Visiting
Hotel**:   Radisson Eastland Hotel Portland, 157 High Street, Portland, ME 04101 (207) 775-5411
                  (A short, but healthy walk to Hadlock Field)
Fan Club: Ramada's Sea Dog Fan Club, Ramada Inn, 1230 Congress St., Portland, ME (207) 774-5611 (Free parking for all Sea Dog games, Transportation discounts, dining and beverage discounts, discount rates on accommodations.)

Directions to stadium:

From the South - use I-295, and take Exit 5 for Congress St. Merge onto Congress, stay left, and make a left at first set of lights (St. John St.) Stay right, and then merge onto Park Avenue.

From the North - Use I-295, and take Exit 6A for Forest Ave South. Take a right at first set of lights, thru Deering Oaks Park, and take a right onto Park Ave.

Hadlock Field is located near the Expo Building on Park Ave.

Portland, Maine

Background

Portland, Maine (population 64,358) was founded over 350 years ago in 1632 in an area known to its Native American inhabitants as Machigonne, or Great Neck. By 1652, the area became part of the Massachusetts Bay Colony, and six years later, the region that is presently Greater Portland, including Portland, South Portland, Falmouth, Cape Elizabeth and Westbrook became known simply as Falmouth. Throughout much of its pre-colonial and colonial history, the region suffered at the hands of the French, the British, and the Native Americans. The area was destroyed in 1675 during King Philip's War by the Native Americans, again by the French and the Native Americans in 1690, and again almost one hundred years later in 1775 by the British during the Revolutionary War. After the Revolution, the area quickly recovered and became known as a major commercial port and shipping center. Some of the early industries focused on the gold and fur trade, but most significant to the region was the abundance of tall, white pine trees, ideal for making large, strong masts for ships.

In 1786, the area known as "The Neck" separated from Falmouth and became the town of Portland. In 1820, Maine finally became a State, and Portland served as its capital until the year 1832. That same year the capital moved to nearby Augusta, and Portland officially incorporated as a city. Industry continued to prosper in the region, and in 1854, Portland was the 7th largest shipbuilding port in the entire United States, and a few years later, the 2nd largest molasses shipping port.

This growth was significantly curtailed by the disastrous Great Fire of 1866, which began during the 4th of July celebration. The Great Fire destroyed one third of the city, taking out most of the public buildings, half the churches, and hundreds of historic houses. Lesser cities might not have recovered from such a catastrophe, but Portland rebuilt itself, incorporating brick reconstruction in the Victorian style homes and buildings still standing today.

As for industry, shipbuilding continued to thrive, and Portland, as the closest deepwater port to Europe, became the home to the U.S. North American Fleet during World War II. It was during that time when over 30,000 shipbuilders mass produced the legendary British Ocean Ships and the United States Liberty Ships, which were large cargo vessels created using all welded construction. Portland continues as the largest industrialized city in Maine, with its major industries of shipping and fishing, and manufacturing of such goods as textiles, forest products, and chemicals.

Portland also serves as the gateway to America's Vacationland. There's just so much neat stuff to do here in this land of natural, rugged beauty. Whether it's a visit to the Portland Head Light (commissioned by President George Washington and lit in 1791); a trip to the Wadsworth-Longfellow Museum; a cruise out to one of the resort islands in

The Lobsterman Statue, downtown Portland

Casco Bay or to nearby Nova Scotia; fine dining and entertainment in Portland's Downtown Arts District; or, of course, fantastic bargain shopping at the outlets in Freeport, Maine, you'll find many fascinating attractions in the region.

Information

Chamber of Commerce/Tourist Bureaus

Convention and Visitor's Bureau
305 Commercial Street
Portland, ME 04101
(207) 772-5800 (Visitors);
(207) 772-4994 (Conventions)

Chamber of Commerce
145 Middle Street
Portland, ME
(207) 772-2811

Stroll along Portland's picturesque downtown shopping district.

Portland's Downtown District
400 Congress Street
Portland Maine 04101
(207) 772-6828

Maine Innkeepers Association
305 Commercial Street
Portland, ME
(207) 773-7670

Downtown Arts District Association (DADA):
(207) 879-0949; (207) 772-5533

City of Portland: (207) 874-8300

Maine Visitor Information: (800) 533-9595 or
(207) 623-0363

Web Site(s): http://www.portland.com; http://www.portland.com/cityhall/

Daytime Entertainment

Guided tours

Mainely Tours
5 ½ Moulton Street
Portland, ME
(207) 774-0808

Summer sightseeing tour vans, running from Mid-May through Mid-October. Tours of Portland and Old Port; Whale Watching; Land & Sea Tours; Shipyard Microbrewery. Airport Transfers, Step-on Guides, and Shuttles and Group Tours available. Service from Visitor Center at 305 Commercial Street; Mainely Tours & Gifts in the Old Port; Holiday Inn By the Bay; Portland Regency Hotel; Radisson Eastland Hotel; Maine Mall and Airport Area; Outer Congress St; South Portland, Westbrook; and Old Orchard Beach.

Historic sites

The Center for Maine History

485-489 Congress Street
Portland, Maine 04101
(207) 774-1822

One acre campus includes the Wadsworth-Longfellow House and gardens (see below), the Maine History Gallery, and the Maine Historical Society Library. Includes extensive historical and genealogical records with more than 125,000 books and over two million manuscripts. Museums contain 8,000 objects, and conducts various programs and exhibits throughout the year.

Gallery (June-Oct.) Tues.-Sun. 10 a.m.-4 p.m.; (Dec.-May) Wed.-Sat. 12 Noon-4 p.m.
Library (Year round) Tues.-Fri. 10 a.m.-4 p.m.

Wadsworth-Longfellow House

Statue of Henry Wadsworth Longfellow on Congress Street

489 Congress Street
Portland, Maine 04101
(207) 879-0427

The boyhood home of the early American poet Henry Wadsworth Longfellow, who wrote such works as "The Wreck of the Hesperus" (1841), "The Song of Hiawatha" (1855), and *Tales of a Wayside Inn* (1863), containing the well-known "Paul Revere's Ride". This house became a Registered National Historic Landmark in 1963 and is the earliest home still standing on the peninsula. Built by Longfellow's grandfather, General Peleg Wadsworth in 1785-86, the house is furnished with actual family belongings and maintained as it would have appeared in 1890.

June-Oct. Open Tuesdays through Sundays, 10:00 a.m. to 4:00 p.m.
December Special Holiday Tours, call for schedule.
Jan-May Limited Hours, call for schedule.

Victoria Mansion

109 Danforth Street
Portland, Maine 04101
(207) 772-4841

Victorian home with original interiors, and antique furnishings.

May-Oct. Open Tues.-Sat. 10 a.m. to 4 p.m; Sun. 1 p.m. to 5 p.m.

Museums

Portland Museum of Art

Seven Congress Square
Portland, Maine 04101
(207) 775-6148

Founded in 1882, the Portland Museum of Art is the oldest arts institution in Maine. Collection of fine and decorative arts includes American works by Winslow Homer, John Singer Sargent, Rockwell Kent, Marsden Hartley, and Andrew Wyeth, as well as European masters like Auguste Renoir, Edgar Degas, Claude Monet, Pablo Picasso, Edvard Munch, and Rene Magritte. The collection is housed in a building designed by I.M. Pei & Partners.

Tues., Wed., and Saturday Open from 10 a.m. to 5 p.m.; Thurs., and Fri. Open from 10 a.m. to 9 p.m.; Sunday Open from Noon to 5 p.m.; Mondays from July through Columbus Day, Open 10 a.m. to 5 p.m.

The Children's Museum of Maine

142 Free Street
P.O. Box 4041
Portland, Maine 04101
(207) 828-1234 Ext. 001

Hands on exhibits for children. Includes working displays on life in Portland, hands on science wonders, and the incredible Camera Obscura - a darkened room with a full 360° view of the city.

Memorial Day through Labor Day Hours (and during school vacations)

Mon. - Sat. 10 a.m. to 5 p.m.; Sun. Noon to 5 p.m.; Closed Friday evenings

Labor Day through Memorial Day Hours:

Wed. - Sat. 10 a.m. to 5 p.m.; Sun. Noon to 5 p.m. Free first Friday evening of each month, 5 p.m. to 8 p.m.

Spring Point Museum

Southern Maine Technical College
Fort Road
South Portland, Maine 04106
(207) 799-6337

Local history museum located at Fort Preble/Spring Point Light.
Memorial Day to October, Open 10 a.m. to 4 p.m. Wed. through Sunday.

The Museum at Portland Head Light

P.O. Box 6260
Cape Elizabeth, Maine 04107
(207) 799-2661

Located in historic Fort Williams, the lighthouse museum is located in the former keeper's quarters and includes original artifacts, navigational aids, lenses, models, and photos. Chronicles history of the Portland Head Light.

June-Oct. Open 10 a.m.-4 p.m.; Apr., May, Nov. & Dec. Open weekends 10 a.m.-4 p.m.

Parks and Gardens

Fort Williams Park

Shore Road
Cape Elizabeth, Maine
(207) 799-7652

Site of the Portland Head Light, Fort Williams Park offers wide grassy areas for picnicking and playing, alongside the rugged cliffs overlooking the waters of Portland Head. Picnic tables, walking trails, great area for flying a kite. Open sunrise to sunset.

Deering Oaks Park

Park & Forest Avenues
Portland, Maine
(207) 874-8793

Nearly adjacent to
Hadlock Field, this park
is a popular place for
gathering before ball
games, to relax in the
shade, or paddle on the
pond. There's a flower
garden, duck pond,
snack bar, and plenty of
room for walking.

Cruises/Charters

Bay View Cruises

Fisherman's Wharf
184 Commercial Street
Portland, Maine
(207) 761-0496

Lobster Bake on the Bay, Seal Watch Cruises, Harbor Lunch Time Cruise, Attitude Adjustment
Cruise, Sunset Cruises (May to September)

Olde Port Mariner Fleet

Long Wharf
170 Commercial Street
Portland, Maine
(207) 775-0727

Deep Sea Fishing
(Shark, Tuna & Blue),
Scenic Cruises, Floating
Irish Pub Sunset Cruise,
Dinner Cruises, Whale
Watching (Seasonal)

Atlantic Seal Cruises

Freeport Town Wharf
South Freeport, Maine
(207) 865-6112

Eagle Island, Seal and
Osprey Watch, Special
Cruises and Charters
available (Seasonal)

Overcast skies over Long Wharf

Casco Bay Lines

Casco Bay Ferry Terminal
Commercial & Franklin Streets
Portland, Maine 04101
(207) 774-7871

Mail Boat Run, Diamond Pass, Sunset Run, Moonlight
Run, Bailey Island cruises, Sunday Music on the Bay
(April to October)

Prince of Fundy Cruises Limited

P.O. Box 4216
International Marine Terminal
468 Commercial Street
Portland, Maine 04101-0416
(207) 775-5616 or (800) 341-7540

Cruises to Nova Scotia ranging from 23 hours to 3 days
(May to October)

Micro-Breweries

Shipyard Brewing Company

No. 86 Newbury Street
Portland, Maine 04101
(207) 761-0807 or (800) BREW-ALE

Brewers of Shipyard Export Ale, Old Thumper,
Blue Fin Stout, Goat Island Light. Located
downtown on the waterfront, tours are available
3 p.m to 5 p.m daily. Shipwear Retail Store
open 9 a.m. to 9 p.m.

D.L. Geary Brewing Company, Ltd.

38 Evergreen Drive
Portland, Maine 04103
(207) 878-BEER

Brewers of Geary's Pale Ale. Traditional British
style brewhouse located off Exit 8 of the Maine
Turnpike. Call to make tour reservations.

Portland City Hall, as reflected by the Post Office

Public Golf courses

Sable Oaks Golf Club

505 Country Club Road
South Portland, Maine 04106
(207) 775-OAKS

18 holes Championship course designed by Geoffrey Cornish and Brian Silva, ranked by Golf Digest as #2 course in Maine. Tee Times accepted one week in advance, Pro Shop opens at 7:00 a.m. Electric carts, Locker Rooms, putting green, Pro shop, lessons, 19th Hole. Statistics:

Gold Yardage 6359, Rating 71.9, Slope 134, Par 70
Green Yardage 6056, Rating 70.2, Slope 129, Par 70
Red Yardage 4786, Rating 68.0, Slope 118, Par 72

Point Sebago Golf and Beach Resort

RR #1
Box 712B
Casco, Maine 04015
(207) 655-2747 or (800) 655-1232

18 hole Championship course located at a lakefront golf resort 22 miles northwest of Portland. Golf School, Golf Learning Center, Vacation Packages, Rental Homes & Trailers, Restaurant, General Store, Nightclub, Boat Rentals, Fishing, Water Sports, tennis courts, Miniature Golf. Seasonal.

Public Beaches

Old Orchard Beach

Old Orchard Beach Chamber of Commerce
P.O. Box 600
Old Orchard Beach, Maine 04064
(207) 934-2500 or (800) FMLY-FUN
http://www.oldorchardbeachmaine.com

Four miles of sandy beaches, boardwalk, amusement park twenty minutes south of Portland. Take Exit 5 or 6 off the Maine Turnpike (I-95) or U.S. Route 1 South from the Maine Mall, and follow the signs to the beach. (Early Portland professional baseball teams used to play in Old Orchard Beach before the Sea Dogs came to Hadlock Field.)

Aquariums and Other Amusements

Maine Aquarium

Route 1
Saco, Maine
(207) 284-4511; 284-4512

Small aquarium 10 miles south of
Portland near Old Orchard Beach.
9 a.m. to 5 p.m.

Aquaboggan Water Park

Route 1
Saco, Maine
(207) 282-3112

Waterslides, wave pool, paddle
boats, miniature golf, Grand Prix
Race Cars, bumper boats, snack
bar, ice cream parlor. Take Exit 5
off Maine Turnpike to Scarborough
Exit 2B, then north on Route 1 for
4 miles. 10 a.m. to 6 p.m. June
through Labor Day.

Palace Playland

Old Orchard Beach, Maine
(207) 934-2001

Waterslide, bumper cars, carousel,
ferris wheel, roller coaster,
funhouse, located just off the
boardwalk.

Discovery Zone Fun Center

50 Foden Road
South Portland, Maine 04106
(207) 772-KIDS

Supervised fun center includes
water walk, obstacle course,
moonwalk, rollerslide, ball bath
wade. Located not far from the
Maine Mall, bring socks.

Balloon Rides

17 Freeman Street
Portland, Maine 04103
(207) 761-8373 or (800) 952-2076

Shopping Malls/Outlets

The Maine Mall

364 Maine Mall Road
South Portland, Maine 04106
(207) 774-0303

Macy's, Filene's, Filene's Basement, JC Penney,
Sears, Lechmere, Food Court, restaurants, over
100 specialty stores. Nearby - Borders Books
& Music, Green Mountain Coffee Roasters
Factory Outlet.

Hours: Mon-Sat 10:00 a.m. to 9:30 p.m.,
Sunday 12:00 p.m. to 6:00 p.m.

Freeport, Maine, USA

Freeport Merchants Association
P.O. Box 452
Freeport, Maine 04032
(207) 865-1212 or (800) 865-1994
http://www.destinationmaine.com/freeport

Most famous for the LL Bean Factory Outlet

[(800) 341-4341], Freeport offers something for every bargain shopper. There are well over 110 shops near Main Street, ranging from large factory outlets to smaller artisan and craft shops. You can find bargains on apparel, arts and crafts, coffees, crystal, china, pottery, footwear, housewares, jewelry, sporting goods and fitness equipment, and all sorts of gifts and one of a kind stores just about twenty minutes north of downtown Portland. When you go, take Exit 20 off I-95 in order to avoid the significant summer shopping traffic on Main Street. Parking could be a problem so plan on shopping early.

Kittery Outlets
I-95 Exit 3, Coastal Route 1
Kittery, Maine
(207) 439-7545 or (800) 639-9645

The Maine Outlet, Kittery Outlet Center, Kittery Trading Post, Tidewater Outlet Mall, Manufacturer's Outlet, and over 120 Factory Outlet stores located one hour south of Portland.

Seasonal Events

Dates are approximate, contact the Visitor Center at (207) 772-5800 for updated schedule information.

June: Old Port Festival, Back Cove Family Day, Greek Heritage Festival.

July: Maine Summerfest, Rotary Club Crafts Festival, Yarmouth Clam Festival, South Freeport Festival.

August: Maine Festival of the Arts, Art in the Park, Italian Street Festival, 6-Alive Sidewalk Arts Festival, Spring Point Festival, Annual Bluegrass Festival.

Lunchtime in downtown Portland

Accommodations/Other

Hotels and Motels:

Visiting Hotel for the Portland Sea Dogs:

Radisson Eastland Hotel Portland
157 High Street
Portland, Maine 04101
(207) 775-5411 or (800) 333-3333
Restaurant & Bar, Top of the East Lounge, Exercise Room, Room Service, Pets OK, AAA & Entertainment Discounts. (The Radisson Eastland is just a vigorous walk away from Hadlock Field.)

Downtown Portland

Ramada Inn & Conference Center
1230 Congress Street
Portland, Maine 04102
(207) 774-5611 or
(800) 2RAMADA
Restaurant & Lounge, Indoor Pool & Sauna, Exercise Room, Pets OK. AAA Discounts. (The Ramada is very close to Hadlock Field, and also is the home for Ramada's Sea Dog Fan Club. The Fan Club offers free parking for all Sea Dog games, shuttle service to Hadlock Field and transportation discounts, dining and beverage discounts, discount rates on accommodations.)

Portland Regency Hotel
20 Milk Street
Portland, Maine 04101
(207) 774-4200 or
(800) 727-3436
Restaurant & Lounge, Exercise Room. (Center of Old Port, middle of Downtown Arts District, and just blocks from waterfront.)

Holiday Inn By the Bay
88 Spring Street
Portland, Maine 04101
(207) 775-2311 or
(800) HOLIDAY
Restaurant & Lounge, Indoor Pool & Sauna, Exercise Room, Water views, AAA Discounts

Susse Chalet Inn
340 Park Ave.
Portland, Maine 04102
(207) 871-0611 or
(800) 5-CHALET
Complimentary Continental Breakfast, Outdoor Pool, AAA Discount.

Embassy Suites
1050 Westbrook Street
Portland, Maine 04102
(207) 775-2200 or (800) EMBASSY
Restaurant & Lounge, Indoor Pool & Sauna, Exercise Room, Kitchens, AAA & Entertainment Discounts. (Near Airport)

South Portland or near the Maine Mall

Portland Marriott at Sable Oaks
200 Sable Oaks Drive
South Portland, Maine 04106
(207) 871-8000 or (800) 752-8810
Restaurant & Lounge, Indoor Pool & Sauna, Golf on-site (Sable Oaks Golf Club), Exercise Room, Pets OK, AAA Discounts.

Sheraton Tara Hotel
363 Maine Mall Road
South Portland, Maine 04106
(207) 775-6161 or (800) 325-3535
Restaurant & Lounge, Indoor Pool & Sauna, Exercise Room.

Comfort Inn
90 Maine Mall Road
South Portland, Maine 04106
(207) 775-0409 or (800) 368-6485
Free Deluxe Continental Breakfast, Outdoor Pool, Pets OK, AAA Discounts.

Howard Johnson Hotel
675 Main Street
South Portland, Maine 04106
(207) 775-5343 or
(800) 446-4656
Restaurant, Indoor Pool, Pets OK, AAA Discounts

Best Western Merry Manor Inn
700 Main Street
South Portland, Maine 04106
(207) 774-6151 or
(800) 528-1234
Restaurant & Lounge, Outdoor Pool, Pets OK, Exercise Room, AAA Discounts

Other

Inn By the Sea
40 Bowery Beach Road
Cape Elizabeth, Maine 04107
(207) 799-3134 or
(800) 888-4287
Restaurant, Outdoor Pool, Tennis, Pets OK, AAA Discounts. (Overlooking the Atlantic Ocean, near to Crescent Beach State Park, private boardwalk to Crescent Beach.)

Black Point Inn Resort
510 Black Point Road
Scarborough, Maine 04074
(207) 883-4126 or
(800) 258-0003
Restaurant & Lounge, Outdoor & Indoor Pools, 18 hole PGA Golf course, Tennis, Health Club.

Harraseeket Inn
162 Main Street
Freeport, Maine 04032
(207) 865-9377 or
(800) 342-6423
Restaurant & Lounge, Jacuzzi's and fireplaces available, afternoon tea, 2 blocks to LL Bean.

Bed and Breakfast Information

If you're thinking of staying somewhere near Main Street in Freeport, you might want to consider a Bed and Breakfast. The Freeport Area Bed & Breakfast Association (FABBA) publishes a brochure listing area Bed and Breakfasts which meet the standards set by the American Bed & Breakfast Association. Contact the FABBA, P.O. Box 267, Freeport, Maine, or call them at (207) 865-1500 or (800) 853-2727 for more information.

Camping Information

Since Maine is America's Vacationland, a great way to see the state is to camp out in the wilderness or near the ocean under the stars. Maine's only National Park is Acadia National Park located about 160 miles north of Portland. At Acadia, you can explore over 38,000 acres of coastline and mountain peaks. Call (207) 288-3338 for Acadia camping information. In the Portland area, you can find plenty of campgrounds in Old Orchard Beach, Freeport, or Kennebunkport, and some of the places to try include the Desert of Maine Campground in Freeport, or the Wassamki Springs Campground in nearby Westbrook. The Maine Campground Owners Association publishes an excellent resource for campers called the Maine Camping Guide, which provides detailed information for Maine, organized by region. You can obtain this Guide by writing to The Maine Campground Owners Association, 655 Main Street, Lewiston, Maine 04240. Or call (207) 782-5874, or visit their web site at http://www.campmaine.com.

Hospital

Mercy Hospital
144 State Street
Portland, Maine
(207) 879-3000

Transportation

Airlines into Portland International Jetport:

Business Express:	(800) 638-7333
Continental Airlines:	(800) 525-0280
Delta Air Lines:	(800) 638-7333
Downeast Express:	(800) 983-3247
Northwest:	(800) 225-2525
Pine State Airlines:	(800) 353-6334
United Airlines:	(800) 241-6522
U.S. Air:	(800) 428-4322

Bus/Taxi/Limo:

Classy Taxi:	(207) 865-0663
Concord Trailways:	(207) 828-1151
Doug's Funny Cab:	(207) 232-7999 (Old Port)
Mermaid Transportation:	(207) 772-2509
METRO:	(207) 774-0351
Vermont Transit Lines:	(207) 772-6587

Car Rentals:

Avis Rent-a-Car:	(207) 874-7500
National Car Rental:	(207) 773-0286
Thrifty Car Rental:	(207) 772-4628

Other Important Phone Numbers:

Portland Police	(207) 874-8300
State Police	(800) 482-0730
Portland International Jetport	(207) 774-7301
Road Information	(800) 675-7453
Harbormaster	(207) 772-8121

Eastern League Statistics

75 Years of Eastern League Champions

Year	Team	Year	Team	Year	Team	Year	Team
1996	Harrisburg	1978	Bristol	1960	Williamsport & Springfield (Co-Champions)	1942	Scranton
1995	Reading	1977	West Haven	1959	Springfield	1941	Elmira
1994	Binghamton	1976	West Haven	1958	Binghamton	1940	Binghamton
1993	Harrisburg	1975	Bristol	1957	Reading	1939	Scranton
1992	Binghamton	1974	Thetford Mines	1956	Schenectady	1938	Elmira
1991	Albany	1973	Reading	1955	Allentown	1937	Elmira
1990	London	1972	West Haven	1954	Albany	1936	Scranton
1989	Albany	1971	Elmira	1953	Binghamton	1935	Binghamton
1988	Albany	1970	Waterbury	1952	Binghamton	1934	Williamsport
1987	Harrisburg	1969	York (Season Leader - Playoffs canceled due to weather.)	1951	Scranton	1933	Binghamton (Season Leader)
1986	Vermont	1968	Reading	1950	Wilkes-Barre	1932	Wilkes-Barre (Season Leader)
1985	Vermont	1967	Binghamton	1949	Binghamton	1931	Harrisburg (Season Leader)
1984	Vermont	1966	Elmira (Season Leader)	1948	Scranton	1930	Wilkes-Barre (Season Leader)
1983	New Britain	1965	Pittsfield (Season Leader)	1947	Utica	1929	Binghamton (Season Leader)
1982	West Haven	1964	Elmira (Season Leader)	1946	Scranton	1928	Harrisburg (Season Leader)
1981	Bristol	1963	Charleston (Season Leader)	1945	Albany	1927	Harrisburg (Season Leader)
1980	Holyoke	1962	Elmira	1944	Binghamton	1926	Scranton (Season Leader)
1979	West Haven (Season Leader)	1961	Springfield (Season Leader)	1943	Scranton	1925	York

Season Leaders indicated where source did not list a Playoff Champion for that year. Regular Season Leaders based on Win-Loss Pct.

NORTHERN DIVISION 1996 STANDINGS					
Club	W	L	Pct.	GB	Attendance
Portland Sea Dogs	83	58	.589	-	408,503
Binghamton Mets	76	66	.535	7 ½	206,589
Norwich Navigators	71	70	.504	12	269,022
New Haven Ravens	66	75	.468	17	254,064
Hardware City Rock Cats	61	81	.430	22 ½	160,765

SOUTHERN DIVISION 1996 STANDINGS					
Club	W	L	Pct.	GB	Attendance
Trenton Thunder	86	56	.606	-	437,446
Harrisburg Senators	74	68	.521	12	230,744
Canton-Akron Indians	71	71	.500	15	213,278
Reading Phillies	66	75	.468	19 ½	384,151
Bowie Baysox	54	88	.380	32	396,086

NORTHERN DIVISION SEMIFINALS	
Binghamton	4
Portland	3
Binghamton	2
Portland	3
Portland	1
Binghamton	6
Portland	4
Binghamton	2
Binghamton	3
Portland	7

SOUTHERN DIVISION SEMIFINALS	
Harrisburg	9
Trenton	2
Harrisburg	2
Trenton	6
Trenton	3
Harrisburg	5
Trenton	2
Harrisburg	5

1996 EASTERN LEAGUE CHAMPIONSHIP	
Portland	3
Harrisburg	15
Portland	2
Harrisburg	3
Harrisburg	5
Portland	8
Harrisburg	6
Portland	1

Playoff Format

"Top two teams in each division, based upon winning percentage, qualify. First place qualifier meets second place qualifier in best-of-five divisional series. First place qualifier hosts games 1-2-5 while second place qualifier hosts games 3-4. Divisional champions meet in best-of-five league championship series. First two games played in Southern Division city, remainder in Northern Division city in even-numbered years. Reversed in odd-numbered years

Portland Wins (3 -2)   Harrisburg wins (3-1)

Harrisburg Senators win 1996 Eastern League Championship (3-1)

{Total 1996 Playoff Attendance (14 games) = 51,801}

Eastern League Single Season Records Batting 1923-1996					1996 Batting Records		
	Player	Team	Year	Record	Player	Team	Record
Games: (142 Game Season) (140 Game Season) (154 Game Season) (154 Game Season)	Curtis Goodwin Robert Reece Robert Bowman Daniel Schell	Bowie Shamokin Schenectady Schenectady	1994 1927 1953 1953	142 143 149 149	Christopher Saunders	Binghamton	141
At Bats:	Granny Hamner	Utica	1947	609	Todd Dunwoody	Portland	552
Runs:	Lawrence Fischer	Harrisburg	1932	134	Jonathon Saffer	Harrisburg	96
Hits:	Don Brown	York	1930	214	Alexander Ramirez	Canton-Akron	169
Doubles:	Dewey Steffens	York	1924	54	Todd Carey	Trenton	34
Triples:	Al Gionfriddo	Albany	1944	28	Alexander Ramirez	Canton-Akron	12
Home Runs:	Ken Strong Rick Lancellotti	Hazleton Buffalo	1930 1979	41 41	Shane Spencer	Norwich	29
RBI:	Ken Harrelson	Binghamton	1962	138	Christopher Saunders	Binghamton	105
Total Bases:	Joe Munson	Harrisburg	1925	355	Todd Dunwoody	Portland	267
Sacrifices:	Mickey Dzurilla Eugene Morrison	Binghamton Elmira	1928 1928	37 37	Essex Burton	Reading	16
Sacrifice Flies:	George Vukovich	Reading	1979	14	Christopher Saunders	Binghamton	11
Walks:	Herschel Held Merrill May	Albany Albany	1949 1947	151 151	Kevin Riggs	Norwich	81
Strike Outs:	Ezell King	Allentown	1959	165	Todd Dunwoody	Portland	149
Stolen Bases:	Larry Lintz	Quebec City	1972	96	Luis Castillo	Portland	51
Batting Avg.	Joe Munson	Harrisburg	1925	.400	Vladimir Guerrero	Harrisburg	.360
Slugging Pct.	Ken Strong	Hazleton	1930	.787	Adam Hyzdu	Trenton	.618
Hit by Pitch	Nick Delvecchio	Norwich	1995	23	Daniel Held	Reading	22
Longest Hitting Streak	Hubert Mason	Binghamton	1925	38	N/A	N/A	N/A

Miscellaneous 1996 Batting Leaders:

Intentional Base on Balls:	Vladimir Guerrero, Harrisburg, 13
Caught Stealing:	Luis Castillo, Portland, 28
Grounded into Double Play:	Daniel Donato, Norwich, 19
Grand Slams:	Ryan Radmanovich, New Britain, 4
Hit for Cycle:	Jose Vidro, Harrisburg, (7/20/96 against Bowie, 4 out of 6)
Home Run/At Bat Ratio:	Tyrone Woods, Trenton, 1/14.2

	Eastern League Single Season Records Pitching 1923-1996				1996 Pitching Records		
	Player	Team	Year	Record	Player	Team	Record
Games:	Carlos Medrano Wayne Gomes	York Reading	1964 1996	67 67	Wayne Gomes	Reading	67
Games Started:	Albert Antinelli Louis Kretlow Pete Magrini	Allentown Williamsport Pittsfield	1959 1948 1965	33 33 33	Jared Fernandez	Trenton	29
Complete Games:	Hugh Mulcahy	Hazleton	1936	31	Carl Pavano	Trenton	6
Shutouts:	Allie Reynolds	Wilkes-Barre	1942	11	Calvin Maduro	Bowie	3
Wins:	Thomas George	York	1925	27	Carl Pavano	Trenton	16
Losses:	Ernest Walters	Elmira	1923	24	Deshane Hale	Bowie	13
Saves:	Albert Reyes	Harrisburg	1994	35	William Hurst	Portland	30
Winning Pct.:	William Macleod	Pittsfield	1965	1.000 (18-0)	Richard Betti	Trenton	.900 (9-1)
Innings:	Hugh Mulcahy	Hazleton	1936	325	Cory Lidle	Binghamton	190.1
Hits Allowed:	Ernest Walters	Elmira	1923	349	Carlton Loewer	Reading	191
Runs:	Ernest Walters	Elmira	1923	206	Carlton Loewer Jared Fernandez	Reading Trenton	115 115
Earned Runs:	Hugh Mulcahy	Hazleton	1936	155	Jared Fernandez	Trenton	101
Walks:	Richard Rozak	Wilkes-Barre	1948	180	Anthony Costa	Reading	92
Strikeouts:	Fred Norman	Binghamton	1963	258	Anthony Saunders	Portland	156
Home Runs Allowed:	Juan Castillo	Binghamton	1993	27	Carlton Loewer	Reading	24
ERA:	Mel Parnell	Scranton	1946	1.30	Carl Pavano	Trenton	2.63

Miscellaneous 1996 Pitching Leaders:

At-Bats Against:	Cory Lidle, Binghamton, 719
Total Batters Faced:	Jared Fernandez, Trenton, 798
Sacrifice Hits Allowed:	Steven Kline, Canton-Akron, 10
Sacrifice Flies Allowed:	Jared Fernandez, Trenton, 9
Hit Batters:	Anthony Costa, Reading, 14
Intentional Walks:	Christopher Neier, New Haven, 9
	Jay Vaught, Canton-Akron, 9
Wild Pitches:	Carlos Chavez, Bowie, 19
Caught Stealing/ Stolen Base Pct.:	Calvin Maduro, Bowie, .818
No-Hitters:	Joe Crawford, Binghamton, against Trenton 5/5/96 (1-0)
	Calvin Maduro, Bowie, against Portland 5/28/96 (5-0)
	Aaron Lane, Bowie, against Norwich 6/25/96 (2-0)
Team Combination Shutouts:	Harrisburg, 8

1996 Overall Fielding Leaders

Position	Player	Club	PCT	Games	Put Outs	Assists	Errors	Total Chances	Double Plays
First	Thomas Davis	BOW	.995	134	1158	95	6	1259	79
Second	Luis Castillo	PRT	.975	108	217	326	14	557	87
Third	Todd Carey	TRE	.941	103	67	238	19	324	21
Shortstop	Kevin Morgan	BNG	.956	107	170	330	23	523	65
Outfield	Todd Dunwoody	PRT	.996	138	254	2	1	257	2
Catcher*	Michael Redmond	PRT	.996	119	814	88	4	906	10
Pitcher	Jared Fernandez	TRE	1.000	30	10	31	0	41	1

* Passed Balls = 8

Miscellaneous 1996 Fielding Leaders:

1996 Fielding Leaders

Position	Games	Put Outs	Assists	Errors	Total Chances	Double Plays
First	Thomas Davis (BOW) - 134; Daniel Held (RDG) - 134:	Thomas Davis (BOW) - 1158	Brian Daubach (BNG) - 115	Daniel Held (RDG) - 12	Thomas Davis (BOW) - 1259	Daniel Held (RDG) - 111
Second	Howard Clark (BOW) - 123	Howard Clark (BOW) - 249	Luis Castillo (PRT) - 326	Christopher Allison (TRE) - 21	Luis Castillo (PRT) - 557	Luis Castillo (PRT) - 87
Third	Christopher Saunders (BNG) - 137	Willis Otanez (BOW) - 106	Christopher Saunders (BNG) - 327	Daniel Donato (NRW) - 25; Christopher Saunders (BNG) - 25	Christopher Saunders (BNG) - 426	James Taylor (NHV) - 30
Shortstop	Juan Bautista (BOW) - 127	Juan Bautista (BOW) - 203	Juan Bautista (BOW) - 354	Juan Bautista (BOW) - 29	Juan Bautista (BOW) - 586	Enrique Wilson (C-A) - 74
Outfield	Todd Dunwoody (PRT) - 138	Bruce Aven (C-A) - 280	Trotman Nixon (TRE) - 14	Derrick Gibson (NHV) - 13	Bruce Aven (C-A) - 289	Trotman Nixon (TRE) - 4; Scott Shores (RDG) - 4
Catcher **	Michael Redmond (PRT) - 119	Michael Redmond (PRT) - 814	Robert Henley (HRG) - 92	Einar Diaz (C-A) - 15	Michael Redmond (PRT) - 906	Robert Henley (HRG) - 11; Walter McKeel (C-A) - 11
Pitcher	Wayne Gomes (RDG) - 67	Cory Lidle (BNG) - 31	Scott Forster (HRG) - 41	Rafael Medina (NRW) - 6	Cory Lidle (BNG) - 65	Shawn Senior (TRE) - 4

** Most Passed Balls = Walter McKeel, (C-A) - 17

1996 Eastern League Honors

Most Valuable Player	Vladimir Guerrero, Harrisburg Senators
Pitcher of the Year	Carl Pavano, Trenton Thunder
Rookie of the Year	Vladimir Guerrero, Harrisburg Senators
Manager of the Year	Carlos Tosca, Portland Sea Dogs

"Star of Stars" Award Winner

All Star Game MVP	Todd Dunwoody, Portland Sea Dogs

1996 All Star Team

First Base	Todd Helton, New Haven Ravens
Second Base	Luis Castillo, Portland Sea Dogs
Third Base	Scott Rolen, Reading Phillies
Shortstop	Enrique Wilson, Canton-Akron Indians
Outfield	Todd Dunwoody, Portland Sea Dogs
Outfield	Vladimir Guerrero, Harrisburg Senators
Outfield	Adam Hyzdu, Trenton Thunder
Catcher	Walt McKeel, Trenton Thunder
Designated Hitter	Rod McCall, Canton-Akron Indians
Pitchers	Carl Pavano (RHP), Trenton Thunder; Mike Welch (RHP), Binghamton Mets; Matt Beech (LHP), Reading Phillies; Tony Saunders (LHP), Portland Sea Dogs

Eastern League Players of the Year
(1962-96)

Player	Yr.	Team	Player	Yr.	Team	Player	Yr.	Team
Vladimir Guerrero	1996	Harrisburg	Pat Adams	1984	Waterbury	Fernando Gonzales	1972	Sherbrooke
Jay Payton	1995	Binghamton	Jeff Stone	1983	Reading	Gene Locklear	1971	Three Rivers
Mark Grudzielanek	1994	Harrisburg	Jim Bennett	1982	West Haven	Greg Luzinski	1970	Reading
Cliff Floyd	1993	Harrisburg	Ron Kittle	1981	Glens Falls	Angel Mangual	1969	York
Russ Davis	1992	Albany	Mark Davis	1980	Reading	Carmen Fanzone	1968	Pittsfield
Matt Stairs	1991	Harrisburg	Rick Lancelloti	1979	Buffalo	Bernie Smith	1967	Williamsport
Jeff Bagwell	1990	New Britain	Jeff Yurak	1978	Holyoke	Tom Fisher	1966	Elmira
Wes Chamberlain	1989	Harrisburg	Harry Spillman	1977	Three Rivers	Owen Johnson	1965	Pittsfield
Rob Richie	1988	Glens Falls	Danny Thomas	1976	Pittsfield	Frank Bertaina	1964	Elmira
Mark Grace	1987	Pittsfield	Dave Bergman	1975	West Haven	Bob Chance	1963	Charleston
Rafael Palmeiro	1986	Pittsfield	Ken Macha	1974	Thetford Mines	Jim Ray Hart	1962	Springfield
Cory Snyder	1985	Waterbury	Tom Robson	1973	Pittsfield			

1996 Eastern League Attendance	
Binghamton Mets	206,589*
New Britain Rock Cats	160,765
New Haven Ravens	254,064
Norwich Navigators	269,022
Portland Sea Dogs	408,503
Bowie Baysox	396,086
Canton-Akron Indians	213,278
Harrisburg Senators	230,744
Reading Phillies	384,151**
Trenton Thunder	437,446

1996 Average EL Daily Attendance (Sorted)			
	1996	Openings	Average
Trenton	437,446	69	6,340
Bowie	396,086	65	6,094
Portland	408,503	68	6,007
Reading	384,151	68	5,649
New Haven	254,064	62	4,098
Norwich	269,022	70	3,843
Harrisburg	230,744	62	3,722
Canton-Akron	213,278	65	3,281
Binghamton	206,589	68	3,038
New Britain	160,765	62	2,593

*   Includes Playoffs
**   Includes 8,825 Attendance during the
      March 31st, 1996 Exhibition against
      Philadelphia Phillies

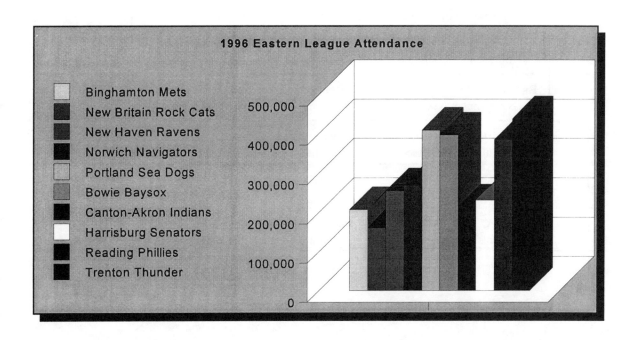

Top 20 E.L. Team Season Attendance						
Club	Year	Total		Club	Year	Total
Bowie	1995	463,976		Albany	1985	324,003
Trenton	1995	453,915		Trenton	1994	318,252
Trenton	1996	437,446		Scranton	1939	317,249
Portland	1995	429,763		Albany	1986	316,034
Portland	1996	408,503		Reading	1993	313,083
Bowie	1996	396,086		Bowie	1994	293,665
Reading	1996	384,151		Reading	1992	287,073
Reading	1995	383,984		Albany	1987	285,016
Portland	1994	375,197		New Haven	1995	283,766
Reading	1994	338,249		Norwich	1995	281,473

Double AA All Star Game History				
Year	Host Stadium	Host Team	Final Score	Attendance
1996	Mercer County Waterfront Park Trenton, New Jersey	Trenton Thunder	National League 6 American League 2	8,369
1995	Fair Grounds Field Shreveport, Louisiana	Shreveport Captains	American League 3 National League 1	6,247
1994	Binghamton Municipal Stadium Binghamton, New York	Binghamton Mets	American League 10 National League 4	6,542
1993	McCarver Stadium Memphis, Tennessee	Memphis Chicks	National League 12 American League 7	6,335
1992	Knights Castle Fort Mill, South Carolina	Charlotte Knights	American League 4 National League 3	4,009
1991	Joe W. Davis Stadium Huntsville, Alabama	Huntsville Stars	American League 8 National League 2	4,022

Canal Park   Akron, Ohio

Illustration Copyright by HOK Sport Facilities Group, Inc., Kansas City, MO.   Reprinted with Permission.

Akron Aeros

Team: **Akron Aeros** (Southern Division)

Stadium: **Canal Park**

        Address: 300 South Main St., Akron, OH 44308
        Phone: (330) 253-5151
        Fax: (330) 253-3300

Team Ownership:

        Operated by: Akron Professional Baseball Club, Inc.
        Principals: Mike Agganis, Greg Agganis
        General Manager: Jeff Auman

Affiliation: Cleveland Indians

Years in Eastern League: 1989-Present

As of the time of writing of this book, in the winter of 1996-7, the Akron Aeros haven't actually played any games at Canal Park. Obviously, this is because 1997 is their Inaugural Season. The prior team, the Canton-Akron Indians called Thurman Munson Memorial Stadium in Canton, Ohio their home field. However, with the close of the 1996 season, the Indians changed their name to the Akron Aeros and then packed their bags and moved into the newest facility in all of the Eastern League, Canal Park just up the highway in Akron, Ohio.

This presents a challenge to the reader of this book (not to mention, the author). I have received very detailed, comprehensive information regarding Canal Park, a stadium designed by Hellmuth, Obata & Kassabaum (HOK), the architects of Camden Yards and Jacobs Field, and I will, of course convey that to you as best as possible.

However, certain aspects of the stadium I can't reveal, because when I researched this book during the summer of 1996, the stadium didn't exist. The best I could do would be to speculate based on the history of the club at Thurman Munson Memorial, so where appropriate I will provide general information. Future editions of this book will correct this deficiency.

Illustration by Akron Aeros. Reprinted with Permission.

Here's my reasoning for giving some information on both stadiums. Canal Park, as you can see in some of my photographs from July 1996, is still under construction at the time of writing this book. In contrast, Thurman Munson had a long, celebrated history in the Eastern League, with an extremely devoted following in both cities, Canton especially. It would be unfair and inaccurate to predict that Canal Park would be operated in the same manner as Thurman Munson, given that the facilities are so different. Nevertheless, after my positive experiences in Canton, I honestly can't see how predictions based on past experience would be a bad thing. Although the City of Akron now is the owner of a brand, new old-style stadium, the ownership of the baseball club remains essentially the same, therefore I have to assume club operations will remain similar as well. But, on the other hand, what do I know? I'm just a fan.

Therefore, I'll let you, the reader, make the call. A caveat, however. Given that the present information I have on Canal Park really is incomplete, it would be wise to contact the Akron Aeros prior to making any plans to attend a home game at Canal Park. As an alternative, I recommend contacting the Akron/Summit Convention & Visitors Bureau at (330) 374-7560 or (800) 245-4254 for more up to date information.

Stadium: **Canal Park**

        Location: Buchtel Avenue and South Main Street, Akron, Ohio.
        Owner: City of Akron, Ohio
        Tenant: 'AA' Eastern League Cleveland Indians Affiliate Club
        Architect: HOK Sport, Kansas City, MO
        Construction
        Manager: Summit Construction, Inc.

Schedule:

Groundbreaking: September 1995
Opening Day: April 1997

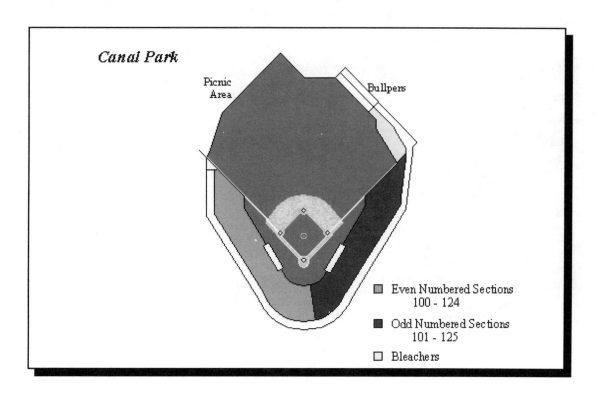

Canal Park

Picnic Area

Bullpens

■ Even Numbered Sections
100 - 124

■ Odd Numbered Sections
101 - 125

□ Bleachers

Stadium Physical Characteristics:

Capacity: 8,500 seats with picnic berm for 500 spectators. Wheelchair and companion seating.

Suites: 25, seating 8 to 12 people.

Building Area: 190,000 square feet total

Clubhouses: 13,000 square feet, including 2 indoor batting tunnels

Team Offices: 5,000 square feet

Restaurant and

Sports Bar: 7,500 square feet - 3 level dining area and outdoor deck with view of field.

Press Box: 3,200 square feet

Novelty Store: 1,500 square feet

Concessions: 45 serving lines

Restrooms: 53 men's fixtures
53 women's fixtures
2 family/disabled toilets

Features: Separated outfield bleacher seating
21 row seating bowl - no cross aisle
Bowl geometry matching Jacobs Field
Camden Yards style bullpens (My notation: These will be located right behind the right centerfield wall - two terraced bullpens where fans can easily watch pitchers warm up.)
Assistive listening system

Electronic scoreboard and message center
Electronic auxiliary scoreboard
Grill/Picnic Areas
Children's play areas
Distributed sound system
ADA Accessible Building

Source:
HOK Sport Fact
Sheet, Kansas City,

View of Canal Park under construction from nearby Ohio/Erie Canal (July 1996).

Site Information:

Area: 8.6 acres

Parking: 40 spaces on-site for
                   players/club
                   12,000 spaces within 10
                   minute walk

Features:

Ohio-Erie Canal Bike/Hike Path
Lock 2 Park
Bicycle parking area
3 entry/ticketing locations
National Inventors Hall of Fame
- 1/8 mile walk

Admission*:

All Reserved: $8.00   (All seats at Canal Park are classified as reserved.)
Reserved for Children 12 and under, and seniors 60 and over: $6.00

1997 Season Seat Plan Information:

A.   High Flyers Club (5 Years): $475.00 per seat per season

Exclusive Features for High Flyers:

Savings: Over 22% off the regular ticket price. Also includes playoff games.

Price Freeze: There is a guaranteed no cost increase for the life that High Flyers retain season
                  tickets. This means the price will remain the same provided they are continually
                  renewed for five, ten, fifteen, even as much as twenty years. In order to insure
                  the price freeze, tickets must be purchased for the 1997 Inaugural Season.

V.I.P. Card: High Flyers receive the following privileges:

        1.   A 10% discount on souvenir Team Merchandise purchased at Canal Park, and a
                  20% off gift certificate, one per seat, good for December purchases.

        2.   For Group or Company outings of 25 or more, a 20% discount off any regular
                  season group tickets, depending upon availability.

3. For youngsters, ages 8 through 17, there is a 10% discounted gift certificate on the costs of Baseball Camps, where your children are instructed by both the players and coaches.

4. Once a season, a special Pre-Game Picnic is held exclusively for High Flyers so you can meet the players and coaches. Complimentary food and beverages are provided.

B. Three Year Term (3 Years): $568.00 per seat, per season

Both Season Seat Plans, High Flyers Club and Three Year Term Seat holders, receive the following special rights and privileges:

Preferred Seats	Guaranteed same seats for every home game.
Playoff Tickets	Free tickets to all home playoff games.
Team Media Guide	Complimentary copy of guide to team records, players and history.
Quarterly Newsletter	Current stadium information and player statistics.
Season Ticket Booklet	Free publication tracking season ticket use.
48 Hour Exchange	Season ticket holders may exchange any future game ticket 48 hours in advance of that game for a ticket to another future game free, depending upon availability.
Rain Outs	If a game is called because of inclement weather, you may exchange the ticket for any other regular season game free, depending upon availability. (No refunds.)
First Right of Refusal	Upon renewal, you may retain the same seats.

To find out more about the Season Seat Plans, call (330) 253-5151 in Akron.

Ticket Office:

Address: 300 South Main St., Akron, OH 44308
Phone: (330) 253-5151
Credit Cards: MasterCard and Visa

Game times:
Weekdays: 7:05 p.m.
Saturday: 7:05 p.m.
Sunday: 2:05 p.m.
Wednesday Home Games in April & May: 3:05 p.m.

(See 1997 schedule. All game times subject to change.)

*[1997 Data. Call (330) 253-5151 for updated Admission prices.]

Approximate distance from Canal Park to Jacobs Field: 39 miles
(Source: Rand McNally TripMaker Version 1.1 1994; Akron, Ohio to Cleveland, Ohio)

Mascot:

Orbit
(Named after a write-in
contest open to area
children 14 years and
younger.)

Team Colors:

Purple, gray, black and red.

**Visiting
Hotel**:

Akron Ramada Plaza Hotel
20 West Mill Street
Akron, OH 44308
(330) 384-1500 or
(800) 2-RAMADA

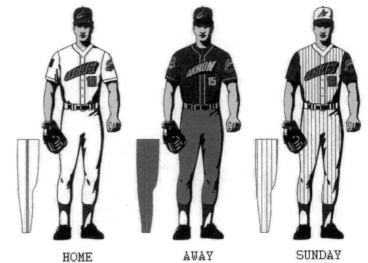

HOME   AWAY   SUNDAY

Illustration by Akron Aeros. Reprinted with Permission.

Fan Club: Fan mail should be addressed to that individual player, care of the Akron Aeros.

Directions to Canal Park:

From I-77, take the Main Street Exit. You want to go north on South Main Street. Continue on South
Main until Exchange, then make a left on Exchange Street. Canal Park is located on the corner of South
Main and Buchtel Avenue.

Comments:

As I mentioned earlier, I visited the site of Canal Park in July 1996, a time when it was still under
construction. There were a couple bulldozers on the future infield, steelworkers balancing on the girders
that would hold the twenty five luxury suites, and hundreds of pipes and reinforced steel jutting out from
every joint, at every
conceivable angle.
However, it wasn't too
hard to figure out the
shape of things to come.
This is a baseball
stadium. If ever that
magic whisper from
"Fields of Dreams" was
going to come true, it
would be so in Akron.
"If you build it, they will
come."

At the time, I couldn't get anywhere near the main entrance on South Main, because of all the safety fences surrounding the area, but I did find my way over to the historic Ohio & Erie Canal, only a pedestrian footbridge away from the future outfield fence in left. From this vantage point, I was immediately struck by the similarities between Canal Park and the other two more famous HOK stadiums, Jacobs Field and Camden Yards. A littler cousin to these, Canal Park is going to be an outstanding addition to the new, old-style, urban parks sprouting up in all levels of professional sports.

Here's how I imagine Canal Park will appear to the average fan entering for the first time on Opening Day (Scheduled for Thursday April 10th, 1997 against the 1996 Eastern League Champion Harrisburg Senators.) You'll find a parking spot somewhere near the stadium, in one of the many parking lots, or perhaps on a nearby street, then walk past the redbrick and sandstone facades to one of the three entry gates, probably the one located on South Main. After a friendly usher takes that day's game ticket, tears it in half, and then gives the other half back to you, you'll enter Canal Park, probably receive some sort of Akron Aeros promotional item, and then be directed to your side of the stadium.

But, you'll be too much taken in by the sights, smells, and sounds of the new ballpark to really pay attention to directions at that point. The first thing you'll notice, is that unlike Thurman Munson Memorial Stadium, as soon as you enter through the turnstiles, you're already at the top level of the stadium! No more climbing the metal staircase up to General Admission; Canal Park's main level concourse will be a wide, open concrete walkway all the way around to the Camden Yards style bullpens in right, and the quaint, pedestrian walkway to the Ohio & Erie Canal in left. From every point along that concourse, you'll have an unimpeded view of this newest of urban ballparks in a intimate, Main Street location.

The field will be bright green, fresh as the first game ever played at Elysian Fields. The smooth, well maintained infield will circle from first to third and back again, as the ground crew waters down the dirt over by shortstop to keep the dust down. Other members of the crew will be laying out the chalk lines for the batters box near home plate, as the two umpires stand nearby with arms crossed, supervising every detail from a close distance. In the outfield, you'll see players having a catch or still stretching out for the

big game against an Eastern League rival. They too will be just as excited as you, playing their first professional game in this new urban arena.

Follow the foul lines out to the asymmetrical fence surrounding the outfield, and your eyes will be captured by the Old Style Clock Tower, and the high tech Jumbotron scoreboard in right center field. At 77' 5" wide by 54' 8" high, this is the largest and newest scoreboard in all of The Minor Leagues. With the easy to read message center, and the traditional matrix scoreboard, you'll be able to keep up effortlessly with all the important statistics of the game including runs, hits and errors, player's position, batting averages, home runs, and rbi's, and of course, the current pitch count against the man at the plate.

Now, you'll hand your ticket to another usher, and he or she will escort you from street level, down towards your seats close to the field. (Don't forget a tip!) The seating areas at Canal Park are remarkably similar to Jacobs Field, what with clear, unimpeded sight lines and no cross aisles, you won't miss a second of the action.

Ohio & Erie Canal, just beyond left field wall at Canal Park

And that will include going to the concession areas along the main concourse. There are 45 serving lines at Canal Park, located within view of the playing field. No more trudging back down the stairs to get a beer and a dog, hoping somehow to still stay in touch with the action on radio or over the loud speakers so you won't miss that next great play. No, at Canal Park, like so many other of the newer Minor League stadiums (Norwich, Bowie, and Trenton), you can get up and go get something to eat without missing even a moment of play.

And finally, the feature that will set Canal Park apart from all other stadiums in the Eastern League will be the year round Restaurant and Sports Bar. The Canal Park Restaurant will have a three level dining area and an outdoor deck with a spectacular view of the field. Of all the other stadiums in the Eastern League, only Bowie has a restaurant open to all ticket holders, however that facility is only open during the regular season. The new Canal Park Restaurant and Sports Bar will be another integral part of the revitalization of downtown Akron ignited by one of the best new stadiums in The Minor Leagues.

Stadium: Thurman Munson Memorial Stadium

Stadium Physical Characteristics

Age: Canton-Akron Indians located here in 1989.

Dimensions:

Left Field Foul Pole:	333
Center Field:	400
Right Field Foul Pole:	333
Playing Surface: Natural grass	

Comments:

Autograph time at Thurman Munson, Summer 1996

Thurman Munson Memorial Stadium felt to me like an old, metal ballpark that had seen a lot of exciting action in this blue collar town. In the late summer of 1996, though, you could tell it's day was near to done. I read where over the years, proper maintenance of the stadium had been called into question, including the major concern of inadequate drainage out on the field. Frankly, after visiting a number of other stadiums in the Eastern League, the maintenance issue appeared valid. And besides, as with any older stadium in these times, poor maintenance and nostalgia both will give way to relocation eight times out of ten. (Being from the Baltimore area and seeing the Oriole games at both the old Memorial Stadium and the new Camden Yards, in my personal opinion, relocation isn't necessarily a bad thing. It can breathe new life into a team, its fans, and a city.)

In Canton, relocation probably was inevitable. Numerous other cities were interested in the Indians 'AA' franchise club, and were it not for the commitment made to build Canal Park, the team could have wound up in the Lehigh Valley region of Pennsylvania, Wildwood, New Jersey or even as far as Springfield, Massachusetts instead of just twenty minutes away in Akron.

I'm sure there's many who hold different opinions. I met some of them at Thurman Munson Memorial those games in July, 1996. It was obvious the Canton fans clearly and dearly loved this old park, honoring one of the best catchers in the last thirty years. You knew it when the Indian fans got to stomping their feet during a ninth inning two out rally, shaking those old metal rafters and the aluminum bleachers in a deafening cheer for the home team so loud and so hard you had to lift your beer up off the deck just to keep it from tipping over. The fervor could even drown the lonely train whistle somewhere off in the northeastern Ohio night.

1997 will be a new day for the club, in a new stadium, and in new surroundings. There'll be plenty memories of Thurman

Munson Memorial still lingering for dedicated fans, but also, plenty of new ones of Canal Park in the years to come. After all, the one and only constant about all of this is baseball. So, shake it all off and come out and catch a game.

Capacity: 5,700

	1993	**1994**	**1995**	**1996**
Attendance	273,639	255,002	195,049	213,278

1996 Average Attendance:

Daily average: 3,281

All Time Attendance Records:

Daily: 7,702 on August 16, 1994
Seasonal: 273,639 in 1993

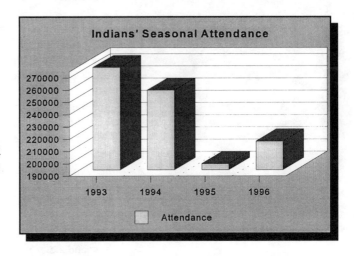

Concessions and Souvenirs

As for the types of concessions available at Thurman Munson Memorial, here it would be unfair to compare to what might be available at Canal Park, without at least giving the Canal Park vendors an opportunity to establish their menus. All I'll say then is that with most stadium concessions, I found that your best bet is always going to be the grilled items. The concessions at Thurman Munson Memorial were no exception. There's just something about a grilled sausage or hot dog which leaves the regular, old weiner from the main concession window in the dust.

My guess is that if Canal Park is at all similar to the newer stadiums in the Eastern League, and it probably will be considering it was designed by HOK Sports, then there will most likely be grill stations and other specialty food areas spread throughout the concession concourse. In addition, we know there's going to be a new restaurant and sports bar at Canal Park, a feature lacking at the old stadium. Therefore, although I'm not aware of the Canal Park concession menu at this time, simply based on my own personal and limited baseball culinary experiences, I recommend you check any grill or specialty menu items first before you make your final concession decision.

View of Field from Concession Stands:

There was no view of the field from the concession areas at Thurman Munson Memorial.

1996 Canton-Akron Indian signing autographs for the fans.

Gift Shop: Yes, there was a souvenir location besides the Customer Service Window on the main concourse. The stand was open from the time the gates opened until approximately fifteen (15) minutes after the conclusion of the game. It was also open non-game days during the week.

Group Information:

Group sizes at Thurman Munson Memorial required a minimum of 25 people. Tickets were discounted at a rate below regular season prices, and the club conceivably could handle a group as large as 1,000 plus. Each group would receive message center and public address recognition; posters to promote the group outing; savings on tickets for Little League teams; no waiting in lines; Honorary First Pitch for groups of 200 plus; and the group leader received two (2) free tickets to any future Canton-Akron Indians game.

Groups could also enjoy Pre-Game Picnics in the picnic area near the right field line. Special menus and rates were available, and the pre-game picnics began one hour prior to the ballgame and continued until the first pitch of the game. Reservations were recommended.

Promotions and Giveaways:

The 1996 Canton-Akron Indians conducted a number of promotions and giveaways during the regular season. There were four nights where the club presented a Fireworks Extravaganza. In addition, fans received such items as schedule posters, schedule cups, logo magnets, roll bags, commemorative pennants, team caps, squeeze bottles, baseballs, beach towels, seat cushions, t-shirts, and much more.

Every Tuesday home game was also Kellogg's Two Scoops Raisin Bran night, and there were ten Knothole Gang Days sponsored by Wendy's throughout the year. (If I haven't already mentioned it, the term "Knothole Gang" refers to an era in professional sports when the outfield fences were made out of wood. The industrious fan on the outside of the park would try to watch the game through the naturally occurring knot holes in the wooden slats.)

The club's policy in 1996 for giveaways and promotions was that fans would receive one item per paid admission ticket. Some giveaways were limited to the number of fans through the gate, and some giveaways were limited to certain age groups. Check the 1997 Promotional Calendar for further information.

In addition, the Canton-Akron Indians conducted a lucky stamp contest in between innings. In order to play to win, you needed to purchase a Canton-Akron Indians Souvenir Yearbook. Contained inside random programs were lucky Indian's stamps placed on random advertisement pages. Lucky winners were announced periodically between innings over the sound system, and you could pick up your prize at the Customer Service area on the concourse beside the main concession stand.

What song played during 7th inning stretch?   "Take Me Out to the Ballgame"

Eastern League Information: No updated information on stats, averages, etc... was posted at Thurman Munson.

Team Information:

Akron Aeros (Southern Division)

History:

Eastern League baseball in Canton-Akron began in 1989 when the Indians began play at Thurman Munson Memorial Stadium. Since that time, the Indians have been in the playoffs in all but just three seasons. A remarkable part of the Tribe's success in northeastern Ohio comes from the pool of talent in the Cleveland franchise. Such great players as Albert Belle, Charles Nagy, Jim Thome and Manny Ramirez honed their skills at Thurman Munson Memorial before eventually making their mark Jacobs Field.

As for the selection of the new team name, Akron Aeros, the club has established Space Science Education as its theme. This is meant to be a tie in with the community's connections to aeronautics, space research and space exploration. For Ohio was the home of the pioneers of modern aviation, the Wright Brothers. In addition, Ohio is the native state of more astronauts than any other state in the nation, including the first American to orbit the earth, Senator John Glenn, the first man to walk on the moon, Neil Armstrong, and one of the first female astronauts, Challenger Mission Specialist Judith A. Resnick.

Therefore, in the spirit of community responsibility, at the time of the writing of this book, the team plans to build a "Challenger Learning Center" for children at Canal Park. This will be in addition to naming each section of the stadium in a way that reflects the notable achievements and history of the space

As a side note, and solely for historical purposes, there was a bit of off season controversy during the fall of 1996 surrounding the selection of the new team name. On October 10th, 1996 the club announced that it had chosen the new team name Akron Blast, with the mascot named Kaboom. As reported by the November 6-12, 1996 edition of USA Today Baseball Weekly, local fans and officials were concerned that this selection was insensitive, considering that astronaut Judith A. Resnick, who perished along with six other astronauts in the January 28th, 1986 Challenger tragedy, was an Akron native. Team Owner Mike Agganis responded quickly to the community's concerns and on October 29th, 1996 issued a press release announcing that he would change the team name. In cooperation with President William Troubh of the Eastern League, the National Association, Akron Mayor Don Plusquellic and the Akron City Council, Mr. Agganis encouraged fans to help name the team by sending postcards to the club. About one week later, on November 6th, 1996, suggestions from 3,000 fans narrowed the choices to Aeros, Quest and Spirit. This was announced in the Akron Beacon Journal, and fans were to phone in their choices. On November 8th, 1996, the club announced that the winner was the Akron Aeros. The renaming of the club mascot was conducted with the same sense of community involvement, with children 14 and under registering their selections at area Acme stores. Each participating child received a free voucher from the club good for one reserved ticket. During the winter of 1997, the new Aeros mascot was named "Orbit". This rapid response to legitimate concerns not only is commendable, but also demonstrates that the Aeros are committed as much to the community as they are toward bringing Quality Minor League Baseball to Akron.

program. With that in mind, the Akron Aeros now look forward to establishing a new history in Canal Park, opening with the 1997 season.

Eastern League Championships: none

(In 1992, Canton-Akron narrowly lost to Binghamton Mets in Eastern League Championship finals, 3 games to 2.)

Famous Players who went on to the Major Leagues:

Albert Belle (1989, '90); Charles Nagy (1989, '90, '93); Jim Thome (1991, '92); Manny Ramirez (1993); Brian Giles (1992, '93); Lee Tinsley (1991, '92); Troy Neel (1989); Julian Tavarez (1993); Dave Mlicki (1992, '93).

Cleveland Indians Minor League Organization			
Team	**League**	**Level**	**City & Phone**
Cleveland Indians	American League	Major League	Cleveland, OH (216) 420-4200
Buffalo Bisons	American Association	AAA	Buffalo, NY (716) 846-2000
Akron Aeros	Eastern League	AA	Akron, OH 44308 (330) 253-5151
Kinston Indians	Carolina League	A	Kinston, NC (919) 527-9111
Columbus Redstixx	South Atlantic League	A	Columbus, GA (706) 571-8866
Watertown Indians	New York-Penn League	Short A	Watertown, NY (315) 788-8747
Burlington Indians	Appalachian League	Rookie	Burlington, NC (910) 222-0223

Sunset over Thurman Munson Memorial Stadium, Canton, Ohio. Summer 1996.

Akron/Canton

Goodyear Park, downtown Akron.

Background

Akron (Pop. 223,019) is an industrialized city in northeastern Ohio, and is also the county seat of Summit County. Originally part of the western frontier of the United States, the first inhabitants were the nations of Native Americans who camped and carried their canoes on the portage path between the Cuyahoga and Tuscarawas rivers. This natural hub of transportation was then settled around 1807, and in 1825, a village was founded by Simon Perkins at the highest elevation of the future Ohio and Erie Canals. The name Akron comes from the ancient Greek, "akros" meaning "high place." It was about this time that the first stretch of the Ohio & Erie Canal was begun, connecting Cleveland and Akron. The 395 foot rise required 44 lift locks to complete. By 1832, when the 308 mile canal was completed, the trip across Ohio had been shortened to just four days, and the state rebounded from impending bankruptcy to become the third most successful state in the nation.

The community of Akron grew at a modest pace as milling and manufacturing companies, such as Quaker Oats, dominated the early 19th century Akron industries, but things really began to blossom when Dr. B.F. Goodrich opened a rubber manufacturing plant here in 1870. Soon thereafter, probably somewhere between 1910 and 1920 when Akron's population bounced from 69,000 to 210,000, Akron became known as the Rubber Capital of the World. Today, the economy of Akron still depends on the major tire and rubber manufacturers, but also on other such diverse industries as aerospace, metals, plastics, electronics, and high-tech polymer research and development. Much of this research takes place at the University of Akron. One of the largest campuses in the state, the University of Akron is renowned for its research into polymer science and polymer engineering, as well as for its programs in industrial/organizational psychology.

Canton (Pop. 84,161) the county seat for Stark County, also is an industrial city about twenty miles south of Akron. Founded in 1805 by Bezaleel Wells, a Baltimore, Maryland native, Canton was apparently directly named after the estate of one Captain John O'Donnell outside of Baltimore, and indirectly, after the Chinese

A watchful guardian of justice outside the Summit County Courthouse

port city of Canton. The early settlers in the region were Pennsylvania Dutch, and like many of the cities in northeastern Ohio, economic prosperity in Canton was tied to the Ohio and Erie Canal. In fact, at one point in its history, Canton was larger than Cleveland. Two of Canton's most famous native sons were President William McKinley, who practiced law here and is buried at the McKinley National Memorial, and one of the greatest athletes of this century, Jim Thorpe, who played for the Canton Bulldogs and is enshrined here at the Pro Football Hall of Fame (built in 1963, a required destination for any true sports fan).

You'll find a number of interesting attractions in this chapter, all the way up and down the Ohio & Erie Canal. And don't forget to bring your golf clubs, because this area has more public courses nearby than any other town discussed in this book. From the Hall of Fame in Canton, to Inventure Place in Akron, up the Cuyahoga Valley to Jacobs Field and the Rock and Roll Hall of Fame in Cleveland, northeastern Ohio has much to offer.

Stadium Park, Canton, Ohio.

Information

Chamber of Commerce/Tourist Bureaus

Akron/Summit Convention & Visitors Bureau
John S. Knight Center
77 E. Mill Street
Akron, OH 44308
(330) 374-7560 or (800) 245-4254

Canton/Stark County Convention & Visitors Bureau
Tourist Information
2141 George Halas Drive, N.W.
Canton, OH 44708-2630
(330) 452-0243 or (800) 552-6036

Convention & Visitors Bureau of Greater Cleveland
50 Public Square
Tower City Center, Ste 3100
Cleveland, OH 44113
(216) 621-4110 or (800) 321-1004

State of Ohio Tourist Information: 1 (800) BUCKEYE

Web Site(s):

Akron:

http://www.config.com/ohio/summit/akron/ (nonofficial)
(Official site under construction)

Canton:

http://www.canton-ohio.com/cvb/cvb.html

Cleveland:

http://www.cleveland.com/ultrafolder

Ohio:

http://www.travel.state.oh.us/

Daytime Entertainment

Guided tours

Akron Discovery Tours

Akron Convention Specialist
122 E. Mill Street, Suite 208
Akron, OH 44309
(330) 535-5296 or (800) 851-5296

Tours of the Rubber City, theme packages, spouse tours. Open 8:30 a.m. - 5:30 p.m.

Carriage Trade

8050 Brandywine Road
Northfield, OH 44067
(216) 650-6262 or (216) 467-9000

Horse drawn carriage rides through the Cuyahoga Valley National Recreation Area.
Office hours Mon. - Fri. 9 a.m. - 5 p.m.

Jacobs Field Tours

Jacobs Field
Indians Team Shop
Ontario Street
Cleveland, OH
(216) 241-8888 or (216) 420-4400

45 minute tour of Jacobs Field. May 1st
to September 30th, Monday through
Saturday (except day games, special
events, and holidays), every half hour
from 10 a.m. to 2 p.m. Tours usually sell
out so make reservations.

Historic sites

John Brown Home

Summit County Historical Society
550 Copley Road
Akron, OH 44320
(330) 535-1120

1830's era home of famed abolitionist John Brown, man who led the raid of the arsenal at
Harper's Ferry, Maryland in 1859. Exhibits on Brown's life. Perkins Stone Mansion,
Greek revival mansion built in 1837 by son of Akron's founder is across the street.

Tuesday to Sunday 1 p.m. - 5 p.m.

McKinley National Memorial

McKinley Museum
800 McKinley Monument Drive,
N.W.
Canton, OH 44708
(330) 455-7043

The final resting place for
President William McKinley and
his immediate family, the memorial
is set on top of a hill and offers
spectacular views of the lush,
green parks nearby. Adjacent to
the memorial is the McKinley
Museum, Discover World, Hoover-
Price Planetarium, and the
Ramsayer Research Library.
Located in Monument Park, and adjacent to Stadium Park which includes: JFK Memorial Fountain, padded
walking and jogging path, babbling brook, room for bikers and rollerbladers, playground, exercise trail,
mini stadium, and tennis courts. (Open till 11 pm.)

Museum hours: Mon. - Sat. 9 a.m. - 5 p.m.; Sun. Noon - 5 p.m.

Museums and Attractions

Pro Football Hall of Fame

2121 George Halas Drive N.W.
Canton, OH 44708
(330) 456-8207 or (330) 456-7762

The place to celebrate the greatest heroes of the gridiron, the Pro Football Hall of Fame is a must
see for every sports fan. From the building's distinctive profile, past the statue of legendary Jim
Thorpe, all the way to the Hall of Heroes, you and your family will marvel at the best who have
ever played the game. The Hall of Fame also includes: a fantastic Photo-Art Gallery; the
Exhibition Rotunda; the Enshrinee Mementoes Room; Super Bowl Mementoes; Super Bowl
Series Room; Mementoes of the Modern Era; the QB-1 Call-the-Play Theater; and the brand new,
Cinemascope theater at Gameday Stadium. Snack bar, Pro Football Research Center, and
Museum Store.

If you're one of the lucky ones to be in
the area during Enshrinement Week, here are
some of the 1996 events that took place
throughout the Canton area: Jackson-Belden
Food Fest; Balloon Classic Invitational and
Balloon Glo; Kickoff Parade through downtown
Canton; Concert & Fireworks Display at nearby
McKinley National Memorial; Ribs Burnoff;
Enshrinees Civic Dinner; Grand Parade through
Canton; Enshrinement into the Hall of Fame;
and the NFL Game at Fawcett Stadium.

Summer Hours Daily from 9 a.m. to 8 p.m.

Inventure Place

National Inventors Hall of Fame
221 S. Broadway
Akron, Ohio
(330) 762-6565 or (800) 968-IDEA
http://www.invent.org

Second greatest attraction in downtown Akron (after the Aeros, of course), Inventure Place includes the National Inventors Hall of Fame honoring the contributions of our country's great inventors, and the Inventors Workshop which encourages young creative minds towards enhanced self-discovery. Focus on the creative aspects of learning, explorations in imagination and ingenuity. Hands on exhibits, interactive educational programs, workshops, overnight camp-ins for children groups, special events and displays. Restaurant and Inventure Place store.

1996 Summer Hours: Monday - Saturday 9 a.m. - 5 p.m.; Sunday Noon - 5 p. m.; Hours subject to change, call ahead to confirm.

Rock & Roll Hall of Fame & Museum

One Key Plaza
Cleveland, OH 44114
(216) 781-7625 or (800) 493-ROLL
http://www.rockhall.com/

Museum devoted to the legends of Rock & Roll. Collection includes such items as: John Lennon's Sgt Pepper's jacket, Rickenbacker guitar, handwritten lyrics to select songs; Buddy Holly's high school diploma; Elvis' leather outfit and guitar from the classic 1968 Comeback show; Jimi Hendrix's original handwritten lyrics to "Purple Haze"; and, Pete Townsend's acoustic guitar, used in composition of songs for The Who's "Tommy".

Summer Hours: Wed. - Sat. 10 a.m. - 9 p.m.; Sun. - Tues. 10 a.m. - 5:30 p.m. No cameras of any kind, photographic or video, are permitted within the museum.

Great Lakes Science Center

601 Erieside Ave.
Cleveland, OH 44114
(216) 694-2000
www.greatscience.com

Hands-on science museum located on Cleveland's waterfront. Includes: Science Phenomena Exhibition with a real Indoor Tornado; Great Lakes Environment Exhibition with a model Sick Earth hospital display; the Tech Floor where you can pilot a blimp; a variety of interactive experiments; six story OMNIMAX Theater with IMAX films; Science Store; and restaurants.

Hours: Daily from 9:30 a.m. - 5:30 p.m.

Parks and Gardens

Cuyahoga Valley National Recreation Area

Canal Visitor Center
7104 Canal Road
Valley View, OH 44125
(216) 524-1497 or (800) 445-9667 (Ohio only)

Thirty three thousand acres of scenic beauty alongside 22 miles of the Cuyahoga River, the CVNRA offers a natural place for recreation such as hiking, biking, golfing, horseback riding trails, and fishing; picnic areas throughout the length of the park; artistic events at the Blossom Music Center; nature watching; and, just plain and simple opportunities for relaxation and spiritual renewal. One of the primary attractions is the popular Ohio & Erie Canal Towpath Trail. This trail is level and hard packed for any visitors using wheelchairs, strollers, bikes and/or rollerblades.

There are two other visitors centers in addition to the Canal Visitor Center; Happy Days Visitor Center and the Hunt Farm Visitor Information Center, and there are numerous entry points to the area. You should obtain a free Park Area Map ahead of time if you're not familiar with the area.

Cuyahoga Valley Scenic Railroad
P.O. Box 158
146 West Main Street
Peninsula, OH 44264-0158
(800) 468-4070

Scenic rail journeys through the heart of the Cuyahoga Valley. Stops include the Canal Visitor Center, village of Peninsula, Hale Farm & Village, Quaker Square, and Inventure Place. Call for schedules and information.

F.A. Seiberling Naturealm Visitors Center
975 Treaty Line Road
Akron, OH 44313
(330) 867-5511

Nature exhibits include woodlands and marshlands, a pond tunnel, the role of man and the environment, a bird watch room, auditorium, and Arboretum.

Weekday Hours: 8 a.m. - 4:30 p.m.

Stan Hywet Hall & Gardens
714 N. Portage Path
Akron, OH 44303
(330) 836-5533

English country manor home owned by co-founder of Goodyear Tire and Rubber Company open for tours, with scenic 70 acres of landscaped gardens.

Summer Hours: Daily 10 a.m. to 4:30 p.m.; Grounds from 9 a.m. to 6 p.m.

Portage Lakes State Park
5031 Manchester Road
Akron, OH 44319
(330) 644-2220

Just south of downtown, lakes carved out of the Ohio countryside by retreating glaciers. Camping, boating, fishing and hunting, swimming, nature trails and picnicking.

Daily from 6 a.m. to 11 p.m. (Swimming only permitted when lifeguards on duty.)

Wine & Chocolate

The Winery at Wolf Creek
2637 S. Cleveland-Massillon Road
Norton, OH 44203
(330) 666-9285

Family owned winery with tastings, and tours when possible.

Tues., Wed. & Thurs. Noon - 8 p.m.; Fri. & Sat. Noon - Midnight; Sun. 1 p.m. - 8 p.m.

Harry London Candies, Inc.
5353 Lauby Road
North Canton, OH 44720
(330) 494-0833 or (800) 321-0444

Chocolate factory tours; Chocolate Hall of Fame; sampling of fresh chocolates; and, largest Chocolate Store in the Midwest.

Store Hours: Mon. - Sat. 8 a.m. - 6 p.m.; Sun. Noon - 5 p.m.
Tour Hours: Mon. - Sat. 9 a.m. - 4 p.m.; Sun. Noon - 3:30 p.m.

Theme Parks & Zoo

Sea World of Ohio
1100 Sea World Drive
Aurora, OH 44202
(216) 995-2121 or (800) 63-SHAMU

Join Shamu, the Killer Whale and all his friends at a theme park which stresses education and conservation, as well as exciting entertainment. Sea World visitors can see: the Seal & Sea Lion Pool; Dolphin Cove; new Patagonia Passage; Shark Encounter; Eagle Point; Penguin Encounter; and a number of great shows like Baywatch action show, Wild Wings Bird Show, Hotel Clyde & Seamore, and of course, Shamu.

Hours: Open Daily at 10 a.m., check schedules for closing times.

Akron Zoological Park
500 Edgewood Avenue
Akron, OH 44307
(330) 375-2550

Over three hundred animals, birds, and mammals in a woodland setting, including Red Pandas, River Otters, African Lions. Petting area, picnic areas, concessions, gift shop.

Summer Hours: Mon. - Sat. 10 a.m. - 5 p.m.; Sun. and Holidays 10 a.m. - 6 p.m.

Public Golf courses

Throughout the rest of this book, I discuss at least one golf course per city, with location, tee time information and course statistics. This is usually easy because most of these towns have two or three decent public courses worth discussing. This chapter is the exception to the rule. There are over 40 courses in Akron, and 39 tournament tested courses in Canton, and there was just no way I could have done them all, or even any one of them, justice. Therefore, I recommend you do the following:

1.   Contact the Akron/Summit Convention and Visitors Bureau at (330) 374-7560 or (800) 245-4254 and ask them to send you a copy of their "Golf & Bowling Directory." This pamphlet lists addresses and phone numbers for 32 public courses in the area, and ten private courses (including Firestone, site of the NEC World Series of Golf).

2.   Contact the Canton/Stark County Convention & Visitors Bureau at (330) 452-0243 or call 1 (800) 533-4302 to request a free copy of "Ohio's Golf Capital: Canton/Stark County." This is a 32 page comprehensive guide to 19 courses in the area. There is some crossover with the Akron/Summit Directory, but the Canton/Stark Guide offers more information than just address and phone number. The Canton/Stark Guide gives you a description of the course as well as including yardages. This guide also lists eight hotels offering Golf Packages and getaways.

      (None of the Akron hotels listed below offer golf packages, but many of the Canton area hotels do. In fact, all of the Canton hotels listed below offer some sort of golf getaway, so if golf is your game, you might want to take a second look at these accommodations. These hotels can be a valuable local resource when you are trying to determine what courses meet your needs and which ones will challenge your skills.)

3.   Finally, if you have a computer with internet connections, check out the excellent golfcourse.com web site located at http://www.golfcourse.com. This site lists even more comprehensive information about select courses around the country, and gives course statistics, history, description, when tee times are accepted, and what time the Pro Shop opens.

Shopping Malls

Quaker Square
135 South Broadway
Akron, OH 44308
(330) 253-5970

Downtown quaint shopping village, restaurants, bars, shops.
Monday - Saturday 10 a.m. - 9 p.m.; Sunday 11 a.m. - 7 p.m.

Chapel Hill Mall
2000 Brittain Road
Akron, OH 44310
(330) 633-1131

Sears, JC Penney, Kaufmann's, theaters, food court, carousel, and over 80 specialty stores.
Monday - Saturday 10 a.m. - 9 p.m.; Sunday Noon - 5 p.m.

Summit Mall
Ghent Road & West Market Street
Fairlawn, OH
(330) 867-1555

Dillard's, Kaufmann's, and over 90 stores.
Monday - Saturday 10 a.m. - 9 p.m.; Sunday 11 a.m. - 6 p.m.

Belden Village Mall
4230 Belden Mall
Canton, OH 44718
(330) 494-5490

Dillard's, Sears, Kaufmann's, food court, restaurants, and over 40 specialty stores.

Monday - Saturday 10 a.m. - 9 p.m.; Sunday 11 a.m. - 6 p.m.

Seasonal Events

Dates are approximate, contact regional tourism offices listed above for updated schedule information.

May: Cherry Blossom Festival; Mayfest at Canal Fulton; May Garden Mart

June: Opening Concert at Blossom Music Center; Antique & Classic Car Show; Boston Mills Art Festival; Strawberry Festival at Canal Fulton; Stark County Italian-American Festival; Founder's Day

One of the primary industries of Akron, the Goodyear office building also includes a museum onsite.

July: Pro Football Hall of Fame Week, Grand Parade, Enshrinement Ceremonies, Hall of Fame Game; Akron Rib Burn Off; Summit County Fair; Akron Arts Expo; Concert in McKinley Park; Olde Canal Days

August: NEC World Series of Golf; All American Soap Box Derby; Cuyahoga Valley Festival

Accommodations/Other

Visiting Hotel for the Akron Aeros:

Akron Ramada Plaza Hotel
20 West Mill Street
Akron, OH 44308
(330) 384-1500 or (800) 2-RAMADA
Restaurant & Lounge, jacuzzi rooms available, free indoor parking, AAA discounts.

Akron:

Akron Hilton Inn at Quaker Square
135 South Broadway
Akron, OH 44308
(330) 253-5970 or (800) HILTONS
Restaurants & Lounge, indoor pool, exercise room, playground, shops, AAA discounts (Silo building listed on the National Register of Historic Places)

Radisson Inn Akron/Fairlawn
200 Montrose Ave
West Akron, OH 44321
(330) 666-9300
Restaurant & Lounge, indoor pool, exercise room, AAA and Entertainment discounts based on availability.

Residence Inn by Marriott
120 Montrose Ave
West Akron, OH 44321
(330) 666-4811
Complimentary breakfast, outdoor pool, kitchens, pets ok, AAA and Entertainment discounts.

Akron West Hilton Inn
3180 West Market St
Akron, OH 44333
(330) 867-5000 or (800) HILTONS
Restaurant & Lounge, indoor and
outdoor pools, exercise rooms, pets
ok, AAA discounts.

Sheraton Suites/Cuyahoga Falls
1989 Front St
Cuyahoga Falls, OH 44221
(330) 929-3000
Complimentary breakfast,
Restaurant & Lounge, indoor pool,
exercise room, sauna, pets ok, scenic
location, AAA discounts.

Holiday Inn Akron/Fairlawn Conference Center
4073 Medina Road
Fairlawn, OH 44333
(330) 666-4131 or (800) HOLIDAY
Restaurant & Lounge, outdoor pool,
exercise room, game room, AAA
discounts.

Holiday Inn Akron South
2940 Chenoweth
Akron, OH 44312
(330) 644-7126
Restaurant & Lounge, outdoor pool,
track & racquet club, game room,
AAA discounts.

Comfort Inn Akron West
130 Montrose Ave
West Akron, OH 44321
(330) 666-5050 or (800) 221-2222
Free continental breakfast, indoor
pool, 48 jacuzzi suites, AAA
discounts.

Days Inn Akron/Fairlawn
3150 West Market St
Akron, OH 44333
(330) 869-9000
Restaurant, outdoor pool, pets
maybe ok, AAA discounts.

Canton:

Best Suites
4914 Everhard Road
Canton, OH 44718
(330) 499-1011 or (800) BEST-INN
Free full buffet breakfast, social
hour, indoor pool, exercise room,
refrigerators, Golf Packages, AAA
discounts.

Comfort Inn
5345 Broadmoor Circle, N.W.
Canton, OH 44709
(330) 492-1331 or (800) 221-2222
Complimentary continental
breakfast, outdoor pool, Golf
Packages, AAA and Entertainment
discounts.

Hampton Inn
5335 Broadmoor Circle
Canton, OH 44709
(330) 492-0151 or (800)
HAMPTON
Free continental breakfast,
exercise room, Golf Packages,
AAA discounts.

Residence Inn by Marriott
5085 Broadmoor Circle, N.W.
Canton, OH 44709
(330) 493-0004
Complimentary breakfast, evening
social hour, indoor pool & spa,
Sport Court, exercise room,
kitchens, Golf Packages, AAA and
Entertainment discounts.

Fairfield Inn by Marriott
5285 Broadmoor Circle, N.W.
Canton, OH
(330) 493-7373
Complimentary breakfast, indoor
pool, Golf Packages, AAA
discounts.

Hospitals

SUMMA Akron City Hospital
525 East Market St
Akron, OH 44309
(330) 375-3000

Akron General Medical Hospital
400 Wabash Ave.
Akron, OH 44307
(330) 384-6000

Aultman Hospital
2600 6th Street, S.W.
Canton, OH 44710
(330) 452-9911

Timken Mercy Medical Center
1320 Timken Mercy Dr., N.W.
Canton, OH 44708
(330) 489-1000

Transportation

Akron-Canton Regional Airport:	(330) 896-2376
Akron-Fulton International:	(330) 375-2888
Cleveland Hopkins International:	(216) 265-6030
AMTRAK:	(800) USA-RAIL
American Trailways Bus:	(330) 376-8524
Greyhound Bus Lines:	(330) 434-5171
Metro Regional Transit Authority (Akron):	(330) 762-0341
Canton Regional Transit Authority :	(330) 454-6132
Akron GI Cab:	(330) 253-2131
Barberton-Summit Taxi:	(330) 825-9933
City Yellow Cab:	(330) 253-3141
Falls Cab:	(330) 929-3121
Niemann Express:	(330) 725-8294
Shuttle One Service:	(330) 686-1505

Hilton Inn at Quaker Square. Sleep in a Silo!

Bowie Baysox

Team: **Bowie Baysox** (Southern Division)

Stadium: **Prince George's Stadium**

Office Address: 4101 NE Crain Highway, Bowie, Maryland 20716
Mailing Address: P.O. Box 1661, Bowie, Maryland 20717
Phone: (301) 805-6000; (301) 956-4004
Fax: (301) 805-6008
Web Site(s):   Currently under construction. Call for details.

Team Ownership:

Operated by: Maryland Baseball Limited Partnership
Principals: Peter Kirk (Chairman), Pete Simmons, Hugh
                   Schindel, John Daskalakis, Frank Perdue.

Affiliation: Baltimore Orioles

Years in Eastern League: 1993-Present

Stadium Physical Characteristics

Age, Built in: 1994
Stadium Owner: Maryland-National Capital Parks and Planning Commission

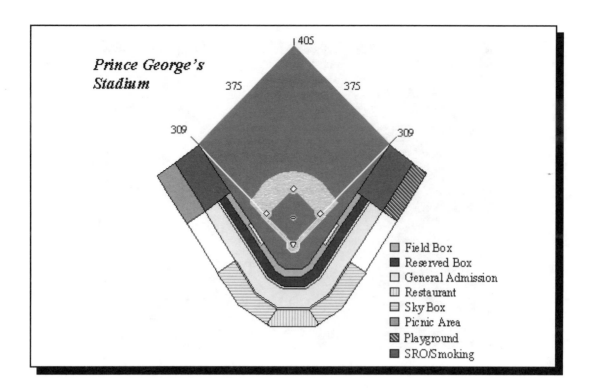

Prince George's Stadium

405
375   375
309   309

- Field Box
- Reserved Box
- General Admission
- Restaurant
- Sky Box
- Picnic Area
- Playground
- SRO/Smoking

Fence height: 8 feet

Bullpens: Inside the fences, and in foul territory.

Playing Surface: Natural grass

Characteristics: Prince George's Stadium is one of the three ballparks in the Eastern League, along with Senator Thomas Dodd Memorial Stadium in Norwich, and the soon to be opened Canal Park in Akron, where the concrete stands are set down into the side of a hill. This means that the fan enters at street level on the main concourse, and finds the stands and the field dug down immediately in front of

them. Prince George's has to be the most open stadium in the league as well, with a large main concourse overlooking the field all the way around, open, grassy lawn areas in left and right field to accommodate overflow standing room only crowds, and a cross aisle separating box seating from general admission. In addition, the Diamond View Restaurant is open to all ticket holders, and provides amazing views of the game from high above home plate. This openness is the catalyst for the consistently high, league leading attendance records set every season at Prince George's Stadium.

Prince George's Stadium is also a "Stay Alert!" park (a phrase borrowed from Stadium Announcer Bud Freeman.) No overhang over the stands, home plate netting that doesn't extend back to the press box, and a 'A' frame roof where balls that look like they're leaving the park roll back into the stands, ...PG Stadium is a good place for a souvenir, or for a conk on the head if you don't Stay Alert!

Total Capacity: 10,000 plus

Box:	3,000
General Admission:	4,500
Lawn:	2,000 plus
Upper Level:	500

	1994	1995	1996
Attendance	293,665	463,976	396,086

1996 Average Attendance:

No. of openings:	65
1996 Daily Average:	6,094

All Time Attendance Records:
Daily: 14,008 on August 17, 1996
Seasonal: 463,976 in 1995

Skyboxes: 14 [12 with 24 seats, 2 with seating for 30]

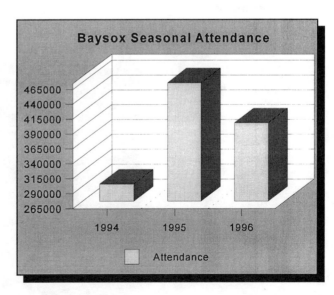

Type of Seating:

The Box Seats all are comfortable individual seats providing both armrests and cupholders. (The Baysox program indicates box seats are 21 inches wide, and provide 34 inches of leg room.) General admission seating is aluminum bleachers. The best thing about General Admission at Prince George's is that you have a lot of mobility throughout the stadium. If you're uncomfortable with your seat selection, for whatever reason, it's very easy to move to another part of the stadium.

Covered Seating: Not available in stands. The concession concourse is under cover from first base around to third base and provides standing room only viewing of the field. In addition, you can enjoy the game from the Diamond View Restaurant which is not only indoors, and more importantly during the hot and humid Maryland summer, air conditioned.

Restrooms:
Ladies:	3 (2 more near the Diamond View on second level)
Men:	3 (2 more near the Diamond View on second level)
Changing tables: Yes	

Customer Service Window: Behind home plate

Smoking Policy:

Not allowed in stands, but there are two lawn areas near right and left field which permit smoking.

First Aid:

Behind home plate, near the Security Office.

Wheelchair & Handicapped Seating:

Access to all areas of the stadium.

Telephones:	Only 2, one on first base concourse, one on third base concourse.
ATM:	Yes, near the Baysox Gift Shop behind home plate.
Scoreboard:	There are two large electronic scoreboards. The board behind left center field is electronic and is the primary game scoreboard. The board behind right center is a graphic scoreboard, and can also show live video of players and fans in between innings. (Keep an eye on this scoreboard, the face you see may be your own!)
Game Clock:	Yes.
Sound:	Overhead, high quality sound system.
Sunsets?	Between third base and left field.
Autographs:	Yes, before the game on the first base side.

Concessions and Souvenirs

There are one hundred feet of concession sales on each side of the main concession concourse, with 32 points of sale.

Best stadium food: There are two finalists for best stadium food at Prince George's, the Open Pit Beef BBQ Sandwich, and the Hot Link Sausage. The Pit Beef BBQ is just really, really good. It's sliced smoked beef served on a warm bun. Sold at the Specialty Beers window on the third base side, you can add a dash of horseradish and some BBQ sauce, and you'll find that it is definitely worth the price. (Don't confuse the Open Pit Beef BBQ with the BBQ sandwiches also sold at the same stand. The regular BBQ is cheaper, and more difficult to recommend.)

As for the Hot Link Sausage, this has to be my favorite. Although it violates my general rule that grilled items are always the best (Prince George's doesn't really have a traditional open grill area, in the sense that say Binghamton, Harrisburg or Trenton does), the Hot Links, as well as the Italian Sausage, are my choice for best concessions in the park. Both should be served with peppers and onions, and are excellent with a good squirt of spicy mustard. I also recommend the Fries. An excellent value, they are consistently hot, salty and just plain great. (Of note - I remember during the first full season at Prince George's Stadium finding a decent crab cake for sale at the Specialty Beers Window. However, I don't believe that Maryland delicacy was on the menu during 1996, at least not after the Fourth of July. It would be a shame if this staple of every Marylander's summer diet was permanently removed from the menu. Hopefully, it is a temporary exclusion and by the time you're reading this, Crab Cakes will again be available at PG Stadium.)

Other Concessions:

There are a number of other concessions which are sold as grilled, in addition to the sausages. These are the Grilled Chicken Breast, Cheeseburgers, Hamburgers, and finally the Garden Burger. (Of this last item, obviously, I'm not a vegetarian so my opinion probably is skewed here, but even after smothering the Garden Burger with onions, relish, mustard and ketchup, it still managed to taste healthy.) Prince George's also sells a Jumbo All Beef Hot Dog, Junior Hot Dog, Corn Dog, Nachos (both regular and Grande), Pretzels, Peanuts and Candy.

There is also a popular Sweet Shop located on the first base side concourse which sells funnel cake, cotton candy, the Baysox helmet sundae, ice cream cones, Italian Ice, and Dove Bars.

Concessions in stands: Beer, sodas, peanuts, Icey Italian Ice, cotton candy.

Hot Dog: Of the different types of Hot Dogs sold, I'd chose the Jumbo Hot Dog as your best value. At one inch thick, and maybe six inches long, if you want a dog, this is your puppy.

Peanuts: $2.00 (Only stadium where I saw vendors toss a bag both accurately and for distance.)

Beer: Beer sales stop at end of 7th inning. Valid ID required.

On tap: Pete's Wicked, Pete's Summer Brew, Amstel Light, Heineken, Miller Lite, Miller, Budweiser, Coors Light. (Specialty beers listed below.)

In stands:

Bud Light, Miller, Miller Light, Red Dog, Coors Light (don't ask for Zima here!)

Microbrews:

Located at Specialty Beer window on third base side, 1996 sales included Pete's Wicked, Sam Adams, Oregon Raspberry Wheat, Oregon India Pale Ale, Blue Ridge Wheat, New Amsterdam Black & Tan. All were on tap.

Non-alcoholic: Available
Wine: Bacardi
Breezers

**View of Field
from Concession Stands:** Yes, there is a large open concession concourse located at the top of the stands from which you can see the game. If you're in line, all you have to do is turn your head and you'll see the field. (Unlike some other stadiums though, you won't hear the play by play radio broadcast of the game in the concession line.)

Restaurant:

Diamond View Restaurant

The Diamond View is located on the second level of Prince George's Stadium, high above home plate. The restaurant seats 130, but can accommodate groups of up to 250 people. Viewing is excellent with large glass windows providing an unimpeded view of the field. There is also balcony level seating which lets you get even closer to the action. The menu differs from that on the first level concourse, and there is a bar serving a variety of beers, wines and non-alcoholic drinks. Most importantly, the Diamond View Restaurant is not only available for group outings, but is also open to all ticket holders.

Menu: Chicken Wings, Chicken Tenderloins, Potato Skins, Nachos, Spiced Shrimp, Turkey Sandwich, Stacked Beef Sandwich, Grilled Chicken Sandwich, Grilled

Cheese Sandwich, Baysox Burger, Deli Dog, Chicken Caesar Salad, Basket of Fries. Desserts include Cheesecake, Homemade Pie, Ice Cream, and Baysox Brownie. The Diamond View Bar serves domestic, imported and microbrew beer including Sam Adams and Budweiser on tap. In 1996, you could also purchase Mountain View Chardonnay, Merlot and Cabernet, as well as assorted flavors of Bacardi Breezer wine coolers.

The Diamond View Restaurant is also proud to offer a Sunday Brunch prior

to every Sunday Home Game. The Brunch menu includes: carving station with Virginia smoked ham; crepe station; omelet station; fresh Belgian waffles; sausage; home fried potatoes; fresh fruit; bagels; assorted pastries; and a juice bar.

Picnics: Picnic area in left field, usually reserved for groups. If not reserved, there are picnic tables available in the shade.

Gift Shop:

The Baysox Gift Shop is located behind home plate just as you enter the stadium. There is a wide selection of Baysox memorabilia for sale, including t-shirts, sweaters, windbreakers, hats, bats, balls, pennants, and much more. The store also sells items associated with other Minor League clubs, and on occasion, autographed bats and balls.

Admission*:

Baysox Prices	
General Admission	$6.00
Reserved Box Seats	$8.00
Field Box Seats (First 4 rows - infield)	$9.00
Luxury Club Seats	$12.00

Season Ticket Plans Available	
Full Season (71 games) Field Box	$639.00
Full Season (71 games) Box Seat	$497.00
Box Seat Mini-Plan (22 games)	$154.00
Box Seat Mini-Plan (12 games)	$84.00
General Admission Book (12 games)	$50.00
Youth/SC/Mil G.A. Book (12 games)	$30.00

Special rates for Kids and Seniors:

$3.00 for Children ages 6 through 12, Seniors 60 and over, and Active Military (with ID).

Free Admission (in General Admission seating only) for children 5 and under, Little Leaguers coming to the game in cap and jersey, and for Bowie Boys and Girls Club.

Group Information:

The Baysox offer a variety of group options. Your group can either reserve a block of box seats or general admission, a skybox with hostess service, or even the Diamond View Restaurant. You can also make plans to have a picnic early in the picnic area near left field. With this many options, groups are insured of having a great time at Prince George's Stadium.

Group Benefits include Reserved Group Seating (Box Seats, Restaurant, and Sky Box only); a public address welcome; complimentary gift to the group leader for groups over 50; recognition on the scoreboard for groups over 50, and a chance to participate in the First Pitch Ceremony for groups over 100.

Group Rates:

Box Seats: For groups of 24-99, you can get reserved Box Seats all together, for only $7.00. For 100+, it's $6.00 per. In addition, every member of the group receives a 10% discount coupon which can be redeemed at the Baysox Gift Shop.

General Admission:

General Admission Rates		
Quantity	Adult	Youth/SC/Mil
24-99	$4.50	$2.50
100+	$4.00	$2.00

Group members allowed to sit anywhere in General Admission, which is a First Come/First Seat area. Youth ages 6-12, Seniors 60 and over, Military must have active military ID.

Luxury Suites:

The Baysox can accommodate groups up to 24 in one of the special, climate controlled Luxury Suites, with hostess service, overlooking the game. Suite rental costs $400.00 in April and May, and $500.00 from June through September. Included in this price are three reserved parking spaces. Although there is a special menu available in the Luxury Suites, the rental price does not include the cost of food. All suite rentals depend upon availability.

Diamond View Restaurant:

Diamond View Group Pricing				
Group Size	April/May		Jun/Jul/Aug/Sep	
	Adult	Youth	Adult	Youth
24 to 49	$25.00	$13.00	$30.00	$18.00
50 plus	$20.00	$13.00	$25.00	$18.00

Restaurant prices include food and balcony seat. Beer and wine available for additional charge. 1996 Data: Call (301) 805-6000 for updated prices.

Diamond View Group Buffet includes: two entrees; carving station (roast turkey and roast top sirloin); pasta du jour; salad bar; fresh fruit; baked rolls; vegetable; potato or rice; dessert; Iced tea and soft drinks.

[*1997 Data: Prices subject to change. Call (301) 805-6000 for more information.]

Ticket Sales:

Address: Main Box Office, Prince George's Stadium, 4101 N.E. Crain Highway, Bowie, Maryland 20716

Phone: (301) 805-2233

Credit Cards: Visa, MasterCard, American Express, Discover

Hours Ticket Window Open:

Non-Game Days: 9:00 a.m to 4:30 p.m. (Mon. - Fri.)
Game Days:

Window: 10:00 a.m to middle of 5th inning.
Phone Orders: 10:00 a.m. to 4:30 p.m. (Mon.-Sat.); 10:00 a.m. to 11:30 a.m. (Sunday home games).

Other General Admission Outlets:

Chesapeake Crown, Pointer Ridge Shopping Center, 1500 Crain Highway, Bowie, MD 20716 (301) 249-1256

Kaufmann's Tavern, 329 Gambrills Road, Gambrills, MD. 21054 (410) 923-2005

Walmart, 150 North Solomon's Island Road, Prince Frederick, MD 20678 (410) 535-3790

Upgrades: General Admission tickets may be upgraded to Box Seats at the Main Ticket Window, depending upon availability.

Exchanges: Box Seat Tickets may be exchanged for Box Seats to another regular season home game, depending upon availability, at the Main Ticket Window up to at least 24 hours in advance of the date printed on the ticket. After the 24 hour deadline, Box Seat tickets may be exchanged for General Admission tickets to regular season home games.

Rain Check Policy:

Box Seats: If a game is canceled due inclement weather, Box Seat tickets may be exchanged for Box Seat tickets to a future regular season game, depending upon availability. No cash refunds.

General Admission: If a game is canceled due to inclement weather, General Admission tickets may be used as a raincheck to future regular season home games, provided it has first been validated before leaving Prince George's Stadium. No cash refunds.

Game times:

Weekdays:	7:05 p.m.
Saturday:	7:05 p.m.
Sunday:	1:05 p.m.

Time Gates open:

1:05 before game time

(See schedule for day games. All times subject to change.)

Parking: Free (There is also a Paid Permit lot closer to the stadium on the first base side.)

Other

For the kids:

Prince George's Stadium is a great place for baseball, and a great place for kids. Prince George's has a beautiful, custom carousel overlooking the Baysox bullpen, a fun playground with attractive, old fashioned equipment, a speed pitch, and a Kid's Stand, all located on the main concourse near right field. In addition, all Baysox fans from 5 to 14 years of age can join the Junior Baysox. Every Junior Baysox receives a special t-shirt, Baysox certificate, and a membership card. And every Sunday home game is Junior Baysox Sunday, with great contests and prizes, Junior Baysox members are admitted for only 25¢ if they wear their Junior Baysox T-shirt. And finally, with it's open concourse and grassy lawns, if the older kids and teenagers start to get restless during a slow game that's developing into a pitcher's duel, the kids can find some time away from the folks, and vice versa, while still remaining in view. All in all, Prince George's provides great, all around, fun family entertainment for all ages.

Promotions and Giveaways:

During 1996, the Baysox sponsored six post game fireworks extravaganzas. In addition, the Baysox gave away such souvenir items as magnetic schedules, Cal Ripken posters, baseball cards, auto shades, caps, seat cushions, photo albums, player photos, even a car at the end of the season. The Baysox also hosted many special events, including but not limited to visits from the Orioles Bird, the U.S. Navy Band Country Current, the Blues Brothers, Sport, the Dynamite Lady, and, of course, Morganna, the Kissing Bandit, among others. Prince George's Stadium was one of 15 stadiums in 1996 to host a warmup game for the USA Olympic Baseball Team as part of the 1996 NationsBank USA Baseball Team Tour. And also, once again Prince George's Stadium hosted the Congressional Baseball Game, pitting U.S. Congressional Republicans versus Democrats on the baseball diamond in Bowie, instead of the floor of the Capitol 15 miles away in Washington, D.C.

As for other events, every Sunday home game was Junior Baysox day, sponsored by Bowie Blade News, McDonald's of Bowie, and Dr. Gallagher, with special admission, contests, and prizes for Junior Baysox members. Mondays saw fans receive special CPI Photo giveaways. Tuesday games were the ones to attend if you wanted to register a chance to win a car from East West Lincoln Mercury. Safeway and

Giant sponsored 2-for-1 nights Tuesdays and Wednesdays, respectively. Also, on Wednesdays, bringing two Kellogg's Raisin Bran box tops with you was good to admit four people for only $2.00. And finally, last but by no means least, every Wednesday at Prince George's was Washington Homes Grand Slam Wednesday where one lucky fan had a chance to win a brand new home.

In between innings:

There were a number of giveaways and contests in between innings at Prince George's Stadium. These included the J-Mart nightly putting contest atop the home team dugout; the Allstate kiddy car race every Tuesday, Thursday and Saturday night game; and the Middle Atlantic Marketing Association's Dairy Dash for kids around the bases. Also, the Baysox usually launched souvenir items like t-shirts and sweatshirts into the crowd using a huge, special Sling Shot. But your best chance to win at Prince George's Stadium required you purchase a Baysox Souvenir Program. Located within randomly selected programs, the Baysox players and staff would sign certain merchant's advertisements, and if you add a lucky program with a Baysox signature, you could redeem it for a prize at the Information Window behind home plate.

What song played during 7th inning stretch?

"YMCA" (Although the announcer does lead the crowd in singing "Take Me Out to the Ballgame" early in the game.)

Radio Station Broadcasting Game:

WNAV 1430 AM; WRC AM 980 (Weekends)

Special:
Prince George's Stadium in 1996 hosted a special exhibit honoring the Negro Leagues. "Rough Diamonds: The Mid-Atlantic Negro Leagues and Sandlot Heroes", sponsored by the Maryland-National Capitol Park and Planning Commission, was located along the first base side concourse in a special viewing area. The exhibit paid tribute to some of the great, unsung heroes of baseball, including Josh Gibson, Oscar Charleston, Leon Day, Buck O'Neill, Satchel Paige , Jackie Robinson, as well as honoring local teams from Prince George's County and nearby areas.. There were classic photographs, valuable memorabilia, replica uniforms and equipment on display. In addition, there was a learning exhibit demonstrating the birth of a baseball and a bat, educational programs, games and storytelling for the kids.

Eastern League Information: Eastern League Information is run nightly on the right center scoreboard.

Team Information

Bowie Baysox (Southern Division)

History:

The Bowie Baysox first season was played at Memorial Stadium in Baltimore during 1993, due to delays in construction of Prince George's Stadium. The start of the 1994 season saw the Baysox still as a nomadic team without a home field and play alternated between Baltimore and the University of Maryland in College Park, until the club found its way home to Prince George's in June of 1994. Due to severe winter weather which further delayed completion of the stadium, the Baysox played in a playable, but unfinished stadium for the remainder of the season. However, with Opening Day in 1995 came a complete ballpark with all the traditional amenities and then some, and the Baysox went on to set an all-time Eastern League attendance record.

Eastern League Championships: None

1994:   Bowie lost to Harrisburg in Southern Division Semifinals (3-2)

Famous Players who went on to the Major Leagues:

Calvin Maduro (1996); Kimera Bartee (1995); Armando Benitez (1994); Brent Bowers (1996); Rocky Coppinger (1995); Jim Dedrick (1993, '95); Cesar Devarez (1993, '94); Curtis Goodwin (1994); Jeffrey Hammonds (1993, '95); Jimmy Haynes (1994); Matt Howard (1995); Scott Klingenbeck (1994); Rick Krivda (1993); Alex Ochoa (1994); Jack Voight (1994); Gregg Zaun (1993); Harold Baines (1993 - rehab); Mike Devereaux (1993 - rehab); Sid Fernandez (1995 - rehab); Jeff Manto (1995 - rehab); Mike Mussina (1993 - rehab); Sherman Obando (1993 - rehab); Fernando Valenzuela (1993 - rehab); Andy Van Slyke (1995 - rehab).

Baltimore Orioles Minor League Organization			
Team	**League**	**Level**	**City & Phone**
Baltimore Orioles	American League	Major League	Baltimore, MD (410) 685-9800
Rochester Red Wings	International League	AAA	Rochester, NY (716) 467-3000
Bowie Baysox	Eastern League	AA	Bowie, MD (301) 805-6000
Frederick Keys	Carolina League	A	Frederick, MD (301) 662-0013
Delmarva Shorebirds	South Atlantic League	A	Salisbury, MD (410) 219-3112
Bluefield Orioles	Appalachian League	Rookie	Bluefield, WV (703) 326-1326
Gulf Coast Orioles	Gulf Coast League	Rookie	Sarasota, FL (813) 923-1996

Approximate distance from Prince George's Stadium to Camden Yards: 27 miles
(Source: Rand McNally TripMaker Version 1.1 1994; Bowie, MD to Baltimore, MD)

Mascot:	None. (Only EL team without a mascot, probably should consider holding a contest and let Junior Baysox choose a team mascot.)
Team Colors:	Warm red, teal and black
Visiting Hotel:	Days Inn, 2520 Riva Road, Annapolis, MD 21401 (410) 224-2800
Fan Club:	All fan mail should be directed to that player in care of the Bowie Baysox.

Directions to stadium:

Prince George's Stadium is located in Bowie on Route 301, between Route 50 and Route 197 (Collington Road).

From the intersection of Routes 50 and 301, follow 301 South then take a left at the second light into Prince George's Stadium.

From points south, proceed north on 301. The entrance to Prince George's Stadium is on the right at the first light after MD 197.

Bowie/Annapolis

Background

Bowie, Maryland (Pop. 37,589) has a history which revolves around Belair Mansion. Originally part of lands deeded to Lord Calvert in 1658, Governor Samuel Ogle was the man who eventually built the Belair Mansion and stables around 1743. A large Georgian estate amid rural tobacco country, the mansion and stables have been famous for their contributions to thoroughbred racing, an important Maryland tradition to this day.

While Belair Estate continued to thrive, nearby the tobacco farming community of Huntington was growing at a modest pace, especially after the introduction of the railroad in the 1870's. That town of Huntington was renamed in the 1880's after Maryland Governor Oden Bowie, incorporated officially as a town in 1916, and remained a small, rural community until significant development events occurred in the

1950's. The Levitt Company bought the Belair Mansion and 2,000 of the surrounding acres around the estate in 1957, and the Bowie City Council subsequently annexed that estate land under city jurisdiction. Levitt built over 9,000 homes on the former grounds of the Belair Estate, and all of this residential suburb became known as the City of Bowie after incorporation in 1963. The Belair Mansion was donated to the city's care a year later.

Historic Belair Mansion

Today, Bowie is still a bedroom community for Washington and Baltimore, but also, recent development efforts are transforming the city's character. Since the construction of Prince George's Stadium, residents have seen new office buildings going up, new homes, hotels and restaurants coming to town, and several brand, new shopping centers just about across the street from the stadium. Situated geographically almost in the center of Maryland, the residential city of Bowie is less than a half hour's drive from the state capital at Annapolis (15 miles); the largest city in the state, Baltimore (20 miles); and our nation's capital, Washington, D.C. (12 miles). Proximity to all these popular tourist destinations should make Bowie an attractive possibility when you plan your next vacation to the vicinity.

As for nearby Annapolis (Pop. 33,187), the town originally called Providence became the state capital in 1694, after the capital was moved from the first settlement of Maryland, Historic St. Mary's City. Renamed after Princess Anne, Annapolis also served as the nation's capital from November 26, 1783 to June 3, 1784. It was during this time that the historic State House, the oldest continually used capitol in the country, hosted meetings of the Continental Congress; witnessed the resignation from the Continental Army of General George Washington; and was the location for the ratification of the Treaty of Paris, which formally ended the American Revolution. Annapolis today is also considered by many to be a sailing capital, and that's not limited to the Midshipmen from the United States Naval Academy (1845). On any given day from late spring through early fall, you're bound to encounter all sorts of recreational boating wonders. Whether it's a short cruise on the Severn River or Spa Creek from City Dock, attending a boating festival or two (including the U.S. Sailboat Show and the U.S. Powerboat Show in early October), or whether it's just sipping a margarita and watching the sailors and powerboaters strut their stuff down Ego Alley, Annapolis is another exciting attraction worth considering.

Information

Chamber of Commerce/Tourist Bureaus

Greater Bowie Chamber of Commerce
6770 Race Track Road
Bowie, MD 20715
(301) 262-0920

Annapolis/Anne Arundel County Conference & Visitors Bureau
26 West Street
Annapolis, MD 21401
(410) 280-0445

Historic Annapolis Foundation Welcome Center
77 Main Street/City Dock
Annapolis, MD
(410) 268-5576

Baltimore Area Convention & Visitors Association
301 East Pratt Street
(USS Constellation Pier)
Baltimore, MD 21202
(410) 837-4636 or (800) 282-6632

Washington, D.C. Convention & Visitors Association
1212 New York Ave., N.W.
Suite 600
Washington, D.C. 20005
(202)789-7000

Web Site(s):

Bowie: http://www.cityofbowie.org

Annapolis: http://www.capitalonline.com

Baltimore: http://www.markpoint.com/balmer.htm
http://www.hyperstuff.com/md/balt/

Washington, D.C.:
http://www.washington.org/ ;
http://www.house.gov/Visitor.html

Daytime Entertainment

Guided tours

Annapolis City Dock

Discover Annapolis Tours

Visitors Center
26 West Street
Annapolis, MD 21401
(410) 626-6000

One hour mini-bus tour of
Historic Annapolis. Call for
schedule information.

Annapolis Tours

Three Centuries Tours of Annapolis
48 Maryland Ave., P.O. Box 29
Annapolis, MD 21404
(410) 263-5401

Walking two hour tour of USNA and Historic
Annapolis. Summer departures: 10 a.m. from
Loews Hotel; 10:30 a.m. from Visitor Center,
26 West St.; 1:30 p.m from Information Booth
on City Dock.

Historic Annapolis African-American Heritage Audio Walking Tour

Historic Annapolis Foundation
77 Main Street/City Dock
Annapolis, MD
(410) 268-5576

Walking tour begins at museum store.

Orioles Ballpark Tours

Oriole Park at Camden Yards
Eutaw & Camden Streets
Baltimore, MD
(410) 547-6234

One hour fifteen minute tours of Camden Yards.
Offered every day but afternoon home games,
depending on weather conditions. Seasonal hours:
Mon. - Fri. Every hour from 11 a.m. to 2 p.m.; Sat.
Every half hour from 10:30 a.m. to 2 p.m.; Sun.
Every half hour from 12:30 p.m. to 2 p.m. Off
season hours: Call.

Gray Line Sightseeing Tours

Union Station, Bus Level
50 Massachusetts Ave., NE
Washington, D.C. 20002
(202) 289-1995

Historical Tours

R & R Pedicabs, Inc
Annapolis Marriott Waterfront Hotel
80 Compromise Street
Annapolis, MD
(410) 841-6235 or (301) 261-8453

Guided tour in a leisurely pedicab. Six days a
week from 11 a.m. to 2 a.m.

Overlooking Eutaw Street at Camden Yards from the Right
Field Bleachers

One dozen different tours offered, including: popular L'il Trolley Tour of D.C. (leaving from over 15
departure stations); Double Decker Tour; Black Heritage Tour; Interiors of Public Buildings Tour; Multi-
Lingual Tour; Mount Vernon & Old Town Alexandria Tour; also offering day trips to Colonial
Williamsburg, Monticello, Harper's Ferry, and Gettysburg. Call for brochure.

Historic sites

Bowie:

Belair Mansion
12207 Tulip Grove Drive
Bowie, MD 20715
(301) 262-6200 ext. 3067

Today's heart of Bowie, this Georgian-style mansion built around 1745, is listed on the National Register of Historic Places and has been recently restored. Open Sundays from Noon - 4 p.m.

Belair Stable Museum
2835 Belair Drive
Bowie, MD 20715
(301) 262-6200 ext. 3060

Famous for producing Gallant Fox and Omaha, the father-son combination that both won the Triple Crown, and Nashua, 1955's "Horse of the Year," the stable's history extends over two hundred years as the breeding ground for some of the finest racehorses in history. Open Sundays in May, June, Sept. And Oct. From 1 p.m. - 4 p.m.

Huntington Railroad Museum
Huntington Heritage Society, Inc.
P.O. Box 183
Bowie, MD 20719-0183
(301) 805-4616 or (301) 262-6200

Baltimore and Potomac Railroad Company station at junction of rail lines linking Washington, D.C. and Southern Maryland. Located near Historic Old Bowie, an area of quaint, old shops and antique dealers. Call for schedule information.

Annapolis:

Maryland State House
State Circle
Annapolis, MD
(410) 974-3400

The State Capitol is the oldest continuously used legislative capitol in America. Served as capital of United States from 1783 to 1784. Open Daily.

Hours 9 a.m. - 5 p.m.; Tours 11 a.m., 2 p.m., 4 p.m.

William Paca House & Garden
186 Prince George Street
Annapolis, MD 21401
(410) 263-5553

Maryland State House

National Historic Landmark. Restored Georgian-style home of a signer of the Declaration of Independence. 18th century residence overlooks a magnificent two acre garden, with terraces, fish-shaped pond, and wilderness garden. Summer Hours: Mon. - Sat. 10 a.m. - 4 p.m.; Sun. Noon - 4 p.m.

United States Naval Academy

Armel-Leftwich Visitors Center
52 King George Street
Annapolis, MD 21402
(410) 263-6933

Established first as a naval school by Secretary of Navy George Bancroft in 1845, the Naval Academy (known to sailors everywhere as The Yard), is the university and training grounds for future Naval and Marine officers. Any tour of the USNA should include: the Visitors Center; Tecumseh Court; The Chapel and The Crypt of John Paul Jones; and the USNA Museum located in Preble Hall.

Visitor Center Summer Hours: 9 a.m. - 5 p.m. Visitors Entrance to the USNA is located at the end of King George Street. The USNA is an open, public installation, and visitors are asked to observe all Naval Academy Regulations.

Museums

The Smithsonian Institution
1000 Jefferson Drive, S.W.
Washington, D.C.
(202) 357-2700 or (202) 357-2020 (Dial-A-Museum)

The most venerable museum institution in the world, the Smithsonian is fourteen museums in all (plus the zoo), with nine conveniently located on the Mall. Some are listed below:

Arts & Industries Building
900 Jefferson Drive, S.W.

National Museum of American History
Constitution Ave., 12th - 14th St., N.W.

Freer Gallery of Art
12th & Jefferson Drive, S.W.

National Museum of Natural History
Constitution Ave. at 10th St., N.W.

Hirshhorn Museum & Sculpture Garden
Independence Ave. At 7th St. S.W.

National Portrait Gallery
8th and F Streets, N.W.

National Air & Space Museum
6th Street and Independence Ave., S.W.

National Postal Museum
2 Massachusetts Ave., N.E.

National Museum of African Art
50 Independence Ave., S.W.

Renwick Gallery
17th and Pennsylvania Ave., N.W.

National Museum of American Art
8th and G Streets, N.W.

Arthur M. Sackler Gallery
1050 Independence Ave., S.W.

The Smithsonian Institution

Daily hours for Smithsonian Museums 10 a.m. to 5:30 p.m. Summer hours may be extended. Closed Christmas.

Directions from Bowie: Parking is limited so take the Metro Rail Orange Line from the New Carrollton Station to the Smithsonian Station.

U.S. Holocaust Memorial Museum

100 Raoul Wallenberg Place
(Independence and D St., S.W.)
Washington, D.C.
(202) 488-0400

Dedicated to the memory of the more than 6 million Jews who perished in concentration camps during World War II, this provocative museum has proven, along with the Vietnam Memorial, as one of the most stirring, and disturbing, memorials in all of Washington.

Hours: 10 a.m. - 5:30 p.m. Daily. Call for reservations and information.

National Gallery of Art

Constitution Ave, 4th Street to 6th Street, N.W.
Washington, D.C.
(202) 737-4215

West Building focus on pre-20th century works from Europe and America. East Building houses 20th century works, plus significant temporary exhibitions.

Summer Hours: Daily from 10 a.m. - 7 p.m. (June through Labor Day)

Babe Ruth Museum

216 Emory Street
Baltimore, MD 21230
(410) 727-1539

National Historic Landmark, where Babe Ruth

Vietnam Memorial

was born. Includes Orioles' Museum, and Maryland Baseball Hall of Fame.

Summer hours 10 a.m. - 5 p.m. (Closes 7 p.m. when Orioles' are at home)

Maryland Science Center

601 Light Street
Inner Harbor
Baltimore, MD
(410) 685-5225

Hands on activities/exhibits, IMAX Theater, Davis Planetarium, demonstrations, science store.

Summer Hours: Mon. - Thurs. 10 a.m. - 6 p.m.; Fri. - Sun. 10 a.m. - 8 p.m.

Parks and Gardens

City of Bowie Parks

City Hall
2614 Kenhill Drive
Bowie, MD 20715

Allen Pond Park, Northview Drive

85 acre park with playground, picnic area with grills, large pond with seasonal boat rentals, biking, jogging, walking & exercise trails, ballfields, basketball courts, amphitheater, ice arena (seasonal). From PG Stadium, take 301 South, turn onto 197 North (Collington Road), left on Northview Drive, park is roughly a mile on the right.

Whitemarsh Park, Route 3 South

210 acres, ballfields, playground, picnics, hiking and biking trails. From PG Stadium, take Route 301 north, continue straight on Route 3, u-turn left on Sylvan Drive or at Route 450, signs for park on right.

Blacksox Park, Mitchellville Road

70 acres, Specially dedicated baseball fields, play area, tot lot, trails. From PG Stadium 301 South, to 197 North (Collington Road), first left on Mitchellville Road, near intersection with Northview Road.

Chesapeake Marine Tours & Charters, Inc.

Slip 20, City Dock
P.O. Box 3350
Annapolis, MD 21403
(410) 268-7600
http://member.aol.com/boattours/cmt.html

Probably the best, and certainly the most popular cruises in Annapolis, CMT offers a variety of tours designed to accommodate any sort of schedule. Located on City Dock, CMT offers the following:

Annapolitan II: 7 ½ hour day cruise to scenic St. Michaels and the Chesapeake Maritime Museum.
Providence: 90 Minute narrated 6 mile cruise of Severn River.
Harbor Queen: 40 Minute narrated cruise of Harbor and Severn River.
Miss Anne: 40 Minute narrated cruise of Spa Creek.
Rebecca: Adventure cruise to Thomas Point Lighthouse.
Jiffy Water Taxi: Taxi on Spa and Back Creeks.

Call for schedule information, or check out their excellent web site.

Waterfront at Annapolis Marriott

Running Free, Inc.
P.O. Box 3254
Annapolis, MD 21403
(410) 263-7837

A variety of opportunities to boat on the Bay, the primary attraction is the *Schooner Woodwind*, a 74', classic wooden sailing yacht. The schooner is available for 2 hour cruises, overnight breakfast stays, and occasionally, private charters. Also leaving from the Marriott Waterfront are 22' Daysailors, for rent or lessons, 17 ½' and 19' inboard Powerboats for rent, and 2 hour guided Sea-Kayak tours. Call for schedules and reservations.

Overlooking Spa Creek from the City Dock, downtown Annapolis.

Beginagain

City Dock
Annapolis, MD
(410) 626-1422

36' sloop with three cruises daily during the season. Call for schedule.

Annapolis Power Boat Rentals

222 Severn Avenue
Annapolis, MD
(410) 280-3700 or (800) 315-3535

Located in Eastport, across Spa Creek, rent a 14', 17', 19' or a 21' power boat. Call for rates and availability.

Family Theme Parks

Adventure World

Central Avenue (Route 214)
P.O. Box 4210
Largo, MD 20775-4210
(301) 249-1500

Over 50 rides, water slides, shows, and games on 115 acres, including Tower of Doom, Mind Eraser, Python, Renegade Rapids, Paradise Island, wave pool, Day at the Circus.

Located on Route 214, three miles from Route 301. Summer Hours: Park opens at 10:30 a.m., except for one week in May and two weeks in June when the gates open at 10 a.m.

Public Golf course, driving ranges, miniature golf.

Enterprise Golf Course

2802 Enterprise Road
Mitchellville, MD 20721
(301) 249-2040

18 hole course named after the carrier, the U.S.S. Enterprise, and built in 1976. Tee times are not accepted in advance, first come first served. Pro shop opens at 7 a.m. Driving range, putting green, snack bar & 19th hole. Statistics:

Blue : Yardage 6586/6546, Rating 71.7, Slope 128, Par 72
White : Yardage 6209/6164, Rating 70.1, Slope 124, Par 72
Red: Yardage 5157/5140, Rating 69.6, Slope 114, Par 72

Bowie Golf & Country Club (Semi-Private)

7420 Laurel-Bowie Road (Route 197)
Bowie, MD 20715
(301) 262-8141

18 holes built in 1959. Advance tee times are not accepted, but since it's semi-private, call ahead anyway. Pro Shop opens at 7 a.m. Driving range, putting green, snack bar & 19th hole. Statistics:

Blue Yardage 6142, Rating 69.8, Slope 114, Par 70
White Yardage 5838, Rating 67.7, Slope 110, Par 70
Red Yardage 5106, Rating 69.6, Slope 113, Par 73

Night Hawk Golf Center

814 MD Route 3 South
Gambrills, MD 21054
(410) 721-9349

9 hole Par 3 public course (Yardage 733, Par 27); Driving Range; Batting Cages; Miniature Golf; Arcade; Miniature Basketball course; Pro Shop. Open 9 a.m. to 7 p.m.

Aquariums/Zoos

National Aquarium in Baltimore

Pier 3
501 East Pratt Street
Baltimore, MD 21202
(410) 576-3800

Aquarium building includes: Ray exhibit; Maryland watershed; Jellyfish; Puffins; Children's Cove; South American Rainforest; Atlantic Coral Reef; Sharks; Seals. Marine Mammal building includes: Dolphin Shows; Lifesize Humpback Whale Model; Underwater Dolphin view; Exploration Station; Discovery Corner; Pavilion Cafe; Aqua Shop.

Hours: July & August: Sun. - Thurs. 9 a.m. - 6 p.m.; Fri., Sat. 9 a.m. - 8 p.m.
Sept. - June: Sat. - Thurs. 10 a.m. - 5 p.m.; Fri. 10 a.m. - 8 p.m.

National Zoological Park

3001 Connecticut Ave., N.W.
Washington, D.C.
(202) 673-4800 or (202) 357-1300

163 acre National Zoo includes: Outdoor views of lions, white tigers, leopards, cheetahs; Elephant House with elephants, rhinos and giraffes; Gibbon Exhibit; Great Ape House with lowland gorillas and orangutans; Monkey House; Small Mammal House with meerkats; Pandas; Reptile House with cobras and pythons; Invertebrate Exhibit; Valley Trail with red wolves, seals, and beavers; Bird House with Indoor Flight Room; concessions, and gift shop.

Summer Hours: Grounds: 8 a.m. to 8 p.m. (Apr. 15- Oct. 15)
               Buildings: 9 a.m. to 6 p.m. (May - Sept. 15)

Shopping Centers/Malls

Bowie New Town Center
Route 50 and Route 301
Bowie, MD

Two brand new shopping centers are located on the corridor from Route 50 south on Route 301 to Excaliber Road and they include the Gateway Center (Borders, Sports Authority, Target) and Collington Plaza (Giant, Radio Shack and WalMart).

Bowie Mainstreet
Route 450
Bowie, MD

Three shopping centers, Free State Mall (Sears, Fair Lanes Bowl), Market Place (theaters), and Hilltop Plaza (Super Crown, Outback Steakhouse) are located in the Central Shopping District on Route 450, between Routes 197 and 3.

Annapolis Mall

2002 Annapolis Mall
Annapolis, MD 21401
(410) 266-5432

Hecht's, Nordstrom, JC Penney, Montgomery
Ward, food court, theaters, over 40 specialty
stores.

Hours: Mon - Sat. 10 a.m. - 9:30 p.m.; Sun.
11 a.m. - 6 p.m.

Annapolis Harbour Center

Route 2 & Aris T. Allen Blvd (Rt 665)
Parole, MD
(410) 266-5857

Barnes & Noble, Office Depot, Tower
Records, Fresh Fields, theaters, and over
thirty stores.

Hours: Mod. - Sat. 10 a.m. - 9 p.m.; Sun.
Noon - 5 p.m.

Harborplace & the Gallery

200 East Pratt Street
Baltimore, MD 21202
(410) 332-4191

Three Inner Harbor Malls, include Light Street Pavilion,
Pratt Street Pavilion and The Gallery.

Hours:Mon. - Sat. 10 a.m. - 9 p.m.; Sun. 10 a.m. - 6 p.m.

Inner Harbor, downtown Baltimore (30 Minutes from Bowie)

Seasonal Events

Dates are approximate, contact regional tourism offices
listed above for updated schedule information.

April: Annapolis Spring Boat Show; Annual
         St. John's-Navy Croquet Match

May: Heritage Day in Bowie; Annapolis
         Waterfront Arts Festival; Chesapeake
         Bay Bridge Walk; Commissioning Week at USNA

June: BowieFest; Annapolis JazzFest; USNA Flag Day

July: Fourth of July Celebration (Bowie, Annapolis, Baltimore, & Washington); John Paul Jones Day;
         Annapolis Small Boat Festival

August: Mid-Atlantic Wine Festival; Maryland Renaissance Festival

All Summer long: Sunday Evening Concert Series at Allen Pond; Theme cruises on Harbor Queen

Accommodations/Other

Visiting Hotel for the Bowie Baysox :

Days Inn
2520 Riva Road
Annapolis, MD 21401
(410) 224-2800 or (800) 638-5179
Free light breakfast, outdoor pool, Entertainment Discounts.

**Comfort Inn Hotel &
Conference Center**
U.S. 50 & 301
P.O. Box 730
Bowie, MD 20718
(301) 464-0089
Restaurant & Lounge, outdoor pool,
whirlpool suites, AAA & AARP
discounts. (Located across street
from Prince George's Stadium.)

Rip's Country Inn
3809 North Crain Highway (Route
301 & Route 197)
P.O. Box 1469
Bowie, MD 20717-0069
(301) 805-5900 or (800) 359-RIPS
Restaurant, Lounge, Delicatessen &
Store, Outdoor Park & Playground,
closest accommodations to Prince
George's Stadium (walking
distance), AAA discounts.

**Annapolis Marriott
Waterfront**
80 Compromise Street
Annapolis, MD 21401
(410) 268-7555
Downtown waterfront hotel,
Restaurant & Lounge, exercise
room, AAA & AARP discounts.

Marriott Residence Inn
170 Adm. Cochrane Dr. (Riva Rd.)
Annapolis, MD 21401
(410) 573-0300 or (800) 331-3131
Complimentary Continental
Breakfast & Evening Social Hours,
kitchens, swimming pool, sport
court, AAA & Entertainment
discounts.

Loews Annapolis Hotel
126 West Street
Annapolis, MD 21401
(410) 263-7777 or
(800) 23LOEWS
Downtown, Complimentary
Continental Breakfast, Restaurant
& Lounge, Entertainment
discounts.

Wyndham Garden Hotel
173 Jennifer Road
Annapolis, MD 21401
(410) 266-3131 or
(800) WYNDHAM
Restaurant & Lounge, indoor pool,
health facility, AAA &
Entertainment discounts, near
Annapolis Mall.

Historic Inns of Annapolis
16 Church Street
Annapolis, MD 21401
(410) 263-2641 or (800) 847-8882
Four inns: Maryland Inn, Governor
Calvert House, Robert Johnson
House, State House Inn located
downtown near State Capitol.
Entertainment discounts.

**Annapolis Holiday Inn Hotel
& Conference Center**
210 Holiday Court (Riva Road)
Annapolis, MD 21401
(410) 224-3150 or
(800) HOLIDAY
Restaurant & Lounge, outdoor
pool, affiliated with nearby gym,
AAA & Entertainment discounts.

Econo Lodge
Rt 50 & 301, P.O. Box 730
Bowie, MD 20718
(301) 464-2200
Outdoor pool, AAA discounts
(Restaurants nearby, near Comfort
Inn and P.G. Stadium.)

Herrington Inn
Herrington Harbour Marina Resort
P.O. Box 150, Route 261
Rose Haven on the Bay
Friendship, MD 20758
(301) 855-8399; (800) 213-9438
Secluded resort on Chesapeake
Bay, about thirty five minutes
southeast of Prince George's
Stadium. Restaurant & Lounge,
outdoor pool, tennis courts, beach,
marina.

Hospitals

Bowie Health Center
(Emergency Only)
15001 Health Center Drive
Bowie, MD 20716
(301) 262-6150
(Hours 8 a.m. to Midnight)

Anne Arundel Medical Center
64 Franklin Street (Franklin & Cathedral)
Annapolis, MD 21401
(410) 267-1000

Transportation

Baltimore/Washington
International: (410) 859-7100 or
(800) 492-4572
Washington National: (703) 419-8000
Washington Dulles
International: (703) 661-2700
AMTRAK: (800) USA-RAIL
(New Carrollton, MD)
Washington Metro
Rail & Bus: (202) 637-7000

MARC Commuter: (800) 325-RAIL
(Bowie State University)
Greyhound-Trailways: (800) 231-2222
A-A Taxi Service: (410) 674-6660
Bowie Cab: (301) 390-9091
BWI Shuttle (Annapolis): (410) 859-0800
Annapolis Transit: (410) 263-7964
Annapolis Harbor Master (410) 263-7973;
VHF Channel 16
Annapolis Water Taxi VHF Channel 68

Harrisburg Senators

Team: **Harrisburg Senators** (Southern Division)

Stadium: **Riverside Stadium**

     Office Address: Riverside Stadium, Harrisburg, PA 17101
     Mailing Address: P.O. Box 15757, Harrisburg, PA 17105
     Phone: (717) 231-4444
     Fax: (717) 231-4445
     Web Site(s):   http://www.fanlink.com/hburg_senators (Official);
     http://www.minorleaguebaseball.com/teams/harrisburg

Team Ownership:

     Operated by: Harrisburg Civic Baseball Club, Inc.
     Owned by: City of Harrisburg (One of only municipalities in the country to own and operate a professional team.)
     General Manager: Todd Vander Woude

Affiliation: Montreal Expos

Years in Eastern League: 1924-35; 1987-Present

Stadium Physical Characteristics

     Age: 1987
     Stadium Owner: City of Harrisburg

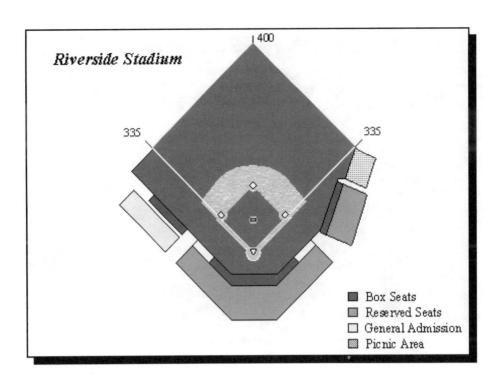

Riverside Stadium

400

335   335

■ Box Seats
■ Reserved Seats
☐ General Admission
▨ Picnic Area

Bullpens: Inside the fences, and in foul territory.

Playing Surface: Natural grass

Characteristics: The most unusual characteristic of Riverside Stadium is its location. The stadium is in the middle of an island on the Susquehanna River. Once referred to as a "pipe dream" only ten years ago, City Island is an amazing venue for family entertainment. Not only do the 1996 Eastern League Champions call City Island home, but so do a number of other appealing attractions. These include a miniature golf course, boat rental facilities, a train ride around the island, Riverside Park, an old fashioned steam ship ride on the Susquehanna, an arcade, batting cages, and the list just goes on an on. It's quite easy to spend an entire day on City Island. Come early on game day, and rollerblade, bike, walk, play a little miniature golf, take a paddle boat ride, or whatever. You can relax and have fun all day and then sit back and enjoy some great Eastern League baseball at Riverside Stadium that evening.

Capacity: 6,302

	1995	1996
Attendance	240,488	230,744

1996 Average Attendance: 3,722

All Time Attendance Records:

    Daily: 6,541 on August 13, 1996
    Seasonal: 250,476 in 1993

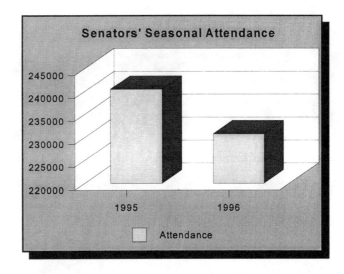

Type of Seating: Most of the seating at Riverside Stadium is on aluminum bleachers. Box seats, however, in sections 2 through 16 provide individual seating with armrests and cupholders. Note: General Admission areas fill up very fast, usually within ½ hour after game time. If you don't have reserved seating, arrive early.

Covered Seating: Covered Seating is available behind home plate, in sections 103 through 109.

Restrooms: Ladies: One (1)
    Men: One (1)
    Changing tables: Yes

Customer Service Window: Customer Service is available in the Senator's Office behind homeplate, and up the stairs located next to the pay phones. Lost and Found also located here.

Smoking Policy:

Smoking is unfortunately allowed in the stands, however the Senators have set aside nonsmoking seating in sections 201 through 204.

First Aid:

First Aid and ambulance services are located near the souvenir trailer on the first base side concourse.

Wheelchair & Handicapped Seating:

Located on the first base side behind Box Seat sections 2 through 6.

Telephones: Pay phones are located on the third base side concourse near Customer Service.

ATM: There is an ATM machine located on City Island near the Arcade.

Scoreboard: Electronic scoreboard in right center field. Limited information displayed, though.

Game Clock: Digital clock in left center.

Sound:

Quality sound system in stands, however there are a lot of echoes. (At the three games I attended, the club hired decent local bands to play before the game. Come out early and hear some good music.)

Sunsets? Behind home plate, on the first base side.

Autographs: Senators players are very accessible about autographs. From 5:45 to 6:00 p.m. there is an autograph session along the main concourse. In addition, you can snag some autographs along the first base line until approximately fifteen minutes before game time.

Concessions and Souvenirs

Best stadium food:

Harrisburg sells many items which I would rate above average or excellent. In fact, it's difficult to say which is the best concession at the stadium. At the top of my list are all the grilled sandwiches. There are grill stands on both sides of the concourse. The grill near third base

sells grilled Footlong Hot Dogs and Pork BBQ, while the grill near first base sells spicy, grilled Italian Sausage, hamburgers and cheeseburgers, and Chicken BBQ. You can also find a tasty Meatball Sub if you're in that sort of mood. Right up there with this list, believe it or not, are the French Fries served up at the Bricker's Famous Fries cart near first base.

To be honest, at most of the other stadiums in the Eastern League, I found it easy to distinguish the concessions and narrow down my best pick. Harrisburg was the exception. The Chicken BBQ sandwich was a tender and juicy piece of chicken breast. It was so good, they could serve the meat alone on a plate. The bun was really my only complaint, this sandwich would have been my choice if the bun was toasted. The Pork BBQ also was delicious. Again, this too might have been better served on a warm, toasted bun, and maybe in a bigger portion, but the flavor of the BBQ was outstanding. As for the Fries, these I had served up with Chicken Strips, and the combination was great! The fries were the type best served with a spritz or two or three of vinegar, and the chicken was fried, hot, and tasty. It could have used some honey mustard or some sort of special sauce, however.

That leaves my favorite two concessions. First, the Italian Sausage This is an excellent choice, grilled outdoors over by first base, the sausage was crunchy on the outside like it's supposed to be, and hot and juicy on the inside with just the right hint of spice. It was well worth the economical price.

But, my favorite concession at Harrisburg was the Footlong Hot Dog, grilled up for you right as you enter the stadium on the third base side of the concourse. The line was so long for this concession, that it was difficult to navigate through the crowd while carrying this tempting delicacy and a tall, cold, draft Yuengling. The best way to describe the Footlong, is imagine your best effort ever at grilling dogs on the barbecue in your own back yard. This is better.

In short, you can't go wrong with any concession choice at Harrisburg. For the most part, it's one of the best overall selections in the Eastern League.

Concessions in stands:

Vendors sell soft pretzels, peanuts, sno-cones, beer, soda and lemonade in the stands.

Hot Dog:

If you're not that hungry, the regular hot dog here isn't bad. But, I can't emphasize enough, Harrisburg's grilled Footlong Hot Dog is a bargain that can't be beat.

Harrisburg Senators 199

Peanuts:	$2.00

Beer: (Beer sales stop at end of the 7th inning.)

On tap: Yuengling, Miller Lite, Busch, Coors Light, Bud, Bud Light

In stands: Labatt's, Molson, Coors Light, Rolling Rock, Yuengling, Heineken, Amstel Light, Red Dog

Microbrews: A wide selection of Pete's Wicked Beers, Molson Ice, Heineken, Amstel Light

Non-alcoholic: Available.

Wine: Wine coolers available.

Desserts: Sno-cones, cotton candy, funnel cakes.

Restaurant: There is a Pizza Hut Restaurant area underneath the right field stands. Here, you can order a hot, personal size pan pizza and a cold drink, and sit down at a table to enjoy your meal. Note, however, this is a popular area for birthday parties and small picnics, so if you want a table, get there early.

View of Field from Concession Stands: No, not really.

Gift Shop: There are two souvenir windows at Riverside Stadium. The larger window is located in the trailer behind first base. There is a smaller booth, near the third base concourse area. At both of these locations, you can find copious amounts of Senators memorabilia, including, on occasion, autographed items, as well as other Minor League souvenirs.

Admission*:

Prices	
General Admission	$5.00
Reserved Seats	$6.00
Box Seats	$7.00

Special rates for Kids and Seniors (General Admission)	
Youth (12 and under)	$3.00
Seniors (60 and over)	$3.00

Special Ticket Rates	
Box Weekender Plan	$175.00
Reserved Weekender Plan	$150.00
Reserved Seat Coupon Book (20 Coupons)	$100.00
Adult Bonus Book (10 tickets)	$40.00
Youth/Senior Bonus Book (10 tickets)	$25.00

Group Information:

Special rates available for groups of 25 or more, selected dates only. Groups of 40 or more can arrange a pre-game picnic at an additional charge.

General Admission Rates		
Group Size	Adult	Youth/Senior
25-149	$3.50	$2.50
150-499	$3.00	$2.00
500 plus	$2.00	$2.00

Group Leader Incentives	
Group Size	Gift Certificate
25-99	Two Reserved Seat Tickets
100-199	Four Reserved Seat Tickets and one Senators Baseball Hat
200 plus	Eight Reserved Seat Tickets and two Senators Baseball Hats

Reserved and Box Seat Rates		
Group Size	Reserved	Box
25 plus	$4.50	$5.50

Picnic Area: The "Bullpen Cafe" is open to groups of 40 or more, accommodating as many as 300 guests. The following menus are available for your selection:

Bullpen Cafe	
Menu	Cost Per Person
Hot Dogs and Hamburgers	$12.00
Barbeque Breast of Chicken	$14.00
BBQ Chicken and Pork Ribs	$18.00
Steak and Baked Potato	$20.00

All menus come with baked beans, cole slaw, pasta salad, lemonade, iced tea, plus a Reserved Seat Ticket for that game. There is a $100.00 Non-refundable deposit required.

Birthday/Team Parties:

The Harrisburg Senators are proud to host Birthday and Team Parties for groups of 10 or more. Every guest will receive one slice of pizza, one small soda, and a slice of birthday cake. In addition, the price includes a Reserved Seat for that game, a free Speed Pitch coupon, a special visit from a Senators Team Member, as well as a visit from Uncle Slam, the Senators Team Mascot. Price is just $10.00 per person.

[*1996 Data: Prices subject to change. Call (717) 231-4444 for more information.]

Ticket Sales: Orders called in at least one week before game are mailed, all other phone orders may be picked up at the Will Call Window. (Note, on game day, the Senators often set up a Will Call table near the upper ticket booth, to avoid unnecessary delay.) The Senators ticket office is also open at Riverside Stadium from 9:00 a.m to 4:30 p.m weekdays, as well as during any Senators home game.

Address: Harrisburg Senators Baseball Club
P.O. Box 15757, Harrisburg, PA. 17105

Phone: (717) 231-4444 or Fax (717) 231-4445

Credit Cards: Visa, MasterCard, American Express, Discover

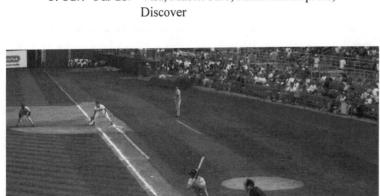

Rain Check Policy:

If any home game is canceled (less than 5 innings played, or 4 ½ innings if Senators are ahead) due to inclement weather, the tickets purchased for that game may be exchanged for tickets of equal value for future regular season games, depending upon availability. No cash refunds are given.

Game times:
Weekdays:	7:05 p.m.
Saturday:	7:05 p.m.
Sunday:	1:05 p.m.

(See schedule for day games. All game times subject to change.)

Time Gates open: 1 ½ hours prior to game time.

Parking: There is a $1.00 fee charged for Parking on City Island.

Other

For the kids:

As mentioned earlier, there are a number of other attractions available on City Island should you decide to arrive early for a ballgame. These include the City Island Trolley, carriage rides, a marina providing paddle boat and Hydrobikes for rent, Water Golf - a miniature golf course overlooking the Susquehanna, riverboat ride, Riverside Park, pavilion

and Trading Post, arcade, and last but not least batting cages. These attractions are all located immediately outside Riverside Stadium. Inside the stadium, kids can test their arms at the Speed Pitch on the third base side concourse.

Promotions and Giveaways:

In 1996, the Senators sponsored a number of special promotional days. There were six extravagant nights of Fireworks displays for all fans after the game. The Senators also gave away such special souvenir items as caps, baseballs, schedule magnets, travel mugs, bats, t-shirts, sport mugs, oven mitts, beach tote bags, helmets, photo albums, autographed baseballs, umbrellas, ice jugs, seat cushions, team photos, youth jackets, replica jerseys, wall clocks, batting gloves, sunglasses, backpacks, can coolers, baseball cards, school kits, baseball gloves, and mini bats. (This is one of the more lucrative giveaway stadiums in the entire Eastern League!)

Check future schedules for dates and availability. Not all fans receive all items, since they may be limited to age and/or first number of fans to arrive at Riverside Stadium.

In addition, certain days of the week at Riverside Stadium are traditional promotional days. In 1996, all Sunday and Tuesday home games were Hardees/WRVV/WHP Radio Family Days. All Monday home games were Burger King Bargain Mondays, offering a bargain for families of four. Each family of four could pick up a coupon at participating Burger Kings valid for four reserved seats, four hot dogs, and four sodas for the price of $19.95. Every Thursday at the park was PA Lottery Million Dollar Thursday where the PA Lottery gave 150 instant lottery tickets to random fans based on lucky program contests. Finally, Fridays were the Mellon Bank Friday Jazz Concerts. Mellon Bank sponsored a free jazz concert on the concourse behind home plate, beginning at approximately 5:30 p.m. at every Friday home game.

In between innings:

The Harrisburg Senators also sponsor some of the most rewarding in-game promotions. The coolest was the AAA Travel "Let's Make a Deal" contest. One lucky fan is picked at random out of the stands to play. That fan automatically received four reserved tickets to a future home game. Then, the announcer gave the lucky fan a choice of receiving an item contained within an envelope, or another mystery item inside a huge, approximately four by four by four foot box driven out on to the infield in between innings. The night I was there, the fan chose the large box. He received a gallon of mustard. Had he picked the envelope, he would have received two tickets to Jamaica. Tough choice, indeed.

Friday night Jazz Concert, behind Home Plate. Downtown Harrisburg is located across the Susquehanna in the background.

This is what happens when you forget to pay your taxes...

Other in-game promotions included the Aetna Health Plan "Diamond Dash", where after Sunday home game, fifty kids between the ages of 5 through 12 were selected to run the bases; a Phillip's Office Products Target Toss, where one fan could win up to $5,000; the Mid-Atlantic Milk Marketing "Dairy Dash" around the bases with Uncle Slam for the chance to win a life-size Cal Ripken Milk Growth poster; a Movie Merchants Video Quiz during the sixth inning; and also the Harrisburg Sports Nightly Sling Shot, probably the best chance to win an in-game freebie, with Senators staff launching t-shirts and other items into the crowd.

The list of in-game promotions at Riverside just goes on and on. There were two contests tied directly to the performance of the Senator players during the game. During the bottom of the sixth inning, if any Senators player hit a home run then one random fan could win the Burger King cash jackpot. The jackpot started at $50.00 and was increased $10.00 every game without a homer during the sixth. And finally, if a Senator player could hit a home run through a small target in the Sutliff Chevrolet/Geo Billboard any time during the game, one lucky fan could win a brand new car.

Don't forget to buy a program as you enter Riverside Stadium. The Senators conduct other giveaways with valuable prizes, but you have to have a lucky program containing a Harrisburg stamp somewhere inside in order to win.

What song played during 7th inning stretch?   "Take Me Out to the Ballgame."

Radio Station Broadcasting Game: WKBO 1230 AM

Eastern League Information:

Riverside Stadium posts the current Eastern League Standings and Senators' records near the Speed Pitch booth on the third base side concourse.

Team Information

Harrisburg Senators
(Southern Division)

History:

Professional Baseball, of one form or the other, dates in the Harrisburg area before the turn of the century. Eastern League information indicated Harrisburg had a Minor League team from 1924 through

1935, however, there is also data available on the Senators Web Page which suggests the history of Harrisburg professional baseball is even richer than expected. Apparently the first Harrisburg Baseball Club organized in 1901 and included the likes of "Chief" Bender, a future Hall of Famer who pitched for the outrageous salary of $125.00 per month.

Starting in 1907, the local team began play in the class "D" Tri-State League. This apparently continued, until Newark moved its Class "AA" team to Harrisburg as part of the International League in 1915. I found other reports showing a Harrisburg team starring one Mr. Jim Thorpe, who was then with the New York Giants organization, playing for Harrisburg in this year. There is conflicting information about what league Harrisburg joined in 1924. The Web page says Harrisburg was with the New York-Penn League, which is today a Short A league. Other sources seem to indicate Harrisburg joined the Eastern League in this year. In any event, this Harrisburg team won three League Championships until floods washed away Island Field in 1936.

The modern era of professional baseball in Harrisburg began anew with Opening Day at Riverside Stadium on April 11, 1987. At that time, the Senators were an affiliate of the Pittsburgh Pirates. They drew 212,141 fans in their inaugural season, not to mention an outstanding first season performance, capped with the Eastern League Championship. This performance couldn't be repeated in 1988, however, Riverside Stadium did host both an exhibition game with the Barry Bonds and Bobby Bonilla led Pirates, as well as the Eastern League All Star game. The following season, 1989, the Senators once again reached the Championship series, but were defeated by the Albany Yankees. Although a tough loss, the 1989 club did send players like Orlando Merced, Carlos Garcia, Stan Belinda, Moises Alou, Tony Longmire, and Wes Chamberlain to the majors.

In 1990, the Senators failed to make the playoffs, but did have the privilege of playing in a game before President George Bush June 22nd at Hagerstown, Maryland. This was also the last season Harrisburg was affiliated with Pittsburgh. In 1991, the club began its relationship with the Montreal Expos, and once again, they reached the playoffs but failed to capture the title. 1992 wasn't a bad season, but in 1993, the Senators reclaimed the crown they had won in their inaugural season. This was one of the best seasons ever for

a Harrisburg team as not only did they win the Championship, but Cliff Floyd was named Minor League player of the year and Eastern League MVP by USA Today, Joey Eischen was named the top pitcher, and Jim Tracy was honored as manager of the year, as well as selected to manage the National League team in the Double A All Star Game.

The following year Harrisburg beat Bowie in the 1994 playoffs to advance to the Championship Series against Binghamton, but the Mets had the better pitching during that series and Harrisburg lost. In 1995, the Senators finished last in the Southern Division, but first in the hearts and minds of the citizens of Harrisburg when the city, under the direction of Mayor Stephen Reed, purchased the franchise for $6.7 million. Considering the Senators' stellar performance in the 1996 playoffs against favored Trenton and then defeating Portland 3 games to 1 to take the Championship for the third time in ten years, this municipal investment is one which has clearly paid handsome dividends.

Eastern League Championships:

1996 Eastern League Champions
Harrisburg over Portland (3 games to 1)

1993 Eastern League Champions
Harrisburg over Canton (3 games to 2)

1987 Eastern League Champions
Harrisburg over Vermont (3 games to 1)

Famous Players who went on to the Major Leagues:

Moises Alou (1989, '90); Shane Andrews (1993); Stan Belinda (1989); Juan Bell (1994); Rafael Belliard (1987); Wes Chamberlain (1989); Cliff Floyd (1993); Mark Grudzielanek (1994); Chris Haney (1991); Tony Longmire (1988, '89, '90); Jim Neidlinger (1987, '88); Curtis Pride (1993); Matt Stairs (1991); Vladimir Guerrero (1996); Mike Lansing (1992); Orlando Merced (1989); Carlos Garcia (1989, '90); Rondell White (1992, '93); Jeff King (1987, '88).

Montreal Expos Minor League Organization			
Team	**League**	**Level**	**City & Phone**
Montreal Expos	National League	Major League	Montreal, Quebec (514) 253-3434
Ottawa Lynx	International League	AAA	Ottawa, Ontario (613) 747-5969
Harrisburg Senators	Eastern League	AA	Harrisburg, PA (717) 231-4444
West Palm Beach Expos	Florida State League	A	West Palm Beach, FL (407) 684-6801
Delmarva Shorebirds	South Atlantic League	A	Salisbury, MD (410) 219-3112
Vermont Expos	New York-Penn League	Short A	Winooski, VT (802) 655-4200
Gulf Coast Expos	Gulf Coast League	Rookie	West Palm Beach, FL (407) 684-6801

Approximate distance from Riverside Stadium to Olympic Stadium, Montreal: 511 miles
(Source: Rand McNally TripMaker Version 1.1 1994, Harrisburg, PA to Montreal, Quebec)

Mascot:	Uncle Slam
Team Colors:	Black, Red & White
Visiting	
Hotel:	Harrisburg Hilton and Towers, One North Second St., Harrisburg, PA. 17101 (717) 233-6000
Fan Club:	Harrisburg Senators Fan Club. Fan Mail should be directed to Harrisburg Senators Baseball Club, P.O. Box 15757, Harrisburg, PA 17105.

Directions to Riverside Stadium, City Island:

The entrance to City Island is located in the middle of the Market Street Bridge in downtown Harrisburg. From I-83, you want to exit at Second Street towards downtown. Proceed north on Second Street and then take a left at the third light (Market). Parking is halfway down the bridge on the right hand side. From I-81, exit on Front Street, proceed downtown, then turn right on Market Street towards City Island.

Harrisburg/Hershey/Carlisle

Background

Harrisburg (Pop. 52,376) located in the beautiful Susquehanna Valley is the capital of the Commonwealth of Pennsylvania. Originally settled in 1719 by John Harris as a trading post and ferry crossing called Harris' Ferry, the area was home to diverse Native American tribes until about the time the city was laid out and renamed Harrisburg in 1785. About thirty years later, in 1812, Harrisburg became the state capital and to this day the major employer in the city remains the state government. However, throughout its history, Harrisburg has always been a significant transportation center; from its early days as an important ferry crossing over the Susquehanna River, through the years of the Pennsylvania canal system, and then on through the rise of commercial manufacturing and distribution via rail, highway, and air transport.

The most outstanding feature of the city, and obviously its focal point, is the spectacular Capitol building itself. Dedicated in 1906 and listed on the National Register of Historic Places, this Italian Renaissance-style dome is modeled after none other than St. Peter's Basilica in Rome. The General Assembly offers free tours to as many as 100,000 visitors annually to this statehouse which President Teddy Roosevelt once described as "the handsomest building I ever saw."

To the west of Harrisburg lie first the suburban stretches of Camp Hill, once a scene of battle during the Civil War, and further beyond, the rural community of Carlisle. If you're looking for a more relaxed pace, Carlisle still offers plenty of opportunities to step back in time. Bed and breakfast's abound amidst the farms and antique shops in the yet unspoiled and quiet environment of Cumberland County.

However, if you're looking for more excitement, just east of Harrisburg is the delightful company town of Hershey, Pennsylvania. Milton S. Hershey (1857-1945) was the man behind the famous chocolate bar that bears his name. Three years after he began producing the Hershey bar, Mr. Hershey built his factory in the farm country of Derry Church, and the community was renamed Hershey in 1906. Today, Hershey Foods Corporation is the largest chocolate and cocoa manufacturing plant in the world. Most likely as you roam these quaint streets lit by candy kisses, you'll pick up the scent of those delicious confections known the world over. Chocolate Town, U.S.A. is also home to exciting attractions for young and old, including HersheyPark, Hershey's Chocolate World, and the Hershey Museum.

Information

Chamber of Commerce/Tourist Bureaus

Local:

Harrisburg-Hershey-Carlisle Tourism and Convention Bureau
114 Walnut Street
P.O. Box 969
Harrisburg, PA 17108-0969
(717) 232-1377 or (800) 995-0969

Harrisburg Chamber of Commerce
114 Walnut Street
P.O. Box 969
Harrisburg, PA 17108-0969
(717) 232-4121

Office of the Mayor
Suite 202
City Government Center
10 North Second Street
Harrisburg, PA 17101-1678
(717) 255-3040

The Hershey Partnership
400 W. Hersheypark Drive
Hershey, PA. 17033
(717) 534-3121

Dauphin County Court House

Nearby:

Gettysburg Travel Council, Inc.
35 Carlisle Street
Gettysburg, PA 17325
(717) 334-6274

Pennsylvania Dutch Convention & Visitors Bureau
501 Greenfield Road
Lancaster, PA 17601
(717) 299-8901 or (800) 735-2629 ext. 2067

Web Site(s):   http://www.visithhc.com

See also: http://www.gettysbg.com   (Gettysburg, PA)
http://www.800padutch.com   (Pennsylvania Dutch Country)

Daytime Entertainment

Guided tours

Office of Capitol Visitor Services
General Assembly
Harrisburg, PA
(800) TOUR-N-PA

Capitol Building Guide Service
Third and State Streets
Harrisburg, PA 17125
(717) 787-6810

Center City Sights and City Wide Sights
(Self-Guided)
Contact the Office of the Mayor or the Tourism Bureau for a copy of one or both of these excellent self-guided tour maps.

Historic sites

State Capitol Building, Plaza and Park
North 3rd and State Streets
Harrisburg, PA
(800) TOUR-N-PA

The centerpiece of state government, the Harrisburg Capitol Building was completed and dedicated in 1906. As mentioned, this Italian Renaissance style structure owes its design to Rome's St. Peter's Basilica, and to certain elements of Paris' Grand Opera House. The Plaza and the Park, as well as adjacent Fisher Plaza, all offer excellent opportunities for sightseeing, walking, or simple lunchtime relaxation.

John Harris Mansion
219 South Front Street
Harrisburg, PA
(717) 233-3462

Home of the founder and namesake of Harrisburg. Museum and home to Dauphin County Historical Society.

Hours: Tuesday to Saturday 10 a.m. -4 p.m.

Fort Hunter Mansion and Park
5300 North Front Street
Harrisburg, PA 17110
(717) 599-5751

Overlooking both the Susquehanna River and the not so distant Blue Mountain Range, Fort Hunter includes the restored 19th century mansion, museum, thirty five acres of park areas, picnic areas, playground, and walking trails along the riverfront.
Open May - December, Tues. - Sat. 10 a.m. - 4:30 p.m.; Sun. Noon - 4:30 p.m.

Museums

State Museum of Pennsylvania

William Penn Memorial Building
Third and North Streets
P.O. Box 1026
Harrisburg, PA 17108-1026
(717) 787-4978

Exhibits and displays about the
history, art, and culture of the
Commonwealth of Pennsylvania.
Includes archaeological artifacts,
paintings and decorative arts,
industrial and technological displays,
and a planetarium.

Tuesday to Saturday 9 a.m. - 5 p.m.;
Sunday Noon - 5 p.m.

The Museum of Scientific Discovery

Strawberry Square
Third and Walnut Streets
P.O. Box 934
Harrisburg, PA 17108
(717) 233-7969

Hands-on discovery museum with exhibits on
gravity, human and animal biology, electricity,
plus changing exhibits on other fascinating
aspects of the world of science.

Tuesday to Saturday 10 a.m. - 6 p.m.; Sunday
Noon - 5 p.m.

Art Association of Harrisburg

21 North Front Street
Harrisburg, PA
(717) 236-1432

Contemporary and living artists offering a
diverse range of artistic displays. Changing
exhibits and annual art contests. Focus on
paintings, sculptures, and ceramics.

Mon.-Thur. 9 a.m.-8 p.m., Fri. 9 a.m.-4 p.m.,
Sat. 10 a.m.-4 p.m., Sun. Noon-3 p.m.

Parks and Gardens

Riverfront Park

Susquehanna River Waterfront
Downtown Harrisburg, PA

Five miles of scenic natural
areas running along the
Harrisburg waterfront.
Walking paths, steps to river,
sculptures, plazas and gardens
line this narrow strip on the
eastern side of the
Susquehanna. (Watch for
special events on the
weekends, including small
seasonal weekend flea markets
south of Market Street.)

Two or three ways local residents can cross the Susquehanna River.

River Cruises

Pride of the Susquehanna Riverboat

City Island
P.O. Box 910
Harrisburg, PA 17108
(717) 234-6500

Classic authentic paddlewheel boat. 45 minute cruises, dinner cruises, private charters, luncheon cruises, school and scout tours, family/senior citizen day. Runs May through October. Call for schedule.

City Island Attractions

Located in the middle of the great Susquehanna River, offering a spectacular view of downtown, City Island is a miracle of modern urban redevelopment and renewal. The City of Harrisburg has transformed what was surely an empty and bleak sixty three acre landscape into a thriving downtown entertainment center, breathing new life and opening plenty of attractive possibilities along the community's waterfront. Here on this easily accessible Island, not only can you catch some fantastic Eastern League baseball (excuse enough to visit), but you'll find well over a dozen attractions designed to please all age groups. There's a children's playground for kids at the miniature Harbortown 1840's era canal village; Water Golf set at an idyllic setting

overlooking the Susquehanna; the superior Skyline Sports Complex with room for soccer, softball and volleyball; an indoor arcade plus nearby batting cages; the expansive Riverside Village Park offering quaint shops, light eateries, as well as picnic facilities by the river; nature and jogging trails; all sorts of rides including the Pride of the Susquehanna, horse-drawn carriage rides, miniature train ride, paddle boats of various shapes and sizes, and even bicycle rentals; and, of course, plenty of summertime special events and concerts.

For more information, contact:

**City Island Information Center
and Park Ranger**
Station: (717) 233-8275
Harrisburg
Senators: (717) 231-4444
Pride of the
Susquehanna: (717) 234-6500
**Lil Grabber Narrow
Gauge Steam**
Railroad: (717) 737-0238
Water Golf: (717) 939-3899
Harrisburg Carriage
Company: (717) 234-1686
Family Kite
Shop: (717) 697-4968
Harrisburg
Marina: (717) 763-7654
City Island
Bike Rentals: (717) 652-2904
Water Taxis: (717) 761-2630

City Island is only 1,000 yards from downtown. There are two large parking lots (minimal fee) with plenty of room. You can drive to City Island on the Market Street Bridge, or walk via the historic metal-span Walnut Street Bridge.

Theme Parks

HersheyPark

300 Park Boulevard
Hershey, PA 17033
(717) 534-3090 or (800) HERSHEY
http://www.800hershey.com

As one of the best theme parks on the East Coast, HersheyPark has over fifty rides to excite you, including the brand new, all wooden roller coaster, the Wildcat. There are three other roller coasters, as

well as five water rides, twenty kiddie rides, shows, shops, games, and more all inside the gate. However, there's more than just thrilling rides in store. As world headquarters for the Hershey Foods Corporation, your senses will be tempted at Hershey's Chocolate World, the official visitor's center open year round. Here you'll experience a chocolate factory-simulated tour, complemented, of course, by a free sample of the world's most famous confection. You can also visit ZooAmerica, an eleven acre North American Wildlife Park featuring hundreds of wild animals on display. Other nearby attractions that were important parts of Milton S. Hershey's

dream, include Founder's Hall (home of the largest unsupported dome in America), the Hershey Museum, and the Hershey Gardens. Finally, don't forget to catch great concerts, plays, and other entertaining shows year round at both the Hershey Theater and HersheyPark Arena.

Some Hershey area attractions are open year round, however HersheyPark is open May through September, with gates opening at 10 a.m., and rides beginning at 10:30 a.m. Park closes at different times during the season, call for details.

Public Golf courses

Country Club of Hershey (Semi-Private)
1000 E. Derry Road
Harrisburg, PA 17033
(717) 533-2464

Three 18 hole courses. South Course built in 1927, West Course built in 1930, both designed by Marice McCarthy, East Course built in 1970 and designed by George Fazio. East and West Courses only open to Members and Guests, South Course open to the Public. Tee times accepted one week in advance, Pro Shop opens 7 a.m., grass driving range, snack bar. South Course Statistics:

Blue Yardage 6204, Par 71
White Yardage 5798, Par 71
Red Yardage 4856, Par 72

Hotel Hershey Golf Course
Hotel Road
Hershey, PA 17033
(717) 533-2171

Nine hole 1932 course located at a resort hotel. Tee times accepted one month in advance, Pro Shop opens 7 a.m. Statistics:

Yardage 2680, Par 34

Sportsman's Golf Course
3800 Linglestown Road
Harrisburg, PA 17110
(717) 545-0023

18 hole course built in 1965. Tee times accepted one week in advance. Pro Shop opens 7 a.m. Driving range. Statistics:

Blue Yardage 6541, Rating 73.0, Slope 130, Par 71
White Yards 6128, Rating 70.6, Slope 124, Par 71
Red Yardage 5344, Rating 66.1, Slope 118, Par 71

Springcreek Golf Course
450 East Chocolate Ave
Hershey, PA 17033
(717) 533-2847

Nine hole 1930-era golf course designed by the company. Tee times accepted one week in advance, Pro shop opens 7 a.m. Statistics:

Yardage 2316, Par 33

Shopping Malls/Outlets

Harrisburg East Mall

Paxton Street
Harrisburg, PA 17111
(717) 564-0980

Hecht's, JC Penney, Lord & Taylor, food
court, with over 100 specialty stores.

Hours: Monday to Saturday 10 a.m. - 9 p.m.,
Sunday Noon - 6 p.m.

Capital City Mall

3506 Capital Mall Drive
Camp Hill, PA 17011
(717) 737-8275

Hecht's, JC Penney, Sear's, Food Court,
theaters, and over 100 specialty stores.

Hours: Monday to Saturday 10 a.m. - 9:30
p.m., Sunday 11 a.m. - 6 p.m.

Camp Hill Shopping Mall

32nd Street and Trindle Road
(581 West, Camp Hill Exit for 11 & 15 North)
Camp Hill, PA
(717) 737-6527

Montgomery Ward, Boscov's, Giant Food, theaters,
food court, over 75 specialty stores.

Hours: Monday to Saturday 10 a.m. - 9:30 p.m.,
Sunday 11 a.m. - 6 p.m.

Factory Stores at Hershey

70 Outlet Stores
Hershey, PA 17033
(717) 520-1236

Black & Decker, Bugle Boy, Corning-Revere,
Dockers, Jockey, Legg's, Levi's, London Fog, with
over fifty outlet stores.

Hours: Monday to Saturday 9:30 a.m. -9 p.m.,
Sunday Noon - 6 p.m.

Seasonal Events

Dates are approximate, contact regional tourism offices listed above for updated schedule information.

April: Earth Day, Carlisle Collector Car Flea Market & Corral

May: A Taste of Harrisburg, Capital City Bikefest, Harrisburg Arts Festival and Memorial Day Parade, Antique & Collectibles Show, Carlisle Import-Kit/Replicar Nationals

June: Susquehanna River Celebration, Harrisburg Symphony Barge Concert, City Island Flower and Crafts Festival, Carlisle All-Ford Nationals, All-Truck Nationals

Water Golf on City Island

July: Harrisburg Independence Weekend Festival, Reservoir Park Concert Series, Summer Carlisle, Chryslers at Carlisle

August: Goodguys Carlisle Rod & Custom Classic, Corvettes at Carlisle, Pennsylvania Renaissance Festival (through October - http://www.PaRenaissanceFaire.com)

Sept.: Kipona Festival and Kipona Artfest (Labor Day)

Accommodations/Other

Hotels and Motels

Visiting Hotel for the Harrisburg Senators:

Harrisburg Hilton & Towers
One N. Second St.
Harrisburg, PA 17101
(717) 233-6000 or (800) HILTONS
Free Continental breakfast, Restaurant & Lounge, Indoor pool, fitness center, AAA and Entertainment discounts (Downtown - walking distance to City Island).

Harrisburg/Camp Hill:

Ramada Inn on Market Square
23 South Second St
Harrisburg, PA 17101
(717) 234-5021 or (800) 2-RAMADA
Restaurant & Lounge, Indoor pool, sun deck, fitness center, AAA discounts (Downtown - walking distance to City Island).

Holiday Inn Riverfront
525 S. Front St.
Harrisburg, PA 17104
(717) 233-1611
Complimentary continental breakfast, Entertainment discounts. (Healthy walking distance to City Island).

Harrisburg Marriott
4650 Lindle Rd.
Harrisburg, PA 17111
(717) 564-5511
Restaurant & Lounge, indoor/outdoor pool, fitness club, sauna, golf nearby, Entertainment discounts.

Sheraton Inn Harrisburg East
800 E. Park Dr.
Harrisburg, PA 17111
(717) 561-2800 or (800) 325-3535
Restaurant & Lounge, Indoor Pool, Health Club, Children and Entertainment discounts.

Radisson Penn Harris Hotel & Convention Center
1150 Camp Hill Bypass
Routes 11 & 15 at Erford Road
Camp Hill, PA 17011
(717) 763-7117 or (800) 333-3333
Restaurants & Lounge, Outdoor Pool, fitness center, AAA & Entertainment discounts (Close to retail shopping malls).

Best Western - Hotel Crown Park
765 Eisenhower Blvd
Harrisburg, PA 17111
(717) 558-9500 or (800) 253-0238
Breakfast buffet, Restaurant & Lounge, outdoor lap pool, exercise room.

Holiday Inn Harrisburg East
4751 Lindle Road
Harrisburg, PA. 17111
(717) 939-7841
Restaurant & Lounge, indoor/outdoor pool, fitness center, tennis, 5 hole chip/putt golf, AAA and Entertainment discounts.

Hershey:

Hotel Hershey
Hotel Road
P.O. Box BB
Hershey, PA 17033
(717) 533-2171 or (800) 533-3131
http://www.800hershey.com
Restaurants & Lounge,
indoor/outdoor pool, fitness center,
tennis, 9 hole golf course, 72 holes
of golf nearby.

Hershey Lodge & Convention Center
West Chocolate Avenue & University
Drive
P.O. Box 446
Hershey, PA. 17033
(717) 533-3311 or (800) 533-3131
http://www.800hershey.com
Restaurants & Lounge, Indoor/outdoor
pool, recreational center, tennis, miniature
golf, 72 holes of golf nearby

Bed and Breakfast

Contact either for information:

Pennsylvania Travel Council
902 North Second Street
Harrisburg, PA 17102
(717) 232-8880
E-mail: PaTravCncl@aol.com

Cumberland Valley Bed & Breakfast Association
Web Site: http://www.pa.net/bnb
or contact The Greater Carlisle Area Chamber of
Commerce, 212 North Hanover Street, P.O. Box
572, Carlisle, PA 17103 (717) 243-4515

Campgrounds

Hershey Highmeadow Campground
P.O. Box 866
Hershey, PA 17033
(717) 566-0902
55 acres, 297 sites, elec., water, sewer, picnic tables, grills, two pools, kiddie pool,
playground, game room, store, laundry, shuttle buses to park.

Hospitals

Pinnacle Health Hospital, at Polyclinic Hospital
2601 North 3rd Street
Harrisburg, PA
(717) 782-4141

Harrisburg Hospital
South Front and Chestnut Streets
Harrisburg, PA
(717) 782-3131

Transportation

Harrisburg International Airport   (717) 948-3900
AMTRAK   (800) USA-RAIL
Capital Area Transit Authority   (717) 238-8304
Rohrer Bus Service, Inc.   (717) 957-3811
Hertz Corp.   (717) 944-4081

Reading Phillies

Team: **Reading Phillies** (Southern Division)

Stadium: **Reading Municipal Memorial Stadium**

          Office Address: Rt 61 South/Centre Ave., Reading, PA. 19605
          Mailing Address: P.O. Box 15050, Reading, PA. 19612
          Phone: (610) 375-8469
          Fax: (610) 373-5868
          Web Site(s):   http://www.readingphillies.com (Official? Under construction.);
                                  http://www.minorleaguebaseball.com/teams/reading/

Team Ownership:

          Operated by: E & J Professional Baseball Club, Inc.
          Principals: Craig A. Stein, President
          General Manager: Chuck Domino

Affiliation: Philadelphia Phillies

Years in Eastern League: 1933-5; 1952-61; 1963-5; 1967-Present

Stadium Physical Characteristics

        Age, Built in: 1950
        Stadium Owner: City of Reading (Reading Municipal Memorial
                              Commission)

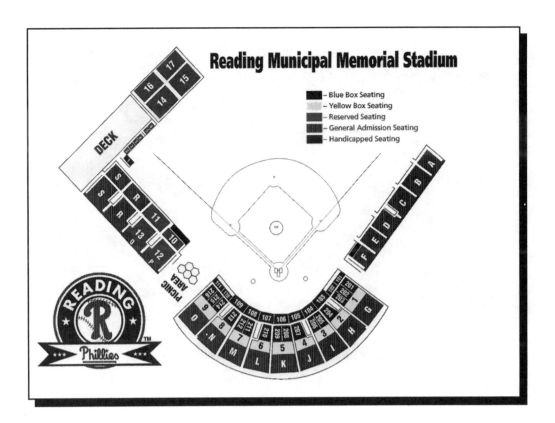

Reading Municipal Memorial Stadium

- Blue Box Seating
- Yellow Box Seating
- Reserved Seating
- General Admission Seating
- Handicapped Seating

Bullpens: Inside the fences, in large foul territory.

Playing Surface: Natural grass

Characteristics:

Tucked underneath a verdant mountainside, this stadium has stood the test of time, over forty years of Eastern League time to be exact. Reading Municipal Memorial Stadium is a surprise to the uninitiated. Like many of the revitalized businesses in this, the Factory Outlet Capital of the World, this stadium has a definite "throw-back" appeal to it. From the classic red brick facade to the lush green fields, Reading Municipal Memorial feels like an historic place to watch America's pastime. The tall and mighty evergreens beyond the centerfield fence clearly will attest to that fact.

There's no hiding the fact that Reading Municipal is an older stadium, however, the town has taken great pride in maintaining this place both as a landmark to the game, and as a modern, entertainment venue. You can sense the pride in the way they care for the field (even in late August, after a full season of rough and tumble play, I didn't see a single patch of dirt on the infield grass).

You can also see the care in the landscaping outside the main entrance and at subtle locations throughout the stadium, the care taken to keep areas like the right field concession patio clean and friendly, even the way they've terraced certain viewing areas to help prevent any impeded views. You'll also find additions here that you won't find at any other stadium in the Eastern League, such as seating behind the left field fence. There's four reserved areas out there beyond the power alley, plus the appropriately named "Dinger's" bar, where groups can come together and maybe catch a

home run. (You can't do that anywhere else in the league currently.) You'll also find aluminum bleachers parallel to the foul lines, which appear to have been added on after it became apparent the popular Phillies could easily fill an 8,000 capacity stadium.

As for the other souvenirs, that is foul balls, Reading Municipal Memorial is most definitely a "Stay Alert" type of park. Almost anywhere you sit, or even stand, you feel close to the diamond. The back stop is tall, but not so wide, so quick fouls will come screaming in off the bat if you're not paying attention. This is true for some of the apparently SRO areas, like in front of the bleachers on the right field line, where you're at eye level with the players, and the smaller overflow SRO area near third base. The only SRO area where you're unlikely to catch anything over than a great view, is the large skyway that surrounds the main grandstands behind home plate. In fact, the only complaint about seating I can think of, is if you do have General Admission tickets, get there early and try to find a spot either behind the backstop, or on the first base line. You'll be closer to the action than the stands in left, plus you won't have to look over the large, blue plastic umbrellas in the group picnic area that separates you from the rest of the stadium. In sum, go ahead and don't be ashamed to bring your old, beatup glove. Even if you don't catch a foul or a dinger, you'll still catch some great memories at Reading Municipal Memorial Stadium.

Capacity: 8,000

	1992	1993	1994	1995	1996
Attendance	287,073	313,083	338,249	383,984	384,151

1996 Average Attendance:

No. of openings: 68
1996 Daily Average: 5,649

All Time Attendance Records:

Daily: 9,112 on May 31, 1996
Seasonal: 384,151 in 1996*

*Includes 8,825 Attendance during the March 31st, 1996 Exhibition against Philadelphia Phillies

Reading has set nine (9) consecutive attendance records.

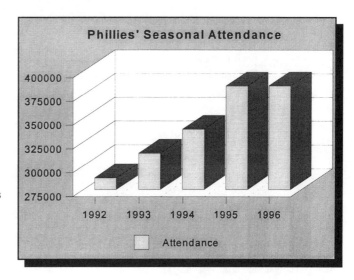

Phillies' Seasonal Attendance

Skyboxes: None.

Type of Seating:

The only complaint about seating here is that there is little room between the rows, and your knees will wind up touching the seat back in front of you. However, there is plenty of lateral room between the seats, especially in Box Seating. Also, there were armrests and cupholders in all Box Seats (Blue and Yellow Box Seating), and the Green Reserved Sections have armrests as well. The General Admission areas are all individual seats.

Covered Seating: There is a small amount of covered seating available high behind home plate. In addition, the skyway behind General Admission (on the Press Box level) is covered. The tables in the picnic area are also covered.

Restrooms: Ladies: 3
Men: 3
Changing tables: Yes, restrooms behind home plate.

Customer Service Window:

Two locations. Main office is just beyond the Souvenir Booth, on the right. During games, there is also an Information Booth open on the Right Field Food Court area.

Smoking Policy:

Prohibited in all spectator seating areas. Permitted on very upper concourse above the grandstands; right field Food Court; walkway behind the picnic area and the left field grandstands; and the Deck, except for the first level of box seats.

First Aid:

No separate office, but paramedics on hand for every game. Ushers will be glad to assist those in need.

**Wheelchair
& Handicapped Seating:**

Yes, wheelchairs are accommodated in both the left field and right field grandstands, on the ends closest to home plate.

Telephones: Two on First Base side concourse.

ATM: No.

Scoreboard: There is a large electronic scoreboard behind the left field fence, and a smaller score board near first base. Watch the left field scoreboard for player stats, as well as updated messages.

Game Clock: Yes, a digital clock on First Base scoreboard, and analog clock on the Pizza Hut sign in left.

Sound: Up and from behind; shows signs of age.

Sunsets?   Behind the Third Base line, close to left field.

Autographs: Yes, you can track down the players as they emerge from the Locker Rooms. Those rooms are the old fashioned kind, built directly underneath and near the ends of the grandstands.

Concessions and Souvenirs

The one thing to keep in mind about the concessions at Reading Municipal Memorial, since most games are crowded, that means the lines for food will be crowded also. There were plenty of concession windows mind you, but still I found myself waiting in long lines throughout most of the game. This problem was exacerbated after the seventh inning when the side concession areas underneath the stands closed early for some reason, and I had to go stand in line at the main windows behind home plate. Also, you can't hear or see the game in line but, for the most part, the wait is worth it. The standard menu at Reading includes hot dogs, Jumbo dogs, Barbeque, Pizza, Meatball Subs, Grilled items (explained below), large hats of fries (the thinnest fries in the Eastern League, by the way), candy, peanuts and a good selection of ice cream.

If the lines are too long underneath the stadium, there are a couple concession stands located at the top of the stands. This one sells Dogs & Snacks.

Overlooking the Grand Slam Grill and other concessions behind the right field bleachers.

Best stadium food:

The very best concessions at Reading Municipal Memorial are located behind the rightfield bleachers at the Grand Slam Grill. Here you'll find a wide variety of grilled items which I guarantee will fill you up nicely. My favorite was the Grilled Chicken Sandwich, which came hot off the grill tender and juicy on the inside, and slightly crunchy on the outside. The grilled hamburgers and cheeseburgers are served smokin' and charred, maybe a little too charred in some cases, but they were also a very good buy. If you're really hungry, the Grand Slam Grill will double up your order. You can get either a Double Cheeseburger, or the special Churger (Chicken and Hamburger together), both of which are mountains of meat that will fill you up so high, you won't need to eat again until October.

The other menu item worth mentioning is the Meatball Sub. This was a meal also, with at least three juicy meatballs, tasty Italian sauce, served warm on an excellent hard roll. This sub smelled so good, that kids in the stands next to me almost could swear they smelled hot pizza nearby. (My only true disappointment with the concessions here, was that considering the club is an affiliate of the Phillies, and is only about an hour from South Philadelphia, I would have really liked to see some cheesesteaks on the menu. Maybe they could get Pat's or Geno's to deliver some steaks with provolone? Preferably Pat's...)

Concessions in stands: Pretzels, Popcorn, Beer, Soda, Cotton Candy, Caramel Corn.

Hot Dog: The hot dog was a major league bargain at only $2.00. It was both long and thick, and crispy and juicy all at the same time. Easy to recommend the Jumbo Dog.

Peanuts: $2.00

Beer: Beer sales end promptly during the 7th inning stretch. You must be 21 or older with ID.

The Phillies will eject anyone who's behavior becomes inappropriate. Plus, anyone who feels they have had too much to drink can go to the Phillies office behind home plate and call a taxi. (On a lighter note, if the lines are too long at the beer-only stands, don't forget, you can usually find a friendly vendor roaming the stands.)

On tap:	Coors, Coors Light, Bud Light, Yuengling, Miller Lite, Miller Genuine Draft
In stands:	Yuengling, Bud, Bud Light
Microbrews:	none
Non-alcoholic:	O'Douls
Wine Coolers:	none

Desserts: Hand-dipped ice cream, Banana Splits, Funnel Cake, Cotton Candy, Sno-Cones.

View of Field
from Concession Stands: No, however, there is a Yogurt Booth and a Dogs & Snacks Booth on the skyway behind the general admission sections of the main grandstands. From up here, you can watch the game while standing.

Gift Shop:

Souvenirs are sold from a window booth near the main entrance. Phillies Memorabilia for both Reading and Philadelphia is on sale during the course of every home game, and you can find a lot of nice pieces to add to your collection. In addition, Reading is one of the only parks in the EL where you can buy a disposable camera at the Souvenir Stand. (Take it from me, you can get nice quality pictures out of these deceptively packaged disposables, and it's good to know they're available if you leave your expensive 35 mm/200 zoom multifunctional camera at home by mistake.)

Note that because of high demand, the souvenir lines can be long and somewhat intimidating, especially for younger fans who can't see over the counter, or who just need a little more time. So, souvenirs are available year round at the Phillies' office during regular business hours.

Admission*:

Ticket Prices	
Box Seats	$7.00
Yellow Box Seats	$6.00
Green Reserved Seats	$5.00
General Admission: Adults (15-61) Child (5-14) Senior (62 and over)	$4.00 $2.50 $2.50
Group Rates (20 or more): Adult Child/Senior	$2.00 $2.00
Children Under 5 (Except Giveaway Days)	Free

Season Tickets	
Full Season Field Box Seats	$325.00
Full Season Box Seats	$280.00

Ticket Books	
12 Adult General Admission Tickets	$30.00
12 Child/Senior General Admission Tickets	$12.00

Mini-Plans (Yellow Box Seats)	
Friday Plan (All Friday games)	$55.00
Saturday Plan (All Saturday games)	$60.00
Sunday Plan (All Sunday games)	$60.00
Lucky Seven Plan (7 Game Variety)	$35.00
Baker's Dozen (13 Game Variety)	$65.00

Group Information:

Reading Municipal Memorial Stadium has some very unique venues for groups. Not only is this stadium the only one in the league with seating behind the outfield fence, the picnic area along the third base side is actually closer to home plate than the left field side bleachers. Picnic groups actually have a better view of the action than some reserved and general admission seating, and that is unusual for the league. The Phillies offer a number of group plans that can accommodate groups ranging from a minimum of 20 people, all the way up to 600! All these plans offer special incentives for your outing, including discount rates on admission, announcement of your group name in lights on the Reading Scoreboard Message Center, availability of group members to take advantage of Phillies Dollars to make concession and souvenir purchases, a variety of special Group Leader Rewards based on amount spent by the group, and a separate Group entrance on the Third Base side. The following is a sample of the types of Reading Group packages available:

1. **Pre-Game Deck Party Buffet:**

    You can arrange to have a pre-game buffet beginning 1 ½ hours prior to the first pitch. This package guarantees reserved seating out in the Left Field Power Alley, Green Sections 16 through 19 (an Eastern League exclusive!), where there are accommodations for 480-600 fans per game, as well as a buffet consisting of hamburgers, hot dogs, pasta, potato salad, lemonade and iced tea, all for the one low price of $12.00 per person. Beer and Soda is not included but is available at an extra charge at Dinger's (aptly named since I saw at least two home runs hit Dinger's red roof during one game). Children under 5 are free. (Reserved seats available for $5.00 per child)

2. **Yellow Group Box:**

Your group can reserve a block of Yellow Box Seats in the prime locations of Sections 1 through 11, all for discounted prices. Children under 5 are free. (Reserved seats available for $5.00 per child)

Yellow Box Group Seating Prices	
20 - 99	$5.50 per seat
100 +	$5.00 per seat

3. **Green Group Reserved:**

This package guarantees that your group of twenty or more will share a block of seats in Green Reserved Seats, Sections 12 through 15, again for the discounted price of just $3.00 per seat. Reading can accommodate groups in Green Reserved as large as 467 people per game, and again, Children under 5 are free, unless they require their own seat.

4. **Red General Admission Groups:**

This package offers significant discounts for groups who just want to have General Admission Seats. Children under 5 are free in this plan:

Red General Admission Group Rates	
20 -225	$2.00 per seat
300 +	$1.50 per seat

Birthday Parties:

Celebrate that special day in a young child's life by making it even more special at Reading Municipal Memorial Stadium. For groups of 10 or more, your birthday child may get to throw out a Ceremonial First Pitch, will get a special announcement in lights on the Scoreboard Message Center, and will receive his or her own autographed Phillies baseball. The prices listed below include a ticket for admission, a baseball painters cap, and $4.00 in "Reading Phillies Dollars" which are good for concessions or souvenirs at the park.

Birthday Parties	
Birthday Reserved Seat Package	$13.00 per person
Birthday General Admission Package	$10.00 per person

[*1996 Data: Prices subject to change. Call (610) 478-TIX1 for more information.]

Ticket Sales:

Address: Tickets, Reading Phillies Baseball Club, PO Box 15050, Reading, PA. 19612

Phone: (610) 478-TIX1

Fax: (610) 478-TIX2

Credit Cards: Visa, MasterCard

Hours Ticket Window Open:

Monday through Friday, 9 a.m. to 4 p.m.; also available at Advanced Ticket Window during every home game.

Rain Check Policy:

If a game is postponed due to rain, you can exchange the raincheck portion of the ticket for a ticket to any future regular season home game, depending upon availability. No Refunds.

Game times: Weekdays: 7:05 p.m.
Saturday: 7:05 p.m.
Sunday: 1:05 p.m.

(See schedule for day games. All game times subject to change.)

Time Gates open: 1 to 1 ½ hours before game time, depending upon promotions.

Parking: Free, but at your own risk. Two lots, one at Municipal Memorial Stadium, and one across the street on Front Street. Arrive early, premium parking spots fill up fast.

Other

For the kids:

"Dad? When's Screwball coming out?" "Mom, where's Screwball?"   At all the games I went to in Reading, invariably I heard one or both of these phrases a couple times each game. One of the more popular activities for kids at Reading (and really, at any stadium with a mascot) is trying to get an autograph from Screwball. This, of course, isn't the only activity for kids, but it is the most popular of the younger set. You can sometimes find Screwball wandering through the stadium early in the game, and you can almost

Screwball signs dozens of autographs every game.

definitely find him (or is it a her?) signing autographs later, over at the Information Booth on the concession patio behind the Right Field side bleachers. While you're over on the patio, let your kids try their luck at the nearby Speed Pitch. It's one of the better ones you'll find in the league. Also, NEW for 1997 is the Phillies' Inflatable Phunland - a 40 foot obstacle course where your kids can crawl, climb, and race to more great excitement! (Don't forget that after Sunday games, a select number of young fans can run the bases after the game. Stop by the Customer Service Booth for more information.)

Promotions and Giveaways:

Reading has some great promotions. Not only were there five (5) spectacular fireworks nights at the stadium, but Reading fans got to see a game between their Phillies and those other Phillies from Philadelphia; a couple visits by "Sport", "That Milk Thing" and the "Phillie Phanatic"; as well as displays of hitting and pitching prowess from legendary baseball greats like Rollie Fingers, Boog Powell, Bill Robinson, and Larry Anderson. (However, don't ask me about "Kiss-a-Pig" Night. It's a good cause, of course, but trust me, you don't want to know.) There was also a travel giveaway where at the end of the season, fans could win a free vacation. In addition to all these promotions, Reading Phillies fans could receive such giveaway items as stickers, batting helmets, replica rings, coloring books, wristbands, lunch bags, Mike Schmidt caps, Larry Bowa Pewter Baseball cards, seat cushions, Eastern League cups, equipment bags, t-shirts, photo albums, glass beer mugs, logo baseballs, frosted mugs, batting gloves, bat and ball carry bags, baseball card albums, baseball cards, insulated sixpack carriers, three ring binders, baseball bats, Mickey Mantle Foundation Baseball caps, lunch bags, and Reading team pictures, all for free.

In between innings:

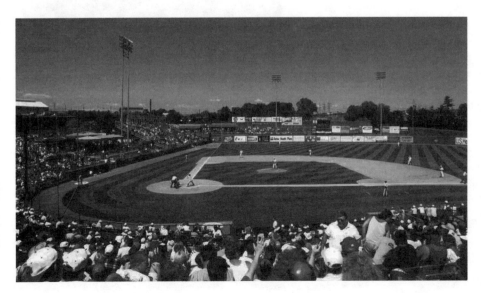

The Reading Phillies host some unique In-Game Promotions. The most novel of them all I thought was the Big Glove Slugfest, where two volunteers donned protective headgear and twelve pound boxing gloves and then started knocking the tar out of each other, in a friendly sort of way of course, for the chance to win some neat prizes.

Other In-Game activities in 1996 included the Herr's Dizzy Bat Spin during the middle of the 5th, where some lucky, unbalanced contestant could win four free bags of chips, four general admission tickets to a future home game, and the chance to humiliate him/herself in front of 6,000 fans; the Rapid Fire Blue Cross Toss; the Strike It Rich Bowling exhibition; the Sir Speedy Pick-a-Prize at the end of the 6th, sort of a Let's-Make-a-Deal where you could win upto $100.00 of souvenir memorabilia; the chance to play softball with Rollie Fingers and Larry Anderson before a regular season home game in the Aetna Health Plans Dream Softball Game; and finally, my favorite, one which all you couch potatoes will enjoy - there was a Best Seats in the House lottery, where two lucky fans were moved up to the La-Z-Boy private lounge near Section 11. (If you're lucky enough to get moved up here, and you already had decent seats in the stands, in my opinion you should do your fellow fans a favor and let someone else trade up, too.)

And of course, not only should you purchase a Souvenir Yearbook for the chance at some lucky signature prizes, you'll also want to hold onto your ticket stubs. The Reading Phillies periodically distribute great prizes to lucky ticket holders throughout the course of the game.

What song played during 7th inning stretch?

"Take Me Out to the Ballgame" (No one really sings because the Phillies are slinging Souvenir T-Shirts into the crowd at the same time. Are you gonna singalong, or try to get a freebie? Me, too.)

Radio Station Broadcasting Game:

WRAW 1340 AM (Flagship); PSR 1230 AM; WPAZ 1370 AM; WGPA 1100 AM.

Eastern League Information:

Posted near inside the main entrance on your left. Includes Phillie's notes so you can keep up on the team's record so far, Club Leaders, Eastern League Records, and the current Season Attendance. In addition, the Reading Phillies will announce current scores for other games being played in the Eastern League, as well as sometimes flash major league scores on the board in left field.

Team Information

Reading Phillies (Southern Division)

History:

You want history? This is the place to be. From the historic Wall of Fame on the first base side of the concourse, to the huge list of Reading Phillies players who've gone on to the major leagues, you can't beat the sense of tradition dwelling at this park.

Minor League Baseball began in this town sometime during the 1880's when there was a franchise in the Interstate League. After the turn of the century, things took on a more professional atmosphere, a more organized atmosphere, and there are as far as I can tell records of at least three professional clubs that played in town. First, there was a club called the Reading Pretzels who played in the Tri-State League, around 1909 or so. Not exactly the most threatening of nicknames, (but a staple of Pennsylvanian delicacy), the Pretzels left opponents like such teams from nearby Altoona, Lancaster, and Harrisburg in knots.

Eastern League play began as early as 1933 in Reading, and many great ones have passed through town on their way to Cooperstown. However, professional baseball hasn't always been the most popular of sports here. For instance, the Reading Indians had attendance problems in the mid-50's, so much so that some old timers can remember when the high school football team drew a larger crowd. Perhaps Reading baseball fans might have turned out in greater numbers to see future greats like Rocky Colavito, and Indians' star Roger Maris, both members of the Reading Hall of Fame.

Indeed, Reading has seen some colossal stars climb up out of the tiny dugouts at Reading Municipal Memorial, including Mike Schmidt, the only player to have his number retired at Reading (No. 24 on the roof), and Greg Luzinski who was as big as ever with the 1970 club. (It's reported that the "Bull" could hit 'em all the way out to the wall, some 500 feet behind the centerfield fence.) Other Reading greats included Ryne Sandberg, and Julio Franco, both of whom have spots in the Reading Hall of Fame. (It's probably only a matter of time before a certain star of the 1983 club joins them, that is, of course, my wife's favorite Phillie, Darren Daulton.)

The real renaissance at Reading Municipal Memorial came when an accountant, Craig Stein, bought the Phillies in 1986 and was at the forefront of owners determined to bring that old time rich feel back to the national pastime. The essence of the philosophy at Reading has to be, let's make everyone feel like a kid again. In that, I have no doubt Mr. Stein, and the rest of the Reading Phillies organization, is succeeding.

Eastern League Championships:

1995: Eastern League
      Champions

Reading defeats New Haven
for Championship (3-2)

1973: Eastern League
      Champions

1968: Eastern League
      Champions

1957: Eastern League
      Champions

Reading Baseball Hall of Fame 1988-1995					
Player	Played	Inducted	Player	Played	Inducted
Mike Schmidt	1971	1987	Bob Wellman	Managed 1968, 74-6	1992
Greg Luzinski	1970	1987	Roger Maris	1955 (Reading Indians)	1993
Joe Buzas	Owner (1977-87)	1987	Whitey Kurowski	Major Leagues 1941-9	1993
Larry Bowa	1967-8	1988	Bob Quinn	GM 1967-8	1993
Ruly Carpenter	President 1967-8	1988	Keith Moreland	1976-7	1993
Dick Wissel	1970-72, '75	1988	Bob Terlecki	1970-1, 73	1993
Bob Boone	1970-1	1989	Carl Furillo	Major Leagues 1946-60	1994
Mark Davis	1980	1989	Andy Seminick	Managed 1970	1994
Frank Lucchesi	Managed 1967-8	1989	Dick Gernert	Major Leagues 1956-62	1994
Paul Owens	Minor League Dir.	1990	Bob Dernier	1980	1994
Andre Thornton	1971	1990	Ozzie Virgil	1979-80	1994
Howie Bedell	1967-9	1990	Bill Dancy	Manager 1983, 84, 88, 94-5	1995
Ryne Sandberg	1980	1991	Joe Altobelli	1952-53 Reading Indians	1995
Dallas Green	1967 (Player-Coach)	1991	Tom Silicato	1972, '75, '77	1995
Ray Starnes	1970-2	1991	Vic Wertz	17 years in Major Leagues	1995
Rocky Colavito	1953	1992	Bob Walk	1979	1995
Julio Franco	1981	1992	Denny Doyle	1968	1996
Jim Olander	1984-6	1992	Jerry Martin	1973	1996
Charlie Wagner	Major Leagues 1938-42, 46	1992	Paul "Cooter" Jones	Reading Indians Reading High Coach	1996
Herb Score	1953	1992	Randy Gumpert	10 years in Major Leagues	1996

Approximate distance from Reading Municipal Memorial to Veterans Stadium: 66 miles
(Source: Rand McNally TripMaker Version 1.1 1994; Reading, PA to Philadelphia, PA)

Mascot: Screwball
Team colors: Red, white and blue

Philadelphia Phillies Minor League Organization			
Team	**League**	**Level**	**City & Phone**
Philadelphia Phillies	National League	Major League	Philadelphia, PA (215) 463-1000
Scranton/Wilkes-Barre Red Barons	International League	AAA	Scranton, PA (717) 963-6556
Reading Phillies	Eastern League	AA	Reading, PA. (610) 375-8469
Clearwater Phillies	Florida State League	A	Clearwater, FL (813) 441-8638
Piedmont Boll Weevils	South Atlantic League	A	Kannapolis, NC (704) 932-3267
Batavia Clippers	New York-Penn League	Short A	Batavia, NY (716) 343-7531
Martinsville Phillies	Appalachian League	Rookie	Martinsville, VA (540) 666-2000

Visiting

Hotel: Wellesley Inn, 910 Woodland Ave., Reading, PA 19610 (610) 374-1500 (Ask them about complimentary tickets to the game for guests.)

Fan Club: All fan mail should be directed to the player, in care of the Reading Phillies.

Directions to stadium:

From Downtown Reading:

Proceed north on Centre Ave. Centre Ave becomes Route 61 North. Reading Municipal Memorial Stadium is located on the left (west) side of Rt 61 South/Centre Ave. just about ¼ to ½ mile before 61 intersects with Rt. 222.

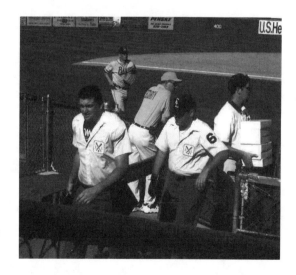

From Pennsylvania Turnpike:

Exit 22: Take Exit 22 to I-176 North. Proceed north on I-176 and then take the Exit for Rt 422 West. Follow 422, and look for signs for 222 North (not 222 Business), Follow 222 North, then exit on Rt 61 South. Reading Municipal Memorial is about ¼ to ½ mile on your right.

Exit 21: Take Rte 222 North, continue on 222 until the exit for Rt 61 South. Take 61 South to Reading Municipal Memorial, about ¼ to ½ mile on your right.

Reading/Berks County

Background

Reading, Pennsylvania (Pop. 78,830) the county seat of Berks County, is known all over the globe as The Outlet Capital of the World. With over 300 factory outlets attracting approximately 10 million shoppers a year, this is more than a mere boast. Located in southeastern Pennsylvania along the banks of the Schuylkill, Reading is a bargain hunter's paradise less than two and a half hours away from New York City, Baltimore and Washington. In fact, the City of Brotherly Love, Philadelphia, is only two exits away on the Pennsylvania Turnpike.

The economic growth of the town through the 19th and 20th centuries owes much to the foresight of Pennsylvania's founder, William Penn, who purchased this strategically located area from the Leni-Lenape people around 1683. Penn's sons, Thomas and Richard laid out the town in 1748, and the county's population quickly grew as immigrants took advantage of the fertile soils and relatively mild climate in the region. The early migration to the region was almost entirely from western Europe, with a strong showing from the Germans by the start of the 19th century. The Pennsylvania Dutch influence is still evidenced by such things as the familiar and purely decorative Hex signs you'll see painted on the sides of the fancy, red barns along some of Berks County's many scenic roads. Perhaps you might even see a few on your way out to visit the homestead of the area's favorite son, pioneer Daniel Boone.

By the Industrial Revolution, Reading had established itself not only as a hub for interstate commerce via the railroads, but also as a major iron producing and manufacturing center in its own right. Today, the Reading area is still more industrialized than the rest of the Commonwealth, with about twenty two percent of its labor force employed in factories. The goods produced today still include the traditional iron and steel, in addition to such diverse industries as electronics, clothing, machinery, hardware, plastics, dairy products, and engineering, insurance, and financial services. In fact, the region's economy is so diverse, there is no single employer responsible for anymore than two percent of the entire workforce.

As for the history of the outlets, the birth of these literally factory-sized stores dates back to the building of the Nolde & Horst Hosiery Mill in 1892. After demand for hosiery declined following World War II, this factory was converted into a multi-tenant manufacturing center. About twenty years later, clothing manufacturers began selling their imperfect stock to employees at bargain prices. This practice proved so popular, that the sale of over-stocked merchandise to the general public quickly became a cottage (or factory, if you will) industry. The Reading Outlet Center is therefore generally acknowledged to be the first factory outlet, with the City of Reading as its capital.

Information

Chamber of Commerce/Tourist Bureau

Reading and Berks County Visitor's Bureau

VF Outlet Village
Park Road & Hill Ave.
P.O. Box 6677
Reading, PA 19610
(610) 375-4085 or
(800) 443-6610

Berks County Chamber of Commerce

645 Penn Street
Reading, PA 19601
(610) 376-6766

Web Site(s): http://www.berksweb.com
http://cityguide.lycos.com/midatlantic/Reading.html

Daytime Entertainment

Guided tours

Contact the listed offices to obtain self-guided tour maps and for further information.

Union Canal Towpath Tour (Self-Guided)
Berks County Park & Recreation Dept.
2083 Tulpehocken Road
Wyomissing, PA 19610
(610) 372-8939

Pennsylvania Dutch Country Hex Sign Area (Self-Guided)
Dutch Hex Tour Association, Inc.
Lenhartsville, PA 19534
(610) 562-8577

Schuylkill River Heritage Corridor (Self-Guided)
Reading & Berks County Visitors Bureau
P.O. Box 6677
Reading, PA 19610
(610) 375-4085 or
(800) 443-6610

Historic sites

The Reading Pagoda Skyline
Skyline Drive
P.O. Box 1615
Reading, PA 19603
(610) 375-6399

At the top of Mt. Penn, you'll find the architecturally misplaced Reading Pagoda, a seven story pseudo-Japanese structure built in 1908 and now owned by the city. The

Pagoda today is the scene of many civic events, and in fact, on the day I visited, I noticed that the site was a lovely place to hold a wedding reception. There are two organizations with offices and gift shops at the Pagoda. The Pagoda-Skyline, Inc. is in charge of the restoration of the Pagoda and the William Penn Memorial Fire Tower (both of which on a clear day are easily visible from Reading Municipal Memorial Stadium). The Berks Arts Council, keepers of the Gallery at the Pagoda, also has a gift shop, exhibits and displays, and they conduct various programs and festivals throughout the year (Call (610) 655-6374 for info on the Arts Council).

Daniel Boone Homestead

400 Daniel Boone Road
Birdsboro, PA 19508
(610)582-4900

The Boone Homestead was settled by the family in 1730. Daniel Boone, arguably one of the greatest frontiersman and wilderness scouts, was born here on November 2nd, 1734. He lived here until he turned sixteen in 1750. Today, this State historical shrine is dedicated to all American youth, with exhibits portraying the early 18th century life of Daniel Boone and of the region's brave settlers.

Open Tuesday - Sunday 9 a.m. - 5 p.m.

Museums

Mid-Atlantic Air Museum

RD 9, Box 9381
Reading, PA 19605
(610) 372-7333

The museum preserves and restores classic aircraft designed, built, and/or flown in the mid-Atlantic region. Collection displayed in Museum hangar and on adjacent outdoor ramp, includes restored WWII B-25 "Mitchell" bomber; 1935 Kellett Autogiro; Martin 4-0-4 "Silver Falcon" airliner; North American F-86 "Sabre"; Messerschmitt BF-108 "Taifun", and the ongoing restoration of a P-61B "Black Widow" night

fighter. Exhibits on aviation history, gift shop, airplane rides on select summer weekends. Take Rt. 183 North, past the Reading Regional Airport Terminal Entrance, then make a right onto Van Reed Rd. and follow signs.

Open daily from 9:30 a.m. to 4 p.m.

Reading Public Museum & Art Gallery

500 Museum Road
Reading, PA 19611
(610) 371-5850

Over 500,000 artifacts and objects
of art, science and history. Displays
and exhibits include paintings,
decorative arts, and sculptures.
Planetarium.

Wednesday to Saturday 10 a.m. - 4
p.m.; Sunday Noon - 4 p.m.

Historical Society of Berks County

940 Centre Avenue
Reading, PA 19601
(610) 375-4375

Pennsylvania German collections, fine and
decorative arts, artifacts, children's hands on
history room, library.

Open Tuesday to Saturday 9 a.m. - 4 p.m.

Parks and Natural Areas

Blue Marsh Lake

U.S. Army Corps of Engineers
R.D. #1 Box 1239
Leesport, PA 19533
(610) 376-6337

Located a very short distance from Reading, up Route 183, Blue Marsh Lake is a fantastic recreational find. Built by the U.S. Army Corps of Engineers and dedicated in 1979, Blue Marsh's primary function is flood control for the towns along the Tulpehocken Creek and the Schuylkill River. However, the lake has become a local recreational favorite with such activities as swimming (no lifeguards), fishing, boating (unlimited horsepower), sailing, water and jet skiing on the huge lake; hiking along the sixteen miles of trails; bird-watching on over 6,000 acres; and picnicking on the soft verdant meadows. There are showers, restrooms, picnic pavilions (which must be rented), charcoal grills, pay phones, and a snack bar open during the summer, as well as three boat launch ramps. To enjoy Blue Marsh Lake, pack yourself a picnic lunch, take Route 183 North from Reading, then turn left onto Palisades Road. The entrance to the Dry Brooks Day Use Area is just up ahead on the right.

Open from 8 a.m. to 8 p.m.

Berks County Heritage Center

2201 Tulpehocken Road
Wyomissing, PA 19610
(610) 374-8839

Gruber Wagon Works, Berks County Heritage Center

Located downstream from Blue Marsh along the 4 ½ mile long Union Canal Bicycle and Walking Trail, this historical interpretation area includes the Gruber Wagon Works, the C. Howard Hiester Canal Center, and Wertz's Red Covered Bridge, among other things. The Gruber Wagon Works, originally built in 1882, was a family run mass producer of wagons. It was placed on the National Register of Historic Places in 1972, moved from its original location in the middle of what is now Blue Marsh Lake in 1976, restored to the condition it would have been in during years of peak production, and declared a National Historic Landmark in 1977. The Canal Center includes exhibits on the Union and Schuylkill Canals, and displays one of the largest collections of canal artifacts in America, including such items as steamboat whistles, anchors, a pilot house, tools, steam engines, and the houseboat *Mildred*. Wertz's Red Covered Bridge dates from 1867 and at 240 feet, is the longest single-span covered bridge in the Commonwealth.

Hours: Tuesday to Saturday 10 a.m. - 4 p.m. Sunday Noon - 5 p.m.

Hawk Mountain Sanctuary

RR 2, Box 191
Kempton, PA 19529-9449
(610) 756-6961

This 2,380 acre nature preserve is the best observation point in the entire United States to witness the autumn raptor migration. Founded in 1934 near Kittatinny Ridge, and as mentioned in Rachel Carson's classic *Silent Spring*, the sanctuary offers a haven for migrating hawks, ospreys, and eagles, at this wonderful "Crossroads of Naturalists." Your best viewing will be in the late summer, after August 15th, through the beginning of December, so bring binoculars (also for rent). There are miles of rugged hiking trails, a museum, visitor's center, and amphitheater. Note, the mountain is smoke-free. There is only limited parking, so arrive early. Hawk Mountain Sanctuary is located approximately twenty miles north of Reading. Take Route 61 North, then proceed northeast on Roue 895,

then turn right onto Hawk Mountain Road. (P.S. If you want to enjoy a nice scenic drive through the Pennsylvania countryside, or better yet if you own a motorcycle, I recommend after you leave Hawk Mountain, continue east until you come to Route 143. 143 will take you back towards Reading, where it intersects with Route 222.)

Trails open dawn to dusk, Visitor Center open 9 a.m. to 5 p.m.

Public Golf courses

Willow Hollow Golf Course

R.D. #1
1366 Prison Road
Leesport, PA 19533
(610) 373-1505

18 holes, closest of those listed to Reading. (North on Rt 183, past airport, but before Blue Marsh.) Tee times accepted two weeks in advance. Pro Shop opens 6:30 a.m. Practice green, locker rooms, 19th hole & snack bar. Statistics:

> Blue Yardage 5810, Rating 67.1, Slope 105, Par 70
> White Yardage 5360, Rating 64.4, Slope 103, Par 70
> Red Yardage 4435, Rating 62.3, Slope 101, Par 70

Rich Maiden Golf Course

RD 2, Box 2099
Fleetwood, PA 19522
(610) 926-1606 or (800) 905-9555

18 hole course, built and designed in 1931 by Jake Merkle. Tee times accepted 3 days in advance. Pro shop opens 6:30 a.m. Bar and Flowering Pot Restaurant. Statistics:

> White Yardage 5450, Rating 63.1, Slope 98, Par 69
> Red Yardage 5145, Rating 65.1, Slope 99, Par 70

Arrowhead Golf Course

1539 Weavertown Road
Douglassville, PA 19518
(610) 582-4258

27 holes divided into Red/White Course (18), and Blue Course (9). John McClean built and

designed the course in 1954. Tee times are accepted one week in advance. Pro Shop opens 6:30 a.m., call after 7 a.m. Putting green, Club House, snack bar. Statistics:

Red/White Course: Yardage 6040, Par 71
Blue Course: Yardage 2638, Par 35

Golden Oaks Country Club (Semi-Private)

10 Stonehedge Drive
Fleetwood, PA 19522
(610) 944-8633

18 holes, semi-private new course built only in 1994 and designed by Jim Blaukovitch. Tee times accepted two days in advance. Pro Shop opens 7 a.m. Driving range, lockers, restaurant & bar. Statistics:

Gold Yardage 7106, Rating 73.1, Slope 120, Par 72
Blue Yardage 6628, Rating 71.2, Slope 114, Par 72
White Yardage 6057, Rating 68.4, Slope 109, Par 72
Red Yardage 5120, Rating 68.5, Slope 108, Par 72

Scenic Rides

Kutztown Airport

Kutztown, PA
(610) 683-5666

Glider Rides (1 or 2 passengers); Airplane Rides (Upto 4 passengers); Open Cockpit Bi Plane Rides (1 or 2 passengers). Mile high soaring excursion; Scenic Tour for Two; Red-Tailed Hawk Flight; 4,000 feet Hands On Intro; Silver Eagle Intro Flight; 2,000 feet Hands On Intro.

Amusement Centers

Schell's Miniature Golf Course

5th Street Highway
Route 222 North
Temple, PA
(610) 929-9660

27 hole miniature course, snack bar. Open 10 a.m.

Blue Falls Grove Water Park

Wiley Road
Off Route 61 North
Leesport, PA
(610) 926-4017

Waterslides, outdoor pool, picnic pavilions, playground. Open 12:30 a.m.

Family Fun Center
Route 61 & 73
Leesport, PA
(610) 926-6161

Arcade, two 18 hole miniature golf
courses, batting cages, bumper boats,
three go-cart tracks, slick track, water
wars, and snack bar. Open 10 a.m.

Carr's Recreation Park
Route 10, 1 ½ miles north of PA
Turnpike Exit 22
New Morgan, PA
(610) 286-4040

Mountain biking, in-line skating,
boating, driving range, rentals.

Crystal Cave
R.D. 3
Kutztown, PA 19530
(610) 683-6765

Cave tours, mini-golf, snack bar,
souvenir shop.

Family Fun Center. Best one listed in the area.

Shopping Malls/Factory Outlets

Reading Outlet Center
801 North 9th Street
Reading, PA 19604
(610) 373-5495 or (800) 5-OUTLET
http://www.shop-roc.com

Big Dog, Britches, Bugle Boy, Coach,
Dockers, Eddie Bauer, Footlocker,
Guess?, Laura Ashley, Levi's, Nautica,
Pier One, Polo/Ralph Lauren, restaurants,
rest rooms, and over 60 outlet stores.

Monday to Saturday 9:30 a.m. - 8 p.m.;
Sunday 11 a.m. - 5 p.m.

VF Outlet Village
801 Hill Avenue
Reading, PA 19610
(610) 378-0408

VF Factory Outlet, London Fog, Donna Karan, Anne
Klein, Liz Claiborne, Vanity Fair, Remington, Oneida,
Izod, Lee, Jantzen, Black & Decker, Reebok, Mikasa,
Designer's Place, Food Court, rest rooms, and over 70
outlet stores.

Monday to Friday 9 a.m. - 9 p.m.; Sunday 10 a.m. - 5
p.m.; Saturdays: until July 30, open 9 a.m. - 7 p.m.; after
July 30 8 a.m. - 9 p.m.

Reading Station Outlet Center
951 North 6th Street
Reading, PA 19601
(610) 478-7000

Brooks Brothers, Calvin Klein, Maidenform, food court, restrooms, and over two dozen outlet stores.
Mon. to Thurs. 9:30 a.m. - 7 p.m.; Fri. 9:30 a.m. - 9 p.m.; Sat. 9:30 a.m. - 7 p.m.; Sun. 11 a.m. - 5 p.m.

The Outlets on Hiesters Lane
755 Hiesters Lane
Reading, PA 19605
(610) 921-8130

Burlington Coat Factory, Kids & Baby Depot, Luxury Linens.

Monday to Saturday 9:30 a.m. - 9 p.m.; Sunday 10 a.m. - 5 p.m.

Home Furnishings Factory Outlet
PA Turnpike, Exit 22
P.O. Box 265
Morgantown, PA 19543
(610) 286-2000 or (800) 226-8011
http://www.herby.com/home/outlets.html

Drexel Heritage, Huffman Koos, Pfaltzgraff, and over a dozen outlet stores.

Daily 10 a.m. to 9 p.m.; Sunday Noon - 5 p.m.

Berkshire Mall
1665 State Hill Road
Wyomissing, PA 19610
(610) 376-8661

Sear's, Bon Ton, Strawbridge's, food court, restaurants, and over 75 specialty stores in this indoor mall. (Grocery store nearby)

Mon. - Fri. 10 a.m. -10 p.m.; Sat. 9 a.m. -10 p.m.; Sun. 10 a.m. -7 p.m.

Fairgrounds Square Mall
North 5th Highway, Rte 222
Reading, PA 19605
(610) 921-9277

Montgomery Ward, JC Penney's, Boscov's, movie theaters, and over 50 specialty stores in this indoor mall.

Daily 10 a.m. - 9:30 p.m.; Sunday 11 a.m. - 5 p.m.

Seasonal Events

Dates are approximate, contact regional tourism offices listed above for updated schedule information.

June: Fiddle & Acoustic Music Fest, World War II Commemoration, Outdoor Midday Concerts, Pennsylvania German Day, Kutztown Pennsylvania German Festival

July:

VF Outlet Village Tent Sale, Independence Week, Midsummer Craft Fair, Annual Apple Dumpling & Township Festival, Great Eastern Invitational Microbrewery Festival, American Indian Festival

August:

Celebration of Music & The Arts, Bavarian Beer Festivals, Pioneer Day, Summer Antique Celebrations & Flea Markets

Reading Outlet Center, downtown Reading.

Accommodations/Other

Hotels and Motels

Visiting Hotel for the Reading Phillies:

Wellesley Inn
910 Woodland Ave
Reading, PA 19610
(610) 374-1500 or (800) 444-8888
Complimentary Continental breakfast, AAA discount.

The Inn at Reading
1040 Park Road
Wyomissing, PA 19610
(610) 372-7811 or (800) 383-9713
Restaurant & Lounge, Outdoor Pool,
fitness center, Entertainment discounts

Sheraton Berkshire
Rt 422 West & Paper Mill Road
1741 Paper Mill Road
Wyomissing, PA 19610
(610) 376-3811 or (800) 325-3535
Restaurants & Lounges, indoor pool,
outdoor putting green, fitness center,
sauna, AAA discounts.

Hampton Inn
1800 Paper Mill Rd
Wyomissing, PA 19610
(610) 374-8100
Complimentary Continental Breakfast
Buffet, fitness center, AAA discounts.

Country Inn & Suites by Carlson
405 North Park Road
Wyomissing, PA 19610
(610) 373-4444 or (800) 456-4000
Free Continental Breakfast, indoor
pool & exercise room, kids free with
an adult, 1 block from VF Factory
Outlets.

EconoLodge of Wyomissing
635 Spring Street
Wyomissing, PA 19610
(610) 378-5105 or (800) 424-4777
Free Continental breakfast, laundry, AAA,
AARP, Corporate & Trucker Discounts.

Reading Holiday Inn
2545 North 5th Street Hwy
Reading, PA 19605-2899
(610) 929-4741
Restaurant & Lounge, outdoor pool, AAA
discounts.

Comfort Inn
2200 Stacy Drive (5th Street Highway)
Reading, PA 19065
(610) 371-0500 or (800) 228-5150
Free Continental Breakfast, fitness center,
AAA discounts.

Days Inn
415 Lancaster Pike West
Reading, PA 19607
(610) 777-7888 or (800) 325-2525

Bed and Breakfast

Contact the Reading & Berks County Visitors Bureau at (610) 375-4085 and ask for a list of the many B&B's located throughout Berks County.

Campgrounds

Contact the Pennsylvania Bureau of State Parks, P.O. Box 8551, Harrisburg, PA. 17105-8511 or call (800) 63-PARKS.

Hospitals

Community General
145 N. 6th Street
Reading, PA
(610) 376-1900

Reading Hospital & Medical Center
6th & Spruce Streets
West Reading, PA
(610) 378-6000

Transportation

Reading Regional Airport:	(610) 372-4666
United Express Airlines:	(800) 241-6522
AAA Reading-Berks:	(610) 374-4531
Carl R. Bieber Tourways:	(610) 683-7333
Roamer Tours & Travel:	(800) 422-8540
Snappy Car Rental:	(610) 777-8887
Werner Bus Lines:	(610) 933-7100 or (800) 532-9800
Reading Metro Taxi:	(610) 374-5111

Trenton Thunder

Team: **Trenton Thunder** (Southern Division)

Stadium: **Mercer County Waterfront Park**

        Address: One Thunder Road, Trenton, NJ 08611
        Phone: (609) 394-TEAM; (609) 394-3300
        Fax: (609) 394-9666
        Web Site(s):   http://www.trentonthunder.com/ (official);
                 http://www.minorleaguebaseball.com/teams/trenton/

Team Ownership:

        Operated by: Garden State Baseball, LP
        Principals: Sam Plumeri, Joe Plumeri, Joe Finley, Joe Caruso, Dick Stanley - Directors;
                 Wayne Hodes, GM and Chief Operating Officer.

Affiliation: Boston Red Sox

Years in Eastern League: 1994-Present

Stadium Physical Characteristics

        Age, Built in: 1994
        Stadium Owner: Mercer County, New Jersey

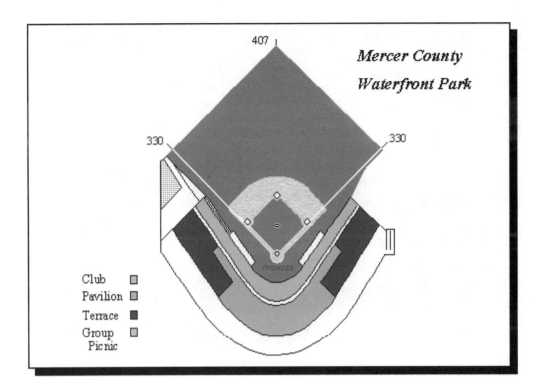

Mercer County
Waterfront Park

407

330   330

Club ▫
Pavilion ▫
Terrace ▪
Group ▨
   Picnic

Bullpens: Inside the fences, along the outfield foul lines.

Playing Surface: Natural grass

Characteristics:

Set on the historic Delaware River, Mercer County Waterfront Park is a great place to catch a game. Like its cousins in Norwich, Bowie, and soon in Akron, Waterfront Park is an example of the open-concourse style of stadium I've described before. Here, things are slightly different because in order to get to the large, open, standing room only capacity concourse, you have to walk up two flights of stairs. (There are ramps and an elevator if you so require.) At the top of the stairs, you don't really see the field right away. There are concession vendors and booths everywhere between you and the seats near the main entrance. Once you get past them, what's spread out before you is a lush, symmetrical playing field right on the banks of the river. (With this proximity to the water, you'd think there'd be drainage problems, but my guess is that the grounds crew have done an outstanding job of prevention and maintenance.)

The wide open concourse area extends all the way from the Picnic Grove in left, to an overlook

area out in right. (From here, you can see the envious folks in their boats and jet skis floating by the stadium, wondering all the while, "What's the score?") The concourse is large enough for an overflow Standing Room Only crowd, and that's really the only type of crowd the Thunder bring in. Don't worry, there's plenty of room to see the game from up here. If you are lucky enough to have a seat however, you'll notice that the stands are solid concrete, with a wide cross aisle between Club and Pavilion seats all the way around. For a cozy, Minor League stadium, this openness is a great design feature, and with no impeded views, you won't have a problem watching the game from anywhere inside Waterfront Park.

Capacity: 6,400

	1994	1995	1996
Attendance	318,252	454,225	437,446

1996 All Star Attendance: 8,369

> 1996 Regular Season Attendance was the largest in EL!

1996 Average Attendance:

> No. of Openings: 69
> 1996 Daily Average: 6,340

All Time Attendance Records:

> Daily: 7,376 on August 17th, 1996
> Seasonal: 454,225 in 1995

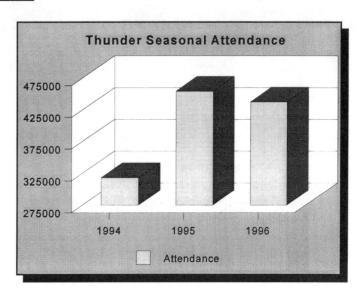

Type of Seating: Club and Pavilion Seats at Waterfront Park include armrests for your comfort. The Terrace seating is aluminum bleachers. (Note - the games I attended in mid-August were sold out, so from first hand knowledge I can only tell you what it's like to stand at Waterfront Park. It's crowded.)

Covered Seating:

> No. However, the concession concourse area is covered. If you need to get out of the weather, there's plenty of room.

Restrooms: Ladies: 2
Men: 1
Changing tables: Yes

Customer Service Window:

> Not inside the stadium. If you need information, you have to go to the ground

level Box Office Window outside the main entrance. (Mercer County Waterfront Park was the only stadium in the EL where I had to go back through the gates to get to Customer Service. Despite this inconvenience, I was able to find members of the Thunder Staff hovering near the Thunder Dugout Store.)

Smoking Policy:

Prohibited. (There is a designated smoking area outside the stands, near right field.)

First Aid:

On the main concourse behind home plate. (Near security.)

Wheelchair & Handicapped Seating: Accessible. There is an elevator near home plate, and a ramp on the third base side. Wheelchair and companion seating available on almost every level at Waterfront Park.

Telephones: Behind home plate on the concourse.

ATM: No.

Scoreboard: Great graphic scoreboard out behind the right centerfield wall. (You can have an approved message posted on the scoreboard by calling (609) 394-3300 at least 72 hours before the game.)

Game Clock: Located on the scoreboard.

Sound: The Thunder spare no expense with audio presentations. Not only was the sound quality clear, but the club has somehow found a wide variety of great audio clips from movies, television and modern music to enhance your entertainment experience.

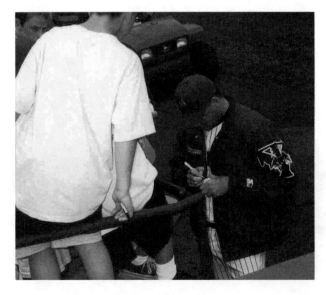

Sunsets? Behind home plate, on the first base side.

Autographs: Yes, along the Club Seats starting at approximately ½ hour before the first pitch.

Concessions and Souvenirs

Best stadium food:

No doubt the best food is available at Loeffler's Sausage Haus on the right field side concourse. I had the grilled (what else?) Italian Sausage. Now, the first thing I want to say about these sausages, and that includes the Bratwurst, Knockwurst, Italian, and the Kielbasa, was the service was outstanding. The guy working the grill didn't just hand me a lukewarm sausage on a bun, he took the time to make sure my meal (and that's what it is, folks, a meal) came hot off the grill. (Service like that will get a nice tip every time.) As for the quality of the Italian, it was hot and spicy, and that's the way I like 'em. Grab yourself a cold beer and one of these babies, and you're set for nine innings!

Other concessions at Mercer County Waterfront Park include a Kid's Meal (Hot Dog, Potato Chips, Soft Drink and Two Baseball Cards); Thunder Dogs (see below); Grilled Chicken Sandwich; Pork Roll (Fried bologna on a bun is an acquired taste, I guess); Hamburger, Cheeseburger, Pizza, Souvenir Bucket of Popcorn; Souvenir Cap of Fries; nachos, pretzels, candy, peanuts and ice cream (Single Dip and Double Dip cones for sale). The most refreshing concession at Waterfront Park came from the Salad Bar. Okay, it's not a salad bar, but they do sell Garden Salads and Fruit Salads from stands along the concourse. (I don't know how well these things sell, but after surviving on hot dogs, french fries and beer for a couple weeks on the road, these were a welcome addition to my diet.) One last thing, try the Lemonade - served with an entire half of lemon, it's a tall, cool refresher on a hot New Jersey night.

Concessions in stands: Soda, Popcorn and Ice Cream.

Card this guy! (Don't worry, Beers of the World also sells soda & peanuts....)

Hot Dog:

The Thunder Dogs are great values. Around eight inches long and at least one inch in diameter, they're quite tasty and quite filling. With just a hint of spice, the Thunder Dog is very, very nice.

Peanuts: $2.50

Beer:

One of the best beer selections you'll find in the Eastern League is right here at Mercer County Waterfront Park. There are Beers of the World stands, a couple special tap stations which were selling souvenir mugs, and even a few vendors walking around the stands. Sales end at the end of the 7th inning, you can only buy two beers per trip, and you must be 21 or older and have a valid photo ID. (There's a beer stand right at the top of the staircase as you enter the stadium. For your information, that stand will back up before the start of the game, primarily for the reason that it's the first one you come to. Unless you enjoy standing in a long line for beer, you'll find plenty of other stands spread out around the concession concourse at Waterfront Park.)

On tap:	Riverhorse, Yuengling, Miller, Miller Lite, Coors Light, Bud Light,
Domestics:	Yuengling, Miller, Budweiser, Rolling Rock
Imports:	Heineken, Amstel Light, Labatts
Microbrews:	Killian's Red, Pete's Wicked (Assorted brews), New Amsterdam (Assorted), Shipyard.
Non-alcoholic:	O'Douls, Sharps
Wine:	Bacardi Breezers (assorted flavors)

Desserts: Cotton candy, hand-dipped ice cream, water ice - assorted flavors.

View of Field
from Concession Stands:

Yes, you can easily keep an eye on the game when you decide to get a Thunder Dog or two. The field is only a head turn away, plus there are televisions broadcasting the action while in line. Mercer County Waterfront Park has a large area devoted to Standing Room Only crowds. This is the concession concourse area that wraps all the way from the picnic area in left field to the Delaware River in right. In fact, many nights during the regular season, the only chance you'll get to see the Thunder is in SRO.

Gift Shop:

Both the Thunder Dugout and the Bullpen have one of the largest selections of merchandise for sale in the Eastern League. The Dugout is the main store located behind home plate, and the Bullpen is the smaller stand along the first base concourse. To be

honest, I was overwhelmed by the Dugout. It's a cool store inside, with everything you could want, including live television broadcasts so you don't miss any of the action. You can find classy looking merchandise ranging from warm comfortable winter coats with the Thunder logo, to a variety of baseball caps you can wear to show off your team spirit. There were banners, bats, balls, seat cushions, in fact, the merchandise lists over 45 great items for sale. (You might even be able to purchase souvenirs from the 1996 All-Star Game by calling the Dugout Store.) The Dugout is open all year, from 10 a.m. to 4 p.m. Monday through Friday, and 10 a.m. to 3 p.m. on Saturdays. On game days, the Dugout closes temporarily at 3 p.m., but reopens at 5:30 p.m until after the end of the game. Call (609) 394-3300 (ext. 114) for more info.

Admission*:

Waterfront Park Admission			
Seats	Individual	Groups 25-99	Groups 100+
Club	$8.00	$8.00	$8.00
Pavilion	$8.00	$6.75	$6.50
Terrace:			
Adults	$5.00	$4.75	$4.50
Children 5-14	$3.00	$3.00	$3.00
Seniors 61+	$3.00	$3.00	$3.00
Children under 5	Free	Free	Free
Standing Room Only	$3.00	Call	Call

Season Ticket Plans Available:

Club Level Season Ticket plans are available for $495.00. As a Season Ticket Holder, you have guaranteed seats for all 71 home games, there is a first right of refusal during the postseason, you get priority consideration when it comes time for seat renewals and upgrades, and finally, you also become part of the reserved parking plan.

Group Information:

Group Outings at Mercer County Waterfront Park sell out quickly, as early as January I'm told, so you must call early to make arrangements. All groups can be announced over the stadium P.A. system, and your group also will be recognized on the scoreboard behind right center field sometime during the game. There are three different ways groups can be accommodated at the games:

1. **Regular Group Outings**:

   Groups of 25 or more can receive discounted ticket prices and preferred seating, subject to availability. Discounted packages are sold on a first come first serve basis, and as mentioned, these are hot items that go quickly. Call (609) 394-TEAM.

2. **Thunder Stadium Restaurant**:

   Groups of 25 or more (upto 110 people) can arrange an outing at the Stadium Club Restaurant. For only $34.00 per person, you will be treated to an all you can eat buffet, which begins ½ before the game and continues for one hour after the game begins. You'll find a cash bar, and some really great views of the action up on the Luxury Suite level of the stadium.

3. **Pennington School Picnic Grove**:

Call the Thunder Group Sales Department for more information on Fundraising, Scout Nights, Luxury Suites, Custom and Group Merchandise, Food Vouchers, and Picnic Groups larger than

There is a wonderfully terraced picnic area out along the left field line at Mercer County Waterfront Park. Here, your group of 25 or more will be treated to an all-you-can-eat meal, which begins ½ hour before the game, and continues for an hour after the game begins. The Picnic Grove is also a great place just to sit and relax with your friends to watch the game. There are two different Picnic Packages available:

The All Star - 25 person minimum	
Without Beer:	$18.00 per person
With Beer:	$23.00 per person
Includes:	Hamburgers, Cheeseburgers, Hot Dogs, Tossed Salad, Potato Salad, Pasta Salad, Pickles, Pretzels, Potato Chips, Cookies, Watermelon, Soft Drinks

The MVP - 100 person minimum	
Without Beer:	$21.00 per person
With Beer:	$26.00 per person
Choice of Three (3):	Hamburgers & Cheeseburgers, Hot Dogs, BBQ Chicken, Italian Sausage BBQ Ribs
Includes:	Tossed Salad, Potato Salad, Pasta Salad, Pickles, Pretzels, Potato Chips, Watermelon, Cookies, Soft Drinks

Special Ticket Plans:

Wendy's Birthday Bash: The Thunder treat your special birthday child like a star at Waterfront Park. One of the neatest things I saw was when Boomer escorted all the birthday boys and girls up on the Home Team Dugout and the entire crowd, estimated well over 6,000, sang "Happy Birthday!" The Birthday Bash is for groups of 10 children or 15 individuals minimum, and the cost is just $10.00 per child. The Birthday celebrant received a special Thunder logo

baseball, and had his or her name shown in lights on the scoreboard. Further, each guest of the Bash received a reserved terrace seat, a hot dog and soda, ice cream, as well as a Thunder team pennant and a free gift from Wendy's.

[*1996 Data: Prices subject to change. Call (609) 394-TEAM for more information.]

Ticket Sales:

Address: Trenton Thunder Baseball, One Thunder Road, Trenton, NJ 08611

Phone: (609) 394-TEAM

Credit Cards: Visa, MasterCard

Hours Ticket Window Open:

Non-Game Days: Mon. - Sat., 10 a.m. - 5 p.m.
Game Days: 10 a.m. to the 4th inning.

Rain Check

Policy: If a game is called due to inclement weather, or if a legal game is not played, tickets may be exchanged at the Thunder ticket office for a ticket of equal or lesser value to any future regular season game, depending upon availability. Suspended or complimentary tickets may not be exchanged.

Game times: Weekdays: 7:05 p.m.
Saturday: April & May - 1:35 p.m.
June - Sep   - 7:05 p.m.
Sunday: 1:35 p.m.

(See schedule for day games. All game times subject to change.)

Time Gates open: 1 ½ hours before game time.

Parking: Ranges from $1.00 to $2.00. Available behind outfield fence, in Riverview Executive Plaza, and across Route 29.

Boomer, the Thunder mascot.

Other

For the kids:

There's a Speed Pitch machine over along the right field concourse where youngsters of like ages can test their arms against each other.

Promotions and Giveaways:

The Trenton Thunder held over fifty promotional nights during the 1996 season. From Fireworks to the occasional Businessperson's Special, from Foam Can Holder giveaways to Back-to-School Night, there were dozens of reasons to come out to Mercer County Waterfront Park during the 1996 season - not to mention, the best winning percentage club in the entire Eastern League! The Thunder welcomed entertainers like the Phillie Phanatic in April, honored Negro League stars of the past in July, hosted the NationsBank USA Baseball Tour vs. Korea and the Double A All Star Game on the same July weekend, and gave away great souvenirs at the front gate all year long. Some of the items you could have received included magnetic schedules, foam can holders, thermal auto mugs, seat cushions, baseball bats, videos, baseball card albums, golf towels, sport bottles, free rolls of film, mini pennants, keychains, beach towels, garment bags, kid's caps, batting helmets, posters, insulated lunch backs, even jewelry! There were a lot of special promotions sponsored by local businesses, including eight vacations courtesy of Caesars Pocono Resorts, two round trip tickets on USAir, two trips from AAA of Central/West Jersey, one trip to Spring Training in 1997, and a car from Bob Maguire Chevrolet/GEO. With all these great promotions, do yourself a favor, pick up a Thunder schedule and come out early to the games next year so you too can be a winner!

In between innings:

For the most part, the Thunder in between inning giveaways are a great addition to all the entertainment on the field. Thunder staff came out with a huge slingshot and tossed real nice souvenir t-shirts up into the crowd. (If you can't catch a fly ball, maybe you'll catch a t-shirt.) There was a Let's-Make-A-Deal contest for the adults, plus plenty of ways to get the kids involved too, including a race against Boomer (the winner

Waterfront Park is one of the few stadiums in the Eastern League which broadcasts live television coverage of the game to various monitors located throughout the park.

won a ten (10) pound candy bar the night I was there), and a Dizzy Bat contest, which is always good for a few laughs.

In fact, the only thing that was a minor disappointment to me were the random giveaways of local sponsor's merchandise. You see, the Thunder between inning giveaways are very different from the way all other clubs in the Eastern League run this type of promotion. Thunder giveaways are tied to randomly selected Seat Numbers, not to lucky numbers, stamps or signatures in the Souvenir Program. If you're one of the many thousands of SRO fans who enjoy the ballgames at Mercer County Waterfront Park, your chances of winning prizes between innings are significantly diminished compared to fans who have seats. I admit this may be petty, but it does seem unfair to the SRO crowd who are just as loyal as the rest of the fans.

What song played during 7th inning stretch?

"Take Me Out to the Ballgame"
(Crowd likes singing along so much, they did it twice.)

Radio Station Broadcasting Game:

WTTM 920 AM (Flagship); WHTG 1410 AM; WIFI 1460 AM; WGHT 1500 AM; (Select games during the 1996 season were broadcast on COMCAST cable as well, WZBN-25)

Eastern League Information:

You can easily stay abreast of Eastern League and Thunder Stats at Waterfront Stadium. You'll find the Thunder pitching and batting leaders posted on the concourse wall behind home plate, as well as the Eastern League current leaders. You will find the starting lineups for the game posted here as well.

Team Information

Trenton Thunder
(Southern Division)

History:

Less than an hour's drive away from the site of the first recorded baseball game held on June 19, 1846 at Elysian Fields, Trenton, not surprisingly, has a baseball history extending back well

before the turn of the century. Trenton was a charter member of the Inter-State Association from 1883 to 1885. This was followed by the deceptively titled Trenton Cuban Giants who played in the Middle States League in 1889. There were professional teams from 1907 to 1914, and from 1936 to 1950 in Trenton. The 1950 Trenton Giants included a young player by the name of Willie Mays.

It took forty four (44) years for professional baseball to return to Trenton, but when it did, it came in with a bang (or ThunderClap I should say). Opening Day was May 9, 1994 and by the end of that inaugural season, the Thunder had drawn in over 318,000 fans in just 51 home dates. During that first season, the Thunder were an affiliate of the Detroit Tigers, and their roster included such notable players as Tony Clark, a heavy hitter who on June 7th of that year, knocked a grand slam 475 feet out into the Delaware River. In 1995, after the change in affiliation to Boston, the Thunder became the first Eastern League club ever to reach 400,000 fans in a single season, finishing the year with an attendance of 454,225. In only three seasons, the Thunder have managed to sell over 1,209,613 tickets. Considering that most of the home games are sell-outs, (53 sell-outs in 1996, including the final 41 in a row) this statistic shouldn't be surprising.

One of the biggest moments in Thunder history, aside from their outstanding 86-56 record (.606 winning percentage) in 1996, was the July 8th Double A All Star Weekend. The City of Trenton, Mercer County, the State of New Jersey, and the Trenton Thunder all had an unprecedented opportunity to show off Mercer County Waterfront Park through a weekend's worth of promotional activities and special events, all culminating with national exposure to a captive baseball audience on ESPN2 the night before the Major League All Star Game in nearby Philadelphia.

Eastern League Championships: None.

    1996:   Best record in Eastern League (.606 winning Pct.)

                 Upset by Harrisburg in Semifinals (3 games to 1)
                 (Harrisburg won 1996 Eastern League Championship against Portland)

    1996:   Hosted Double-A All Star Game.

Famous Players who went on to the Major Leagues:

    Tony Clark (1994); Joe Hudson (1995); Nomar Garciaparra (1995); Jeff Suppan (1995); Bill Selby (1995); Vaughn Eshelman (1995 - rehab); Aaron Sele (1995- rehab); Lee Tinsley (1995 - rehab).

Boston Red Sox Minor League Organization			
Team	League	Level	City & Phone
Boston Red Sox	American League	Major League	Boston, MA. (617) 267-9440
Pawtucket Red Sox	International League	AAA	Pawtucket, RI. (401) 724-7300
Trenton Thunder	Eastern League	AA	Trenton, NJ. (609) 394-TEAM
Sarasota Red Sox	Florida State League	A	Sarasota, FL. (813) 365-4460
Michigan Battle Cats	Midwest League	A	Battle Creek, MI. (616) 660-2287
Lowell Spinners	New York-Penn League	Short A	Lowell, MA. (508) 459-1702
Fort Myers Red Sox	Gulf Coast League	Rookie	Fort Myers, FL. (813) 332-8106

Approximate distance from Mercer County
Waterfront Stadium to Fenway Park: 284 miles
(Source: Rand McNally TripMaker Version 1.1 1994; Trenton, NJ to Boston, MA)

Mascot: Boomer (the Thunderbird)
Team Colors: Kelly green, Royal Blue, Yellow and Black.
Visiting
Hotel: Novotel Hotel Princeton, 100 Independence Way, Princeton, NJ 08540 (609) 520-1200
Fan Club: Fan mail should be addressed to that player in care of the Trenton Thunder. There is a
                   Kid's Club for children from age 4 through 12. Call (609) 394-3300 for information.

Directions to stadium:

From North New Jersey: Take Route 1 South to Route 129 South. Exit Right onto Cass St. West,
                         Waterfront Park is ½ mile on left.

From South New Jersey: Take I-295 North to Exit 60 (Rte 29 North). The stadium is 3 miles up Rte 29.

From NJ Turnpike:

Exit 7A, to I-195 West. I-195 turns into Rte 29 north, continue for 3 miles to the stadium.

From Pennsylvania:

I-95 North, across the Delaware River. Exit 1 in New Jersey is Rte 29 South. Continue on 29 for approximately 6 miles to the stadium.

Trenton/Princeton

Background

Trenton, New Jersey (Pop. 88,675) is a city rich in revolutionary history. As you no doubt recall from early history classes, George Washington led his colonial troops across the Delaware River on Christmas Day, 1776, successfully waging a surprise attack on Hessian and British troops encamped in downtown Trenton at the Old Barracks. Today, Washington Crossing State Park is one of the nicer places in the region to spend a day outdoors, and you can still interact with characters from colonial and revolutionary times at the Old Barracks Museum

Trenton has always been an important point of trade situated on the Delaware River. Early Dutch and Scandinavians traded with Native Americans here, and one of the earliest grist mills was established around 1679 by an English Quaker, Mahlon Stacy. Stacy's son sold part of his father's grant to a Philadelphia merchant, William Trent in 1714, and that area became known as Trenton in 1721. In it's history, Trenton has served as the nation's capital, in both 1784 and in 1799. It became the state capital in 1790, and was formally incorporated as a city two years later.

During the Industrial Age, Trenton's location on the Delaware River and the Raritan Canal, plus the new Camden and Amboy Railroad, made the city a manufacturing powerhouse. John Roebling manufactured steel cable starting around 1849, pottery and ceramics manufacturing was more than successful, and the city's rubber products became known around the world. Today, as the capital of the Garden State, the major employers are still medical, commercial, transportation, manufacturing, and the government. It's no secret that Trenton is still rebounding from serious economic downturns in the mid-20th century, however, for many in the area, and especially trainriders along the Northeast corridor, Trenton's motto will remain, "Trenton Makes, The World Takes."

Downtown Princeton, N.J.

Nearby in Mercer County, is Princeton, New Jersey (Pop. 13,198), one of the many important partners necessary for economic resurgence in the area. Historically, Princeton also shares the honor of once being the seat of government. In 1777, not only did General George Washington defeat the British, but the very first New Jersey legislature met here in Princeton. In addition, in 1783, the Continental Congress met in Princeton's historic Nassau Hall. The area was originally settled in the late 17th century by English Quakers, who first called the town Stony Brook until the name was changed in honor of William III, the Prince of Orange.

Today, Princeton is world renowned not only for its superior academic institutions like Princeton University, (the College of New Jersey became Princeton in 1756), but also, for its research centers, its technology, medical, and pharmaceutical companies, and for its industrial and corporate headquarters located along the Route 1 corridor. There are numerous meeting and convention facilities in the area, and in fact, most of the hotels listed at the end of this section are quite capable of providing full service corporate accommodations.

Information

Chamber of Commerce/Tourist Bureaus

Trenton Convention & Visitors Bureau
Lafayette and Barracks Street
CN 206
Trenton, NJ 08625-0206
(609) 777-1771

Mercer County Division of Economic Development
P.O. Box 8068
Trenton, NJ 08650
(609) 989-6555

Mercer County Chamber of Commerce
P.O. Box 8307
Trenton, NJ 08608
(609) 393-4143

Princeton Area Convention & Visitors Bureau
20 Nassau Street
Princeton, NJ 08542
(609) 683-1760 or (800) FOR-A-CVB

Bucks County Tourist Commission, Inc.
152 Swamp Road
Doylestown, PA 18901-2451
(800) 836-BUCKS

Web Site(s): http://www.prodworks.com/trenton/

Daytime Entertainment

Guided tours

Walk This Way
940 Berkeley Avenue
Trenton, N.J. 08618
(609) 396-9419

Leaves from Trenton Visitors Center, Lafayette at Barrack Street at 1 p.m. on Sundays.

Historical Society of Princeton
158 Nassau Street
Princeton, N.J. 08542
(609) 921-6748

Sunday Walking Tours, Tours by appointment, maps for self-guided tours, information about tours of Princeton University.

Historic sites

New Jersey State Capitol Complex
Trenton, N.J.

The State Capitol Complex includes eight separate facilities located within easy walking distance in the heart of New Jersey's seat of government. The historic sites mentioned below all revolve around the New Jersey State House. Dating from 1792, the State House is the second oldest state capitol in continuous use. Stop by and you might see the Governor at work, or on Mondays and Thursdays, you may be able to view a meeting of the State Legislature from one of the second floor galleries. Adjacent to the State House is the State House Annex, a newer building meant to accommodate the growth of the state government throughout the mid to late 20th century. Many legislative meetings and public hearings are conducted in the Annex. If history and culture are more to your liking than politics, consider visiting the State Museum (see below), the State Library, or the State Archives, all close by at the Capitol Complex. You could also visit the 18th century at the nearby Old Barracks Museum (see below), or the Old Masonic Lodge, or perhaps you might want to find out more about the War Memorial, a grand community center currently undergoing a major renovation.

Hours and Phone Numbers:

State House:	Mon.-Fri. 9 a.m.-5 p.m; Sat. Noon-3 p.m.Information (609) 633-2709.
State House Annex:	Tour info at (609) 633-2709
State Museum:	see below.
State Library:	Mon. - Fri. 8:30 a.m. - 5 p.m (609) 292-6220
State Archives:	Tues. - Fri. 8:30 a.m. - 4:30 p.m. (609) 292-6260
Old Barracks:	see below.
Old Masonic Lodge:	Daily 10 a.m. - 4 p.m. (609) 777-1770
War Memorial:	(609) 984-8484

Trent House
15 Market Street
Trenton, N.J. 08611
(609) 989-3027

Dating from 1719, this summer estate of a wealthy Philadelphia merchant, and the man for which the town of Trenton is named after. This historic mansion has been restored and furnished just as it was in the early 18th century.

Hours: Daily 12:30 a.m. - 4 p.m.

Trenton Battle Monument
Located at "Five Points", the intersection of North Broad and Warren Streets, and Brunswick, Pennington, and Princeton Avenues.
Trenton, N.J.
(609) 737-0623

150 foot tall granite column commemorating Washington's victory at the Battle of Trenton, agreed to be a turning point in the Revolutionary War.

Open Wed. - Sun. With elevator service up to the observation deck.

Museums

Old Barracks Museum

Barrack Street
Trenton, N.J. 08608
(609) 396-1776

This Registered State and National Historic Landmark was built in 1758 in order to house 300 British troops during the French and Indian War. This was the site of important action during the Battle of Trenton, when General George Washington surprised British and Hessian troops encamped here on December 26, 1776.
Adjacent to the Old Barracks is the Officer's House, built in 1759, and the oldest surviving officer's quarters in North America today. Both the Barracks and the Officer's House offer glimpses into military life in the colonies, with historic displays, original furnishings, lectures, exhibits, and character portrayals of 18th century life.

Open Daily from 10 a.m. - 5 p.m. Groups by appointment.

New Jersey State Museum

205 West State Street
Trenton, N.J.
(609) 292-6464, or (609) 292-6308

Regional Native American displays, New Jersey historical art exhibits, 20th century art including works by Georgia O'Keefe, Alexander Calder, John Marin, Louise Nevelson, as well as regional artists, 150-seat planetarium, lectures, children's programs.

Open Tuesday - Saturday 9 a.m. - 4:45 p.m.; Sunday Noon - 5 p.m.

The Art Museum

McCormick Hall
Princeton University
Princeton, N.J. 08544-1018
(609) 258-3787

Collections span the centuries. Includes Greek and Roman ceramics and bronzes, Roman mosaics, Medieval European sculptures and stained glass, Renaissance art, large collections of Chinese, Mayan, and African art.

Hours: Tuesday - Saturday 10 a.m. - 5 p.m.; Sunday 1 p.m. - 5 p.m.

Grounds for Sculpture

18 Fairgrounds Road
Hamilton, N.J. 08619
(609) 586-0616

Unique artistic display showcasing large modern works on a picturesque, naturally landscaped canvas. Outdoor sculpture gardens, courtyards, walls, indoor 10,000 square foot art museum, amphitheater.

Hours: Fri. & Sat. 10:00 a.m. - 4:00 p.m.

Trenton City Museum

Ellarslie in Cadwalader Park
Trenton, N.J.
(609) 989-3632

Regional and local fine and decorative arts, and industrial artifacts. Historic and contemporary porcelains and ceramics. Contemporary arts.

Hours Tuesday - Saturday 11 a.m. - 3 p.m.; Sunday 2 p.m. - 4 p.m.

Parks and Gardens

Washington Crossing State Park

355 Washington Crosing Penn Rd
Titusville, N.J. 08560-1517
(609) 737-0623

The site of General George Washington's famous Christmas Day crossing of the Delaware in 1776, this 800 acre park is just eight miles north of Trenton. 140 acre nature area, picnicking, group camping, fishing, hiking, biking, and horseback trails (no rental facilities). Also includes Visitor Center/Museum, with over 900 artifacts from the Revolutionary War (737-9303); Nature Center, with environmental exhibits and displays (737-0609); Johnson Ferry House, where Washington finalized his strategy prior to the Battle of Trenton (737-2515); and Nelson House, part of the original ferry house (737-1783).

Memorial marking the location where Washington crossed the Delaware.

Canoes

Princeton Canoe Rental

483 Alexander Road
Princeton, N.J. 08540
(609) 452-2403

Rent a canoe at Delaware & Raritan Canal State Park. Open weekends, April - October 9 a.m. - 7 p.m., weekdays June - August 11 a.m. - 5 p.m. Weather permitting.

Theme Parks

Six Flags Great Adventure

Exit 16 off I-195
NJ Turnpike Exit 7A (I-195 East)
P.O. Box 120
Jackson, N.J. 08527
(908) 928-1821
http://www.sixflags.com

Theme Park, Stunt shows, Wild Safari
Animal Park, Bugs Bunny Land, and many
exciting rides. Opens at 10 a.m., call for
seasonal schedule.

Sesame Place

P.O. Box L579
Langhorne, PA 19047
(215) 752-7070

Water rides, shows, games, outdoor play
activities. From Trenton, take Route 1 South
to Oxford Valley Exit, left onto Oxford
Valley Road, right at 4th traffic light. Opens 9
a.m. during mid-summer, 10 a.m. non-peak season. Call for schedule.

You should have no problem finding Sesame Place. It's near
this giant water tower in Langhorne, PA.

Public Golf courses

Princeton Country Club

1 Wheeler Way
Princeton, N.J. 08540
(609) 452-9382

18 holes William F. Gordon designed course. Tee
times are not accepted, Pro Shop opens at 7:00 a.m.
Driving Range. Statistics:

Blue Yardage 6060, Rating 68.8, Par 70
White Yardage 5845, Rating 67.7, Par 70
Red Yardage 5360, Rating 69.9, Par 72

Cranbury Golf Club

49 Southfield Rd
Cranbury, N.J. 08512
(609)799-0341

18 holes, semi-private course. Tee times accepted 7
days in advance, pro shop opens 7:00 a.m.
(Recommend call ahead.) Range, practice green,

lockers, Cranbury Bog Restaurant, bar, grill. Statistics:

> Blue Yardage 6265, Rating 70.0, Slope 117, Par 71
> White Yardage 6004, Rating 69.0, Slope 114, Par 70
> Red Yardage 5395, Rating 72.0, Slope 118, Par 71

Mercer Oaks Golf Course
Village Road West
West Windsor, N.J.
(609) 936-9603

18 holes. Driving Range, Putting Green, bathrooms, small pro shop, snack bar. Call 989-6680 for tee times. Statistics:

> Blue Yardage 7017, Par 72
> Gold Yardage 6630, Par 72
> White Yardage 6305, Par 72
> Red Yardage 5355, Par 72

Aquariums

New Jersey State Aquarium at Camden
1 Riverside Drive
between Federal St. and Mickle Blvd
Camden, N.J.
(609) 365-3000 or (800) 616-JAWS

Shopping Malls/Outlets

Princeton Forrestal Village
Route 1, Forrestal Village Exit
And College Road West
Princeton, N.J.
(609) 799-7400

Dansk, Bass, Oneida, Dress Barn, and over 30 factory outlet stores, three restaurants, food court.

Mon.-Wed. 10 a.m. - 6 p.m.; Thurs. & Fri. 10 a.m. - 9 p.m; Sat. 10 a.m.- 6 p.m.; Sun. Noon - 6 p.m.

Princeton Market Fair
U.S. Route 1 at Meadow Road
West Windsor, N.J.
(609) 452-7777

Barnes & Noble, Oshman's SuperSports, Jos. A. Bank, and over 60 other specialty stores, theaters, restaurants.

Mon.-Sat. 10 a.m.-9 p.m.; Sunday 11 a.m.- 5 p.m.

Quakerbridge Mall
Route 1 and Quakerbridge Road
Lawrenceville, N.J.
(609) 799-8130

Sear's, Macy's, JC Penney, Lord & Taylor and over 100 other specialty stores, theaters, restaurants.

Trenton Downtown Association, Inc.
23 East State St.
Trenton, N.J. 08608
(609) 393-8998

Publishes a guide to downtown retail & dining spots.

Seasonal Events

Dates are approximate, contact regional tourism offices listed above for updated schedule information.

May: Kite Days (Princeton), Capital Music Festival, Princeton YMCA Lobster Bake

June: Heritage Days (Largest ethnic street festival in New Jersey), Trent's Town Faire, June Fete (Princeton), Capital Music Festival, Free Fishing Days, Strictly Art in Princeton, Opera Festival

July: Fourth of July Celebration, Space Days

August: Trenton Jazz Festival

Accommodations/Other

Hotels and Motels

Visiting Hotel for the Trenton Thunder :

Novotel Hotel Princeton
100 Independence Way
Princeton, NJ 08540
(609) 520-1200 or (800) NOVOTEL
Restaurant & Lounge, Outdoor pool, exercise room, room service, Kid's free policy (call), Entertainment discounts.

Princeton Marriott Forrestal Village
201 Village Boulevard
Princeton Forrestal Village
Princeton, NJ 08540
(609) 452-7900 or
(800) 242-8689
Restaurants & Lounges, health club, indoor/outdoor pool, sauna, tennis courts, volleyball court, room service. (Near factory outlet stores.)

Hyatt Regency Princeton
102 Carnegie Center
Princeton, NJ 08540
(609) 987-1234 or
(800) 233-1234
www.travelweb.com/hyatt.html

Restaurant & Lounge, Comedy Club, indoor/outdoor pool, health club, tennis courts, courtesy shuttle, Entertainment discounts.

Summerfield Suites Hotel
4375 Route 1 South
Princeton, NJ 08543
(609) 951-0009 or (800) 833-4353
Buffet breakfast, pool, fitness room, kitchens, convenience store, Entertainment discounts.

Holiday Inn Princeton
4355 Route 1 and Ridge Rd.
Princeton, NJ 08540
(609) 452-2400
Restaurant & Lounge, indoor pool, exercise facility, room service, Entertainment discounts.

The Forrestal at Princeton
100 College Road East
Princeton, NJ 08540
(609) 452-7800 or
(800) 222-1131
Restaurants, fitness center, indoor pool, sauna, tennis, jogging trails.

Nassau Inn at Palmer Square
Palmer Square
Princeton, NJ
(609) 921-7500 or
(800) 862-7728
Restaurants & Lounge, downtown Princeton, across the street from the University.

The Inn at Lambertville Station
Bridge Street & The Delaware
Lambertville, NJ 08530
(609) 397-8300
Restaurant & Lounge, continental breakfast, rustic setting.

Howard Johnson Lodge
2991 Route 1 (Brunswick Pike)
Lawrenceville, NJ 08648
(609) 896-1100 or (800) 654-2000
Free continental breakfast, adjacent restaurant, outdoor pool, discounts for children.

Red Roof Inn
I-295 and U.S. Route 1 North
Exits 67/67A
Princeton, NJ
(609) 896-3388 or
(800) THE-ROOF

Campgrounds

Washington Crossing State Park
355 Washington Crossing-Pennington Road
Titusville, NJ 08560
(609) 737-0623
Four group campsites only with total capacity of 115. 75¢ per person, per night. Fire rings, pit toilets, interpretive center, visitor's center, trails, picnic tables and shelters, playground, fishing.

To obtain a list of state parks, write the New Jersey Division of Parks and Forestry, CN 404, 501 East State Street, 4th Floor, Trenton, NJ 08625-0404, or call either (609) 292-2797 or (800) 843-6420. For other campgrounds in the state, contact the New Jersey Campground Owners Association, 29 Cook's Beach Road, Cape May Court House, NJ 08210. (609) 465-8444, or try http://www.beachcomber.com./Nj/campnj.html.

Hospitals

Helene Fuld Medical Center
750 Brunswick Ave., Trenton
(609) 394-6000

Medical Center at Princeton
253 Witherspoon Street, Princeton
(609) 497-4000

Mercer Medical Center
446 Bellevue Ane., Trenton
(609) 394-4000

St. Francis Medical Center
601 Hamilton Ave., Trenton
(609) 599-5000

Transportation

Trenton-Mercer Airport
Eastwind Airlines   (800) 644-3592
Ronson Aviation   (609) 771-9500

Princeton Airport
    Analar Corporation   (609) 921-7681

Trenton Station
    AMTRAK   (800) USA-RAIL
    NJ Transit   (800) 872-7245

Princeton Jct. Station
    AMTRAK   (800) USA-RAIL
    NJ Transit   (800) 872-7245

NJ Transit - Mercer   (800) 772-2222
Suburban Transit   (908) 249-1100
Greyhound & Trailways   (215) 931-4011
Starr Tours   (609) 587-0626
SEPTA   (215) 574-7800
Stouts Bus Service   (609) 883-8891

Bibliography

1996 Eastern League Final Official Statistics, Howe Sportsdata International, Boston, MA.

Acton, "Fifty Golden Years" Anniversary Booklet of the American Thermos Products Company, 1957.

Barnes, Greater Portland Celebration 350, Gannet, Maine, 1984.

Chadwick, Baseball's Hometown Teams, The Story of the Minor Leagues, Abbeville Press, New York (1994).

DC Access, ACCESSPress, New York.

"Gator Guide", Day Publishing, New London, CT., vol 2. No. 22, August 21-27, 1996.

Gershman, Diamonds, The Evolution of the Ballpark, Houghton Mifflin, New York (1993).

HOK Sport Fact Sheet, Kansas City, MO (816) 221-1576.

Smith, The Valley of Opportunity, A Pictorial History of the Greater Binghamton Area, Donning Co., Norfolk, VA 1988.

USA Sports, The Minor League Baseball Book, Macmillan Travel, New York, NY 1995.

USA Today Baseball Weekly, 9/11-17, 1996, p. 27 (1996 Season Standings).

Microsoft Encarta '95.

Souvenir Programs:

Baysox Program, Vol II, No's 1, 2 & 3 (1996); Baysox Clipper, April 1996.

Binghamton Mets 1996 Souvenir Program.

Canton-Akron 1996 Souvenir Yearbook; Akron Professional Baseball Club, Inc. Press Releases.

Hardware City Rock Cats, 1996 Official Souvenir Scorebook Magazine.

Harrisburg Senators 1996 Commemorative Yearbook.

New Haven Ravens 1996 Game Program, Second Edition.

New Haven Ravens 1996 Group Brochure.

Norwich Navigators 1996 Souvenir Yearbook.

Portland Sea Dogs 1996 Souvenir Program.

Reading Phillies 1996 Souvenir Yearbook.

Trenton Thunder 1996 Official Yearbook.

Chamber Guides & Resources provided by:

Akron Summit Convention & Visitors Bureau.

Annapolis & Anne Arundel Conference & Visitors Bureau.

Bowie Business 1996, Greater Bowie Chamber of Commerce.

Canton/Stark County Convention & Visitors Bureau.

Cooperstown Visitors' Guide, Cooperstown Chamber of Commerce (1996).

Greater New Haven Convention & Visitors Bureau.

Greater Portland Maine Visitor's Guide, 1996-97.

Harrisburg/Hershey/Carlisle Tourism and Convention Bureau.

Mercer Tourism Guide, Mercer County Div. of Eco.Dev., Mercer County Chamber of Commerce.

Mercer Business Magazine.

Mystic Coast & Country Magazine, Spring Summer 1996, The Day Publishing Co. (860) 442-2000.

Norwich Chamber of Commerce.

New Britain Chamber of Commerce Brochures.

New Haven Chamber of Commerce.

Princeton Area Convention & Visitors Bureau.

Internet Web Pages:

http://cityguide.lycos.com/midatlantic/Reading.html

http://gs1.com/Rock/Cats.html

http://statlab.stat.yale.edu/nhol/

http://www.berksweb.com

http://www.courant.com/sports/minor/rocprev.html

http://www.fanlink.com/hburg_senators (Official)

http://www.gators.com

http://www.golfcourse.com

http://www.klx.com/guide/hardware_city.html

http://www.mainelink.net/seadogs (official)

http://www.minorleaguebaseball.com/teams/binghamton

http://www.minorleaguebaseball.com/teams/canton-akron

http://www.minorleaguebaseball.com/teams/hardware-city

http ://www.minorleaguebaseball.com/teams/harrisburg

http://www.minorleaguebaseball.com/teams/norwich/

http://www.minorleaguebaseball.com/teams/new-haven

http://www.minorleaguebaseball.com/teams/portland-me/

http://www.minorleaguebaseball.com/teams/reading/

http://www.minorleaguebaseball.com/teams/trenton/

http://www.ravens.com

http://www.spectra.net/mall/bmets

http://www.trentonthunder.com/

http://www.visithhc.com

Autographs

Order Form

To order a copy of ***It's Raining Rock Cats and Sea Dogs: A Fan's Guide to the AA Ballparks and Towns of the Eastern League***, please return this form and your check or money order to:

Pax River Press
3540 Crain Highway
Box 229
Bowie, Maryland 20716
(301) 805-1757 FAX: (301) 352-8190
e-mail: 74273.310@compuserve.com

Name: _____

Address: _____

City: _____ State: _____ ZIP: _____

Telephone: _____

	Quantity	Price	Subtotal
	_____	@ $24.95	_____
Maryland Residents add 5% Sales Tax			_____
Shipping: $2.25 first book, $1.75 for each additional book			_____
		Total:	_____

Make checks or money orders payable to **Pax River Press**. Please note: We can **not** accept any form of Credit Card payment at this time.

If you are not satisfied with your order, then you may return any books for a full refund - for any reason, no questions asked.

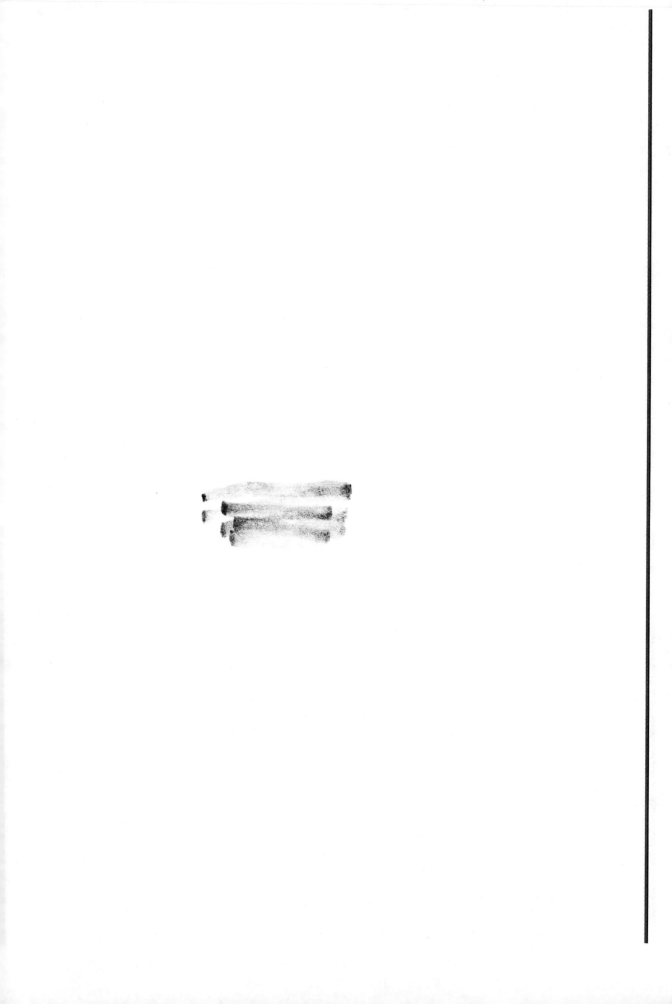